I0086230

Sprouting Valley:
Historical Ethnobotany of the
Northern Pomo from Potter Valley,
California

CONTRIBUTIONS IN ETHNOBIOLOGY

CONTRIBUTIONS IN ETHNOBIOLOGY

Marsha Quinlan and Dana Lepofsky, Series Editors

Contributions in Ethnobiology is a peer-reviewed monograph series presenting original book-length data-rich, state-of-the-art research in ethnobiology. It is the only monograph series devoted expressly to representing the breadth of ethnobiological topics.

Explorations in Ethnobiology: The Legacy of Amadeo Rea
Marsha Quinlan and Dana Lepofsky, Editors

Sprouting Valley: Historical Ethnobotany of the Northern Pomo from Potter Valley, California
James R. Welch

Sprouting Valley: Historical Ethnobotany of the Northern Pomo from Potter Valley, California

James R. Welch

SOCIETY OF ETHNOBIOLOGY

2013

Copyright © 2013 Society of Ethnobiology
All rights reserved

Library of Congress Control Number: 2013939560

ISBN 978-0-9887330-2-2 (paperback)
ISBN 978-0-9887330-3-9 (PDF)

Society of Ethnobiology
Department of Geography, University of North Texas
1155 Union Circle #305279, Denton, TX 76203-5017

Cover photo: John Scott using a fire blower to shape a wooden bowl, Pinoleville Rancheria, 1901. Photograph by John W. Hudson, used with permission. Negative no. CSA1889, The Field Museum, Chicago.

For David W. Peri (1939–2000)

David Peri, a close friend during the last years of his life, provided me with both the idea for this study and the primary archival resources to conduct it. After the City of Ukiah acquired the Hudson-Carpenter estate in 1975, David was hired to do an inventory. During the course of this project, he recognized the unparalleled ethnobotanical value of John Hudson's field-notes. With permission from Lila Lee, administrator for Otis Kendrick, former owner of the Hudson-Carpenter estate, he retained copies of the entire set of documents containing ethnobotanical data with the intention of analyzing and publishing it himself.

In the late 1970s David began efforts to systematize the material on index cards with the assistance of students, whose names regrettably I never located. He never completed the effort and the Hudson ethnobotany study eventually took up permanent residence on several locked shelves at the bottom of a cabinet in his office. Decades later, as he approached retirement, David realized he was unlikely to finish the project and passed the materials on to me, his master's student at the time, so that I might use them for my thesis.

Our close collaboration discussing and assessing this remarkable ethnohistorical and ethnobotanical resource changed my view of the potential of both ethnobotany and anthropology. My work under Dr. Peri's tutelage led me to continue my studies in the doctorate program in anthropology at Tulane University. I was already in New Orleans when news of David's death reached me, just five months after he signed my completed thesis. It gives me immense pleasure to now complete the project that once was as much David's as my own.

Table of Contents

List of Figures

List of Tables

Foreword

The monograph before you is about the use and management of plants by a California in-digenous society, the Potter Valley (Sprouting Valley) Pomo, a subgroup of the Northern Pomo, a little more than one hundred years ago. The Potter Valley Pomo today exist as a small tribe, recognized by the United States as such; this work is about their ancestors' land-scape and traditional knowledge. The sources of the work are mostly vast, disparate data from primary and secondary texts, photographs, and museum collections of that time. Those sources are rooted in early American ethnography of the time period, largely carried out by a contemporary, dedicated student of the Potter Valley Pomo, physician John Hudson. James R. Welch has done an extraordinary job in rendering Hudson's ethnography (and spe-cifically the ethnobotany found in it) into a solidly reliable, beautifully illustrated portrait of people and their landscape. He has captured vividly what would otherwise be an elusive reality of this relationship, in spite of limitations ethnography done more than one hundred years ago tends to impose. James Welch's contribution here is a methodological and empirical breakthrough by way of his reconstruction of that intermediate reality between people and landscape, intangible because it has not been current for a long time, but undeniably rich in its verisimilitude.

The day is past when ethnographers—whether amateur or professional—studied the re-maining knowledge of elders of depopulated, vanquished societies. In the California context as elsewhere, they used to query these mature veterans of Euro-American conquest on what their people were really like before they had been enslaved, shot, or killed by alien disease. In the United States, the method was for many years restricted to our own indigenes, of course, the Native Americans, and before the professionalization of anthropology at the very beginning of the twentieth century, it was exclusively done by ethnographers who did not have specific training or certification in their chosen field of study. Some were government employees. Others were motivated by antiquarian interests. A few—always a minority in any civilization—had genuine gifts of intercultural sensitivity, sharp intellect, and deep insights by which they could visualize beyond the veneer of the obvious. They could examine a cul-ture, people, and associated landscape that could very likely have been as real as these can seem without benefit of time travel. James Mooney was one of these ethnographers; another is the much less well known Dr. John Hudson. Mooney had a high school education; Hudson was a physician. Neither had training in anthropology, but unlike many of the other amateur ethnographers and antiquarians with interests in Americana and indigenous North America, both possessed tremendously good eyes, ears, and noses for the pre-conquest reality of the peoples and environments that mesmerized them. That sense of reality gave them impetus to preserve as faithfully as their skills permitted rare textual and material culture without which any historical understanding of the relevant places and times would be foggy if not indeed opaque today. Yet whatever one wishes to call the method—salvage ethnography or memory culture or urgent anthropology in the service of preserving the human cultural record—few aspire to do it today. There are reasons for that.

In the contribution before you, James Welch overcomes the limitations of dated ethnographic methodology. That methodology was based on a theory that culture could be grasped in its entirety by interpreting selected words, phrases, and text engraved in native speech concerning a recent past, and matching all that to seemingly objective lists of things known about that past by what was deemed to be objective science of the time. These were lists of useful plants employed indigenously as food or medicine or shelter (i.e., ethnobotany); of animals hunted for their meat or hides; of toponyms denoting distinct environments crisscrossed by the people and their beliefs about these; of ceremonies designed to increase abundance of the good, or diminish the incidence of the bad, however cognized. The methodology fell away in ethnography, and in its corollary fields, including ethnobotany, a good while ago. That is because culture is constantly changing, people's memories are fallible, and other problems and topics regarding situating cultures in relation to each other and to a wider, dynamic world ended up replacing directionless empiricism, description, and rote recording of shared ideas and behavior of somewhat distant or even remote forebears of seemingly threatened, soon-to-be extinct societies and traditional knowledge. In the case before us, of course, the Potter Valley Pomo Tribe, though small in size and in corporately owned lands, are with us today.

By the time of the current ethnographic moment, any local society in question itself might no longer be extant even in relic form, either because of the long-term, lingering effects of colonialism (both internal or external) and the assimilation to a cultural singularity brought about by the most current phase of human history, globalization. At least that is not the Pottery Valley Pomo case. The past is clothed in differences of perspective, both spatially (the landscape) and temporally (changing climates of opinion about what is important in an environment, and of a people who live in it). Welch makes use of the past by turning lists, fragments of text, illustrations of the time, collections of herbarium specimens of useful plants and other material culture such as baskets, weapons, fire drills, and the like into a complex, well-woven narrative of the Potter Valley Pomo in this early period. The narrative places them in a landscape context. This is a landscape—draining to the Russian River valley—mostly transformed by our time into vineyards and other agrarian formats. Yet the historic context of canyons, chaparral, marshes, hills, mountains, and other diverse habitats that made up the northern Pomo landscape before those transformations, and the people's uses of fire and other tools in managing it, change the focus of the lens. In the pages that follow, the reader can apprehend aspects of the landscape and the people who inhabited it just before the onset of agraria. James Welch produces a scintillating account that sets a new benchmark of scholarly caliber for studies of the ethnobotanical and ecological past of societies that were once abundantly supplied with traditional knowledge. This is a contribution to ethnobotany that approaches viewing history not in a primitivist way—as though what came before was automatically better than what now exists—but rather sensitively and intelligently, with an eye to broader impacts of benefit to those, descendants and ethnobiologists included, who seek environmental and cultural resuscitation. This book is itself reflective and reconstructive of the sophistication ancestors of the Potter Valley Pomo displayed in their own perception, use, and management of a historic landscape.

William Balée
Tulane University
New Orleans, Louisiana
April 7, 2013

Acknowledgements

Of the many people who helped during the course of this study, I am especially indebted to David Peri for his immeasurable contributions.

Carlos Coimbra Jr., Verle Anderson, and anonymous reviewers provided insightful comments on preliminary drafts. William Balée's encouragement over the years was a source of inspiration to publish this book. Linda Alfano spent many uncomfortable hours over a photocopier and rushed the copies off to the post office so that I could consult them in Brazil, where I now live. Access to these documents was provided courtesy of Sonoma State University Library and with gracious assistance by Lynn Prime.

During a visit to Ukiah and Potter Valley in 2011, Norma Rosales of the Potter Valley Tribe treated me to an entertaining afternoon of storytelling and Gregg Young, Environmental Director for the Potter Valley Tribe, served as an excellent guide, sharing invaluable information regarding the local landscape and recent tribal history. Carlos Coimbra Jr. and Ricardo V. Santos were excellent companions during this trip and made valuable comments on working drafts. Sherrie Smith-Ferri at the Grace Hudson Museum generously guided me through the Hudson-Carpenter ethnographic collections and shared many of her thoughts about the material I consulted and photographed.

The wonderful folks at Contributions in Ethnobiology and the Society of Ethnobiology provided assistance and support at all stages of review, revision, and production. Marsha Quinlan and Dana Lepofsky, editors of the Contributions in Ethnobiology series, deserve special thanks for their helpful comments and inspired dedication to this new initiative by the Society of Ethnobiology. Additionally, I am grateful to Shannon Wood for creating excellent maps and Jonathan Dombrosky for his thorough copyediting.

Particular note must be made of the students at Sonoma State University who assisted with the initial effort to systematize John Hudson's ethnobotanical information in the 1970s under David Peri's supervision. I regret I am unable to acknowledge them by name.

Permissions to reproduce the images in this monograph were generously provided by the Grace Hudson Museum, Bancroft Library, The Field Museum, and Chris K. Kjeldsen.

1. Introduction

Located in the North Coast Ranges of California about 185 km to the north of San Francisco, Potter Valley is the historical homeland of the Potter Valley Pomo, an indigenous community whose members spoke dialects of the Northern Pomo language until recent generations (Figure 1). Known to neighboring indigenous peoples as "Sprouting Valley" (**Ba-lo'kai**) and described by early non-indigenous visitors as one of California's lushest and most productive coastal valleys (Stewart 1943), Potter Valley is situated in a transition zone between the coast and inland mountains (Munz and Keck 1973). With dry hot summers and cold wet winters,

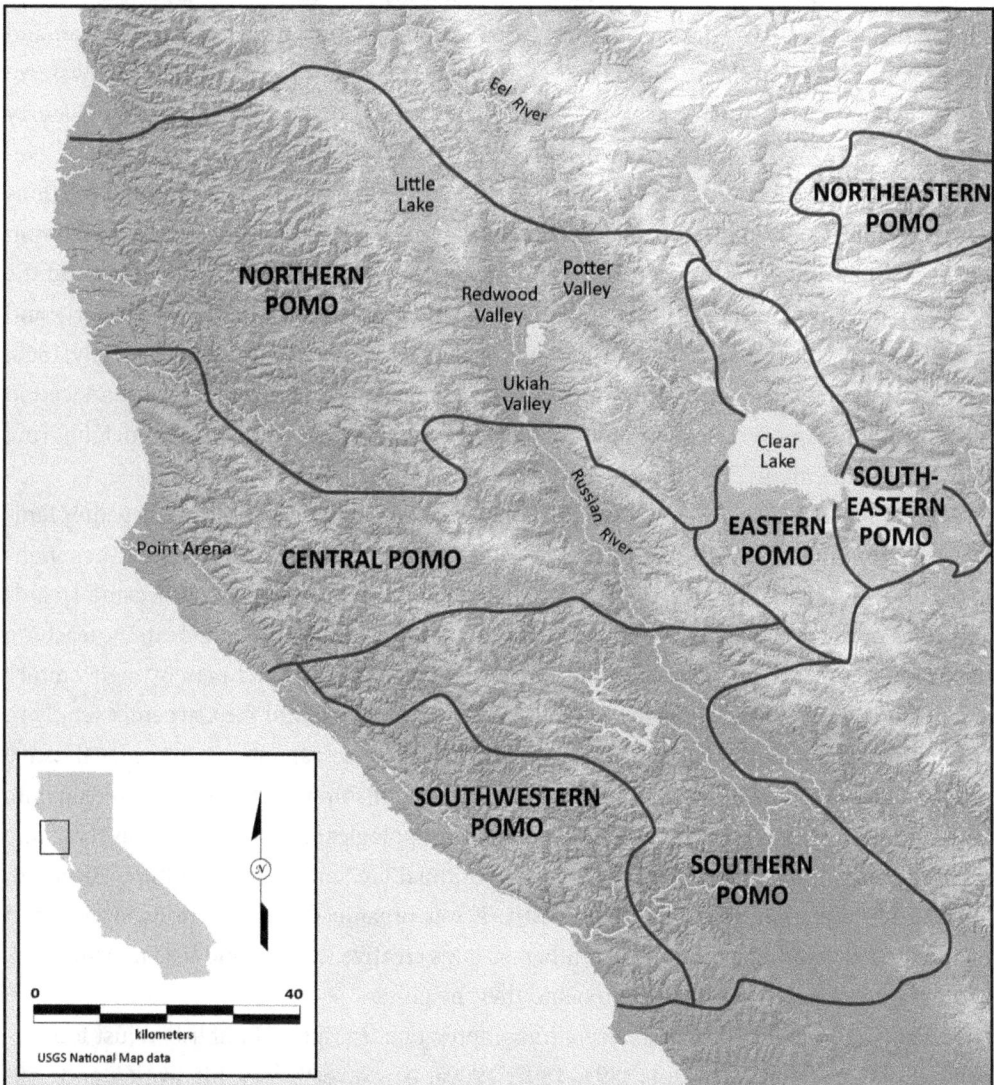

Figure 1. Map of Pomoan lands. Adapted from Barrett (1908a).

the ecologically varied valley and its neighboring territories provided proximate access to enormously diverse seasonal resources and close contact with socioculturally distinct indigenous neighbors (Turner et al. 2003). Within this setting, the sedentary Potter Valley Pomo supported themselves by collecting, hunting, and fishing local resources and dedicated much of their cultural attention to artistic expression and ceremonial activities. Consistent with the physical and cultural richness of their homeland, the Potter Valley Pomo also had extremely diversified knowledge of their local botanical and ecological resources.

In 1850, a thousand or more Potter Valley Pomo lived in five primary settlements along the oak woodlands of the valley floor and travelled seasonally throughout an expansive territory to collect resources in what are now Mendocino and Lake Counties (Kroeber 1925; Stewart 1943). However, events during that precipitous year ushered in a period of rapid change leading to their demographic reduction and dislocation from the valley (Bean and Theodoratus 1978; H. M. Carpenter 1899). On the heels of a devastating assault and massacre by the United States military early that year (Barrett 1952; A. O. Carpenter and Millberry 1914; Heizer 1973), the first non-indigenous settlers arrived in the valley in search of livestock range. Although William Potter and his companions maintained amicable relations with the valley's native residents and interfered minimally as the community recovered from the massacre, within less than a decade the valley was entirely inhabited by settlers and the Potter Valley Pomo were forced to live in impermanent rancherias on private property and provide cheap labor in exchange for this privilege (Bean and Theodoratus 1978). By 1868, the pressures of territorial circumscription, overgrazing, enslavement, and forced relocation had caused the impoverished community to leave the valley and seek refuge in neighboring indigenous settlements (Hudson 1893).

Among Potter Valley's early nineteenth century settlers was the eccentric Carpenter family, who abhorred the systematic persecution of the valley's native residents by their non-indigenous neighbors. After arriving in the valley in 1859, the Carpenters became friends and allies of the Potter Valley Pomo, assisting them legally in avoiding relocation, teaching their children in a local school, and artistically representing the richness of their culture and personal lives (Crawford 2000; K. Holmes 2006). Marrying into the Carpenter family in 1890, homeopathic doctor John W. Hudson (Figure 2) also took an interest in the local native people. Building on the Carpenter's close personal relationship with the Potter Valley Pomo, Hudson began what would become a lifelong anthropological study focusing on their fine art of basketry, foodways, curing practices, ceremonial life, and material culture. Although his research was more scientific than artistic, it was organically related in inspiration and method to his wife's oil painting, his mother-in-law's creative writing, and his father-in-law's photography of the Potter Valley Pomo and their neighbors.

Hudson never finished his primary ethnographic manuscript and published just four articles and short letters (Hudson 1893, 1897, 1900a, b). Nevertheless, his work stands out among contemporaneous ethnographic studies of indigenous peoples in Californian for its

Figure 2. Dr. John W. Hudson, circa 1892. Photograph by A.O. Carpenter. Original in the collections of Grace Hudson Museum, Ukiah, California.

long duration and its basis in predominantly personal rather than professional relationships with consultants. Having never received formal training in anthropology, linguistics, or botany, Hudson nevertheless documented Potter Valley Pomo culture and language with a thoroughness and longevity that was atypical of early anthropology in California. Also unusual for that time was Hudson's keen academic interest in ethnobotany, evidenced in his unpublished fieldnotes by an enormous quantity of data on Northern Pomo plant names and uses.

By the time Hudson began his study, the Potter Valley Pomo had been displaced from their traditional settlements in the valley and endured four decades of persecution. He nevertheless found living members and descendants of this once populous group to have retained extensive traditional knowledge of local botanical resources. Consistent with the principles of salvage ethnography popular at the time (Conn 2004; Gruber 1970), Hudson's research sought to ascertain Potter Valley Pomo culture and plant knowledge as they existed before the disruptions caused by the arrival of non-indigenous settlers.

Hudson strove to conduct ethnographic research with the rigor of prominent anthropologists and museologists with whom he corresponded, but did so according to his own priorities and styles. For example, unlike many professional anthropologists who worked with Pomoan peoples in the late 1800s and early 1900s (e.g., Barrett 1952; Gifford 1926; Kroeber 1911; Loeb 1926), Hudson focused much of his research efforts on the members and descendants of a single local community. Also, he dedicated considerable attention to documenting the minutia of local plant knowledge in diverse cultural domains. At that time, ethnobotany was a largely overlooked aspect of indigenous culture. Many of the well-known ethnographers working in California at the time tended to address plants only in passing or as a basis for cross-cultural comparison (e.g., Barrett 1908b, 1952; Freeland 1923; Gifford 1967; Kroeber 1922; Loeb 1926; Mason 1904). In contrast, Hudson's documentation of Potter Valley Pomo plant knowledge was both topically broad and extremely detailed in many of its particulars. In the course of his research, Hudson recorded over 40,000 Northern Pomo terms, which were described as the earliest and most extensive vocabulary list collected for any indigenous language in California (McMurray and Tharp 1977). Amidst this data are innumerous entries on cultural knowledge of plants used for such diverse purposes as medicine, food, architecture, clothing, art, and ceremonial activities.

Having never organized or taken steps to publish the great majority of his ethnobotanical findings before his death in 1936, these data remained dispersed throughout his unpublished fieldnotes and other writings with all of the inherent limitations that accompanied his amateur ethnographic and ethnobotanical methods. This previously unexplored resource nevertheless contained invaluable and otherwise unavailable information about indigenous plant knowledge at an early time in Mendocino history. Through its focus on a single Pomoan community, Hudson's research brings into detailed relief the local cultural and ecological contexts of peoples that are elsewhere often conflated in anthropological representations as a generic Pomo culture (McLendon and Oswalt 1978). Such lack of ethnographic specificity belies the distinctiveness of historical Pomoan peoples as speakers of seven different languages and members of dozens of politically autonomous communities in varied local landscapes. Hudson's Potter Valley Pomo data therefore provide a renewed opportunity to consider the Potter Valley Pomo community and the Northern Pomo language on their own terms.

In this book I endeavor to explore the historical relationship between Potter Valley Pomo society and the local Northern California landscape through the lens of Hudson's ethnobotanical research. To facilitate access to these previously unsystematized data, I organized the ethnobotanical content of his fieldnotes and other unpublished writings, updated his plant identifications according to contemporary botanical nomenclature, and interpret these findings in terms of what is known historically and ethnographically about Potter Valley Pomo society and its relationship to the Northern California landscape. The results of this effort include an exceptionally robust set of cultural information regarding over 260 taxa of vascular plants, mushrooms, and algae, including many uses not documented elsewhere for Pomoan or other indigenous peoples. This reconstructed Potter Valley Pomo ethnobotany constitutes one of the most thorough records of plant use for any indigenous group in California. Although some other early ethnobotanical studies of native peoples in California offer ethnographically richer accounts of indigenous plant use (e.g., Barrows 1900; Bocek 1984) and others address more plant taxa (e.g., Timbrook 2007), the cultural plant knowledge deriving from Hudson's research and presented in this book is unequalled in the breadth of its data pertaining to a single local community and language.

2. Reconstructing Potter Valley Pomo Plant Knowledge

Amidst John Hudson's writings are several indications of his research goals. As he wrote in the introduction to an ethnographic manuscript, *Poma*, which he hoped to publish with the Smithsonian Institution but did not complete before his death:

> The native tribes here considered occupied the lowlands of Potter Valley, California, on the northeast source of the Russian River, who called themselves **Po'-ma**, or **Tcă ma-po'** (persons from red earth). The following themes record some of the impressions received during a forty year residence among these now reduced and decadent tribes: notable examples of their customs, art and industries, expressly omitting the spectacular, unmeaning modern ceremonies. As the larger part of the material pertains to activities long since obsolete it may be retrieved solely through knowledge of the language, analysis of words and motive, privileges of friendship and by the patient sounding of aboriginal memories.[†]

Evident in this citation is Hudson's explicit ethnographic interest in documenting Potter Valley Pomo society in broad ethnographic terms. The collection of papers in his monograph covers such diverse topics as basketry, food preparation, hunting techniques, childbirth, proper names, and mythology. His first ethnographic article (Hudson 1893) was an important contribution to the study of native Californian basketry because it approached the topic taxonomically and indicated how to calculate market value, thus stimulating public interest in Pomoan basketry and ironically serving to increase the value of his own collection (Colson 1974; McLendon 1993). Hudson successfully published several other articles and short letters addressing shell beads, acorn processing, and drilling technologies (Hudson 1893, 1897, 1900a, b). In each of these examples, his publishing objectives were more ethnographic than ethnobotanical. There is little evidence that he ever intended to publish his copious ethnobotanical data. In fact, the disarray in which he left them suggests he may have undervalued their academic potential. In this chapter, I discuss the strengths and limitations of Hudson's unpublished ethnobotanical data and describe the steps I took to systematize, update, and interpret them.

The contents of Hudson's *Poma* manuscript and his own affirmation that it documents "the totality of Potter Valley Pomo culture" suggest he sought to establish himself as an eth-

---

[†] With the exception of infrequent spelling and punctuation corrections for the sake of clarity, unpublished quotations are reproduced as originally written to preserve their historical integrity.

nographer beyond the constraints of his evident preference for collecting material culture and ethnobotanical data. However, Hudson's research style may not have been as well suited for this purpose. Beginning in 1893, Hudson documented Northern Pomo terms using a vocabulary elicitation schedule provided by Smithsonian Institution Bureau of Ethnology director John W. Powell (1880). This form consisted of 139 pages of English vocabulary lists under such headings as dwellings, colors, and plants with spaces for writing equivalent terms in a study language. Useful for standardizing vocabulary collection by independent scholars of diverse languages due to its systematic format, it nevertheless included many terms that were irrelevant to Potter Valley Pomo society, such as "toga" and "fire-place." Hudson faithfully used this guide until its pages were filled. Thereafter, much of his freeform linguistic notes continued to follow a similar format—long lists of word along the left margin of each page with brief identifying passages to the right.

Hudson seems to have been inspired by this model of language as vocabulary and by a related anthropological model that was popular among anthropological scholars at the time, whereby cultures were analyzed as inventories of discrete traits (e.g. Kroeber 1922; Mason 1902, 1904). Accordingly, his ethnographic and ethnobotanical fieldnotes systematically prioritized vocabulary items accompanied by short passages at the expense of robust cultural description. Additionally, Hudson routinely formulated his brief notes about cultural plant uses and knowledge in the passive voice and thereby rendered the human actors invisible. For example, in a passage describing how the Potter Valley Pomo used split-stick clappers made from manzanita (*Arctostaphylos* spp.), Hudson wrote:

> **ma ki la hai** (thundersticks) syn **madim**. syn **Pa-dax**. A pair of manzanita clappers, slapped together in imitation of lightening stroke & followed by the roar of the **madim** as thunder. It was used in the assembly chamber during the minor ceremony **ma-ki-la**.

An example of writing techniques anthropologists historically used to convey ethnographic authority (Clifford 1983), this passage demonstrates the difficulty in extracting from Hudson's data even the most basic qualifying information about who had plant knowledge or used plants for specific purposes. This limitation resurfaces in my own ethnobotanical descriptions in this book where lack of ethnographic information made it impossible to communicate precisely who (e.g., women, men, elders, mothers, etc.) had specific ethnobotanical knowledge or made certain uses of plants.

Hudson's ethnobotanical investigation of the Northern Pomo from Potter Valley is reminiscent of American ethnobotany's earliest systematic studies, with their roots in economic botany (Davis 1995). In his article *Aboriginal Botany*, often cited as the earliest delineation of the scientific study of ethnobotany, Stephen Powers (1875) described a field of study that addresses the "vegetable world" used by "aborigines," "Indians," and "savages" for any and all purposes. In this initial text, Powers established several of what would later become trademarks of ethnobotanical publications: inventory format, materialist emphasis, and abbreviated sociocultural information. About the time Hudson was engaged in his own research with the Potter Valley Pomo, new ethnobotanical studies were being published that improved on, but also consolidated, the limitations of Powers' approach (Davis 1995). In California, some of the first studies of plant use among the indigenous peoples exemplify Powers' approach, such as those by Chestnut (1902) and Merrill (1923).

Several early scholars took somewhat more robust ethnographic approaches to recording plant knowledge among indigenous peoples in California. For example, David P. Barrows (1900) published on the ethnobotany of the Cahuilla in a manner that prioritized this group's cultural relationship with the local environment and thereby provided greater anthropological context than is evident in Hudson's data. In another example, John P. Harrington documented Chumash and Ohlone ethnobotany in the course of other ethnographic and linguistic studies. Like Hudson, Harrington did not publish his ethnobotanical data from California, although he did publish on the ethnobotany of indigenous peoples elsewhere (Robbins et al. 1916). Compared to Harrington, whose records also contained important gaps (Bocek 1984; Timbrook 2007), Hudson employed methods that resulted in briefer sociocultural description and inconsistent botanical collections.

Another example of Hudson's sometimes overly abbreviated note-taking style is a recurrent lack of information identifying his study locations and sources, including consultants' community and language affiliations. This shortcoming may be related to historical circumstances that served to complexify the distinctions between interrelated groups. When Hudson conducted his field research, the Potter Valley Pomo had already been displaced from their home valley and most lived in other nearby Pomoan settlements (Smith-Ferri 2006). Consequently, when he knew them, many of Hudson's consultants were integrated members of other communities or had mixed community affiliations. For example, in a rare passage from his unpublished manuscript identifying one of his male consultants, Hudson wrote:

> As told by **Ke-wil** (suinom) **Cin-na ta-da-la** (applinem), 1897. Born in Potter Valley 1835. **Da-no ka Ke-ya,** father. **Ca-nel Po-ma,** mother. Sold as slave to Gen. Vallejo at Sonoma, 1846. Guide and servant to Kelsey brothers in Lake Country till their massacre in 1851, following his tampering with their guns. Spoke English, Spanish and many native dialects. Wampum manufacturer and trader by profession and was well known by Sacramento tribes. Told mainly in **Ca-nel** dialect, with a few archaics and Keyan idioms.

Thus, Hudson's tendency to exclude information about his consultants' community and linguistic affiliations may derive from the real complexities they entailed. However, Hudson's imprecision in this regard results in some ambiguity as to whether certain portions of his notes pertain specifically to the Northern Pomo from Potter Valley or to members of other local communities then living in such settlements as Pinoleville, Coyote Valley, and Yokayo. This limitation must be emphasized, because it may have resulted in the inadvertent inclusion in this book of some plant uses or native terms deriving from different Pomoan communities.

The quality of Hudson's data was also limited by his demonstrated lack of linguistics and botany training. Despite attempting to write Northern Pomo plant names according to ortho-graphic conventions then advocated by researchers at the Smithsonian Institution (Table 1), his linguistic transcriptions and glosses suffered from frequent inconsistencies. He similarly strove to improve his plant identifications by sending numerous specimens for identification by reputable California botanists, including Alice Eastwood at the California Academy of Sciences in San Francisco and Willis Jepson at the University of California, Berkeley. How-ever, these requests often received replies without accurate determinations due to the poor quality of his collections. Even when he did receive accurate plant identifications, Hudson often failed to follow through by correlating these scientific names with the imprecise com-mon and genus names that prevail throughout his notes. Nevertheless, the accuracy and completeness of many pages of his fieldnotes were greatly improved by his admirable habit of retyping and subsequently correcting them by hand.

As he described in the introduction to his *Poma* manuscript, Hudson attempted to docu-ment Potter Valley Pomo culture as it existed before the transformations that followed the arrival of non-indigenous settlers in the region. This approach exemplifies what McLendon and Oswalt (1978) characterized as a major problem with Pomo anthropology since Steven

Table 1. Phonetic alphabet employed by Dr. John W. Hudson.

Symbol	Description
â	as in "all"
a	as in "far"
ă	as in "what"
ai	the i sounds in "aisle"
au	as in "out"
c	arbitrarily as in "sh"
e	as in "they"
ě	as in "when"
g	as in "gig"
h	as in "host"
k	as in "kick"
i	as in "pique"
ĭ	as in "pick"
o	as in "note"
q	represented by "kw"
tc	as ch in "church"
u	as in "rule"
ŭ	as in "pull"
w	as in "win"
x	double consonant aspirate (the Greek "x" or German "ch" is approximate)

Powers (1872, 1877), evident in publications by many prominent scholars who endeavored to reconstruct pre-contact Pomoan culture from the memories of living individuals (e.g., Barrett 1917a; Barrett 1917b; Freeland 1923; Gifford 1926; Kniffen 1939; Kroeber 1911). Although this approach to ethnography was typical of the era, its inherently speculative nature combined with Hudson's tendency to not identify his sources and methods makes it particularly difficult to ascertain whether some of his ethnographic passages are reliable.

Even though several of Hudson's research habits may not have facilitated achieving his ethnographic goal of documenting the totality of Potter Valley Pomo culture, they proved a productive strategy for collecting ethnobotanical information. Amidst his ever-growing vocabulary lists, frequent entries were plants and items of material culture made with plants. Following the model of culture as inventory, he gradually recorded an astounding diversity of ethnobotanical entries. Similarly, at a time when collecting Pomoan basketry was very popular among affluent enthusiasts with aesthetic or scholarly interests (Cohodas 1997), Hudson set himself apart by systematically collecting and documenting an unparalleled diversity of materials, weaves, forms, and functions. Also, many of his topics pertained to privileged cultural domains rarely evident in comparable ethnobotanical treatments from that time in California anthropology (e.g., Barrows 1900; Bocek 1984; Chestnut 1902; Merrill 1923; Timbrook 2007).

Hudson's exceptional access to ethnobotanical information seems to have derived from what he described as the "privileges of friendship" he enjoyed with the Potter Valley Pomo. An ongoing interrelationship between Hudson's research and his in-laws' longtime friendships with their indigenous Potter Valley neighbors is evident in the recurrence of themes, images, and people in his ethnographic writings and their creative writings, photographs, and paintings. For example, many of Hudson's consultants also were featured in his wife's paintings and in parents-in-law's photography. Several of these individuals included "Squealing Charlie" Brown, who appeared as "wild man" at the 1894 California Midwinter International Exposition in San Francisco, Jeff ("Powly") Dick and his wife Joseppa Batty, a noted basket maker, Captain Jack, Jennie and John Miller, John Scott, and Tony Me-tok (Figures 3, 4, 5, and 6). Like his in-laws, Hudson also developed close personal relationships with these people and was fondly remembered by them for generously lending money and providing clothes, food, and legal advice.

Initially mediated through the Carpenter's friendships with their native Potter Valley neighbors, Hudson's ethnographic study also benefitted from his own personal and organic relationships with them. These circumstances contributed to the longevity of Hudson's research activities, which spanned over four decades in an era when most anthropological fieldwork in California was accomplished during brief excursions to distant sites. For example, Chestnut's influential study of indigenous ethnobotany in Mendocino County was conducted during just five short visits between 1892 and 1898 (Chestnut 1902). Hudson's enduring focus on a single native community stands out in contrast to Chestnut and other

Figure 3. Pomoan dancers, circa 1895. "Squealing Charlie" Brown in middle, wearing white clothes. Photograph by A. O. Carpenter. Original in the collections of Grace Hudson Museum, Ukiah, California.

Figure 4. Captain Jack Napoleon, Pinoleville, circa 1895. Photograph by A.O. or H.M. Carpenter. Original in the collections of Grace Hudson Museum, Ukiah, California.

Figure 5. John Miller drilling clamshells, Pinoleville Rancheria, circa 1895. Original in the collections of Grace Hudson Museum, Ukiah, California.

Figure 6. Tony Me-tok. Photograph by H.M. Carpenter. Original in the collections of Grace Hudson Museum, Ukiah, California.

scholars of the era who often erroneously blurred the distinctions between Pomoan languages and communities (e.g., Barrett 1908b, 1917a; Freeland 1923; Kroeber 1911; Loeb 1926; Powers 1872; Purdy 1902).

The strengths of Hudson's research circumstances and the limitations of some of his methods are simultaneously evident in his unpublished and unsystematized ethnobotanical data. In order to render this information more accessible and thereby facilitate appreciation of its important contributions, I traced Hudson's plant identifications through historical floras and online databases to associate them with contemporary scientific taxa to the most specific degree of classification possible (Table 2).Vascular plant nomenclature follows *The Jepson Manual, Second Edition* (Baldwin et al. 2012), as systematized in The Jepson Online Interchange: California Floristics (Jepson Flora Project 2012b). Nonvascular plant names (algae, fungi, and lichens) follow Abbott and Hollenberg (1976), Arora (1986), and Tavares (1997). To help resolve Hudson's imprecise common names (for example, "firs" or "acorn") and scientific names (for example, "Allium" or "Angelica"), I cross-referenced possible taxa with information regarding their historical and contemporary distributions in Mendocino and Lake Counties (Calflora 2012).

I also included in my analyses ethnobotanical data from the scant published sources that explicitly address the Northern Pomo from Potter Valley. John Hudson and his mother-in-law, Helen Carpenter, published several articles about the Potter Valley Pomo (H. M. Carpenter 1893a, b, 1899; Hudson 1893, 1897, 1900a, b). According to Hudson, a publication by Powers (1877) presented data partially collected in 1872 in a large settlement at the southern end of Potter Valley. Barrett (1908a) and Stewart (1943) also presented some information regarding Potter Valley. Gifford and Kroeber (1937) include data from several Potter Valley Pomo consultants in their comparison of material culture elements among Pomoan groups. Additionally, Chestnut (1902) published ethnobotanical data that was partially collected from former residents of Potter Valley. The Potter Valley plant information from these sources helped fill in some gaps in Hudson's data and thereby improve the scope of my findings.

After systematizing all available data according to contemporary scientific name, I tabulated them according to multiple variables including botanical family, plant community (vegetation type), and plant use category. The distribution of taxa by plant community follows the *CalFlora Database* (2012), which is based on Munz and Keck (1973), Lum (1975), and Walker (1992). Plant use categories (Table 3) were loosely adapted from Moerman (1998).

In quantifying my results, I conservatively counted only the most unambiguously identified taxa for each plant entry, which I refer to henceforth as primary taxa. For example, Hudson evidently used the word "angelica" for several taxa in the genera *Angelica* and *Lomatium*, but only *Angelica californica*, *Angelica tomentosa*, and *Lomatium utriculatum* could be specifically identified from Hudson's notes. In this case, I included only these three species in my tabulations. In another example, I only counted the single entry *Anthemis* sp. because Hudson's use of the common name dog fennel did not permit more specific identifi-

Table 2. Scientific name changes, showing Hudson's terms, updated taxa, and bibliographical sources used.

Hudson's term	Updated taxon	Sources used
Aesculus glabra	Aesculus californica	(Jepson Flora Project 2012b)
Agoseris plebia (plebeja)	Agoseris grandiflora	(USDA and NRCS 2012)
Alnus californica	Alnus rhombifolia	(Nuttall 1842)
Angelica tomentosa	Angelica californica	(Jepson Flora Project 2012b)
Asclepias mexicana	Asclepias fascicularis	(USDA and NRCS 2012)
Baccharis douglasii	Baccharis glutinosa	(Jepson Flora Project 2012b)
Baccharis viminea	Baccharis salicifolia	(USDA and NRCS 2012)
Beckmannia erucaeformis	Beckmannia syzigachne	(USDA and NRCS 2012)
Brevortia (Brevoortia) ida-maia	Dichelostemma ida-maia	(USDA and NRCS 2012)
Brodiaea capitata	Dichelostemma capitatum	(USDA and NRCS 2012)
Brodiaea congesta	Dichelostemma congestum	(USDA and NRCS 2012)
Brodiaea grandiflora	Brodiaea coronaria, Brodiaea terrestris	(Munz and Keck 1973)
Brodiaea laxa	Triteleia laxa	(USDA and NRCS 2012)
Bromus marginatus	Bromus carinatus	(Jepson Flora Project 2012a)
Bromus maximus	Bromus diandrus	(USDA and NRCS 2012)
Calandrinia menziesii	Calandrinia ciliata	(Jepson Flora Project 2012a; USDA and NRCS 2012)
Calochortus venustus	Calochortus luteus, Calochortus superbus	(Jepson Flora Project 2012a)
Carem kelloggii, Carum kelloggii	Perideridia kelloggii	(Moerman 1998; The Plant List 2012)
Castanopsis chrysophyla	Chrysolepis chrysophylla	(USDA and NRCS 2012)
Caucalis microcarpa	Yabea microcarpa	(Jepson Flora Project 2012b)
Cercocarpus parvifol (parvifolius)	Cercocarpus betuloides	(Jepson 1936)
Cogswellia utriculata	Lomatium utriculatum	(Moerman 1998; The Plant List 2012)
Cornus californica	Cornus sericea	(Hrusa and Calflora 2001)
Corylus rostrata	Corylus cornuta ssp. californica	(Jepson Flora Project 2012b)
Crataegus rivularis	Crataegus gaylussacia	(Jepson Flora Project 2012b; Jepson 1925; G. L. Smith and Wheeler 1992)
Dentaria californica	Cardamine californica	(Jepson Flora Project 2012b)
Diplacus glutinosus	Mimulus aurantiacus	(Jepson Flora Project 2012a; USDA and NRCS 2012)
Drudeophyton kelloggii	Tauschia kelloggii	(Munz and Keck 1973)
Echinocystis sp.	Marah sp.	(Hitchcock et al. 1959)
Epilobium paniculatum	Epilobium brachycarpum	(Jepson Flora Project 2012b)
Eremocarpus setigerus	Croton setiger	(Jepson Flora Project 2012b)
Erythronium gigantea (giganteum)	Erythronium californicum	(Jepson Flora Project 2012b; The Plant List 2012)
Fragaria californica	Fragaria vesca	(USDA and NRCS 2012)
Fritillaria mutica	Fritillaria affinis	(USDA and NRCS 2012)
Gnaphalium californicum	Pseudognaphalium californicum	(Jepson Flora Project 2012b)
Godetia lindleyii	Clarkia amoena	(Best 1996; Jepson Flora Project 2012b)
Hemizonia luzulifolia	Hemizonia congesta	(USDA and NRCS 2012)
Heracleum lanatum	Heracleum maximum	(Jepson Flora Project 2012b)
Hesperoscordum lacteum	Triteleia hyacinthina	(Jepson Flora Project 2012b; Jepson 1909; Moerman 1998)
Hookera coronaria	Brodiaea coronaria	(Moerman 1998; Yanovsky 1936)
Iris cal. (californica)	Iris macrosiphon	(USDA and NRCS 2012)
Juncus effusus	Juncus exiguus, Juncus laccatus	(Jepson Flora Project 2012b)
Kotolo (common name)	Asclepias eriocarpa	(Calflora 2012; Chestnut 1902)
Lathyrus watsonii	Lathyrus jepsonii	(USDA and NRCS 2012)
Lepiota americana	Leucoagaricus americanus	(Vellinga 2000)
Lolium temulentum	Festuca temulenta	(Jepson Flora Project 2012b)
Lupinus micranthus	Lupinus bicolor	(Jepson Flora Project 2012a; USDA and NRCS 2012)
Madia densifolia	Madia elegans	(Jepson Flora Project 2012b; The Plant List 2012)

Table 2 continued.

Hudson's term	Updated taxon	Sources used
Mesembryanthemum aequilaterale (aequilaterus)	*Carpobrotus chilensis*	(Jepson Flora Project 2012a)
Micromeria chamissonis	*Clinopodium douglasii*	(Jepson Flora Project 2012a; USDA and NRCS 2012)
Montia perfoliata	*Claytonia perfoliata*	(USDA and NRCS 2012)
Morchella crassipes	*Morchella esculenta*	(Arora 1986)
Nemophila insignis	*Nemophila menziesii*	(Munz and Keck 1973)
Nicotiana biglovii (bigelovii)	*Nicotiana quadrivalvis*	(Jepson Flora Project 2012b)
Nymphaea polysepala	*Nuphar polysepala*	(Jepson Flora Project 2012a; USDA and NRCS 2012)
Oenothera ovata	*Taraxia ovata*	(Jepson Flora Project 2012b)
Orthocarpus purburascens (purpurascens)	*Castilleja exserta*	(Jepson Flora Project 2012a)
Peucedanum utriculata (utriculatum)	*Lomatium utriculatum*	(Jepson 1936)
Psoralia (Psoralea) macrostachya	*Hoita macrostachya*	(Jepson Flora Project 2012b)
Quamasia leichtlinti	*Camassia leichtlinii, Camassia quamash*	(Coville 1897)
Quercus densiflora (densiflorus)	*Notholithocarpus densiflorus*	(Jepson Flora Project 2012b)
Ranunculus bloomerii	*Ranunculus orthorhynchus*	(USDA and NRCS 2012)
Ranunculus eisenii	*Ranunculus occidentalis*	(USDA and NRCS 2012)
Rhamnus californica	*Frangula californica*	(Jepson Flora Project 2012b)
Rhamnus crocea	*Rhamnus ilicifolia*	(Jepson Flora Project 2012b)
Rhamnus purshiana	*Frangula purshiana*	(Jepson Flora Project 2012b)
Rhus canadensis trilobata, Rhus trilobata canadensis	*Rhus aromatica*	(IPNI 2012; Jepson Flora Project 2012b)
Rubus vitifolius	*Rubus ursinus*	(Jepson Flora Project 2012b)
Salidago cal. (californica)	*Solidago velutina*	(Jepson Flora Project 2012b)
Salix hindsiana, Salix sesselifolia hindsiana	*Salix exigua*	(Jepson Flora Project 2012b)
Salix nigra	*Salix gooddingii*	(Munz and Keck 1973)
Sambucus glauca	*Sambucus nigra* ssp. *caerulea*	(Jepson Flora Project 2012a; USDA and NRCS 2012)
Saururaceae californica	*Anemopsis californica*	(Jepson Flora Project 2012b)
Scirpus campestris	*Bolboschoenus robustus*	(Fernald 1900; Jepson Flora Project 2012b)
Scirpus lacustris	*Schoenoplectus acutus* var. *occidentalis*	(Jepson Flora Project 2012b; S. G. Smith 1995)
Scirpus maritimus	*Bolboschoenus maritimus*	(Jepson Flora Project 2012b)
Scirpus robustus	*Bolboschoenus robustus*	(Jepson Flora Project 2012b)
Scorzonella maxima	*Microseris laciniata*	(Best 1996; Moerman 1998)
Scorzonella procer	*Microseris laciniata*	(Best 1996; Moerman 1998)
Sitanion elymoides	*Elymus elymoides*	(USDA and NRCS 2012)
Symphoricarpos racemosus	*Symphoricarpos mollis*	(Jepson Flora Project 2012b; Munz and Keck 1973)
Thallictrum polyca. (polycarpum)	*Thalictrum fendleri*	(Jepson Flora Project 2012b)
Trifolium tridentatum	*Trifolium willdenovii*	(Jepson Flora Project 2012b)
Trifolium virescens	*Trifolium fucatum*	(Jepson Flora Project 2012b; Moerman 1998)
Urtica californica	*Urtica dioica*	(USDA and NRCS 2012)
Urtica loyalii (lyallii)	*Urtica dioica*	(USDA and NRCS 2012)
Vaccinium oviflorum, Vaccinium ovifolia	*Vaccinium ovatum*	(Jepson Flora Project 2012a; USDA and NRCS 2012)
Viscum album	*Phoradendron villosum*	(Chestnut 1902; Hawksworth and Scharpf 2007)
Zigadenus micranthus	*Toxicoscordion fontanum, Toxicoscordion micranthum*	(Jepson Flora Project 2012b)
Zigadenus venenosus	*Toxicoscordion venenosum*	(Jepson Flora Project 2012b)

Table 3. Plant use categories and descriptions. Adapted from Moerman (1998).

Plant use category	Description
Abortifacient	Substance used to induce abortion.
Adhesive	Glue or gum used to bind other materials.
Analgesic	Remedy for pain (***ko o'***).
Antidiarrheal	Remedy for diarrhea.
Antihemorrhagic	Remedy for internal bleeding.
Antirheumatic	Internal or external treatment for rheumatism, stiffness, pain, or swelling in the muscles or joints.
Antispasmodic	Remedy used to prevent or treat spasms.
Architecture	Material used in the construction of buildings.
Arrow	Material used in the manufacture of arrows used for unspecified purposes. For materials used in arrows with specific applications, see hunting items, fowling items, and game and contest items.
Asthma remedy	Remedy for asthma.
Basketry	Material used in basketry.
Beverage	Product consumed as a beverage or used in preparing a beverage.
Bow	Material used to manufacture bows used for unspecified purposes. For materials used in bows with specific applications, see hunting items, fowling items, and game and contest items.
Bread	Ingredient used for breads or cakes.
Brush or broom	Material used in the manufacture of hair brushes, utility brushes, combs, or brooms.
Bulb or corm food	Bulb or corm that was cooked and eaten as an "Indian potato".
Burn dressing	Substance used to treat burns.
Cathartic	Remedy used to evacuate the bowels.
Ceremony	Material used in ceremony or in the manufacture of items used in ceremony.
Cleaning agent	Soap or other product used to sterilize, clean, or disinfect (but not as a medical treatment for infections).
Clothing	Product used as clothing or in the manufacture of clothing.
Cold remedy	Remedy for colds, cough, or bronchitis.
Colorant	Material used to paint, dye, or color objects.
Communication	Material used in the manufacture of communication devices.
Confection	Product consumed as a candy or sweet.
Container	Material used in the manufacture of vessels, cups, bowls, mortars, pots, or trenchers.
Cooked green	Foliage or stem portion that was cooked and eaten.
Cooking	Material used in food preparation or cooking.
Cordage	Fiber material used for thread, string, rope, or binding.
Counterirritant	Substance used to induce local irritation in order to treat general irritation.
Decoration	Material used in jewelry, body ornamentation, tattooing, or masks.
Dermatological aid	Material used to treat skin conditions.
Disinfectant	Material used as a medical treatment for infections.
Diuretic	Remedy used to increase urine flow.
Divination and doctoring	Item used in curing, divination, or other activities associated with native doctors.
Emetic	Remedy used to induce vomiting.
Emollient	Material used to soften or smooth the skin.
Eye medicine	Remedy used to treat eye conditions.
Febrifuge	Remedy for fevers.
Fiber	Fiber material used for unspecified purposes. Fibers used for specified purposes are included elsewhere.
Fire	Material used to produce fire or for burning.
First aid	Remedy used to treat minor cuts (***shy ba tcher kon***), sores (***shy ba ba choon***), boils (***shy ba cha han***), or bruises (***ya pecho***).
Fishing	Material used for fishing or in the manufacture of fishing devices.
Flavoring	Spice or condiment used to enhance the flavor of other foods.
Food	Unspecified ingredient or food item. Specific foods are included elsewhere.
Fowling	Material used for fowling or in the manufacture of fowling devices.
Fragrance	Substance used as deodorant or perfume.
Fruit food	Fleshy fruit consumed fresh or after minimal processing.
Fungus food	Mushroom consumed as food.

Table 3 continued.

Plant use category	Description
Gaming and competition	Material used in gaming, competition, or in the manufacture of gaming or competition instruments.
Gastrointestinal aid	Remedy for nausea, abdominal pains, or indigestion.
Hair treatment	Substance used to stimulate hair growth or vigor.
Host plant	Plant functioning as a primary home or habitat for other useful plants, animals, or fungi.
Hunting	Material used in hunting or trapping, including charms and other aids.
Insecticide	Substance used to kill insects.
Laxative	Remedy used to accelerate defecation.
Legend	Plant or plant product appearing in legend, oral history, or tales.
Leprosy treatment	Product used to treat leprosy (*bi-ko' bi-ko' du-tal'*).
Matting or bedding	Material used in preparing woven mats, floor coverings, or bed padding.
Medicine	Remedy used for unspecified purposes. Remedies used for specified purposes are included elsewhere.
Mush	Food consumed as mush.
Music	Material used in the manufacture of musical instruments.
Narcotic	Substance used to induce sleep or stupor.
Nut food	Nut product that was eaten raw or after minimal processing.
Packing or carrying	Material used to assist in carrying or transporting loads.
Padding or toweling	Absorbent material used for padding or wrapping.
Panacea	Remedy used to treat a great number of diseases, a cure-all.
Pediatric aid	Material or substance related to the promotion of children's health.
Poison	Substance with the potential to harm or kill a person (*ka-li kom*).
Polish	Substance used to smooth or shine the surfaces of tools or implements.
Psychiatric aid	Substance used to treat mental disorders.
Root food	Root that was eaten raw or cooked.
Salad food	Foliage or stem portions that were eaten fresh as salad.
Salt	Material used in obtaining or preparing salt.
Sea vegetable	Edible seaweed.
Seed food	Seed or grain that was parched and ground into pinole.
Smoking	Smoking substance or material used for smoking paraphernalia.
Snakebite remedy	Remedy used to treat snakebite.
Spirituality	Product with spiritual or "psychic" qualities (*xa*).
STD remedy	Remedy used to treat sexually transmitted diseases, such as gonorrhea or syphilis.
Stimulant	Product used to temporarily increase alertness.
Timekeeping	Instrument used to monitor or tell time.
Tool	Device used for utilitarian purposes such as cutting, digging, climbing, and woodworking.
Trade	Material used in barter or trade.
Ulcer remedy	Remedy used to treat external ulcers.
War	Instrument or object used in battle.
Watercraft	Material used in the manufacture of canoes or paddles.
Women's health	Substance considered to affect women's health, including remedies related to menstruation, pregnancy, or motherhood.

cation, even though it is possible he referred to several members of the genera *Anthemis* and *Chamaemelum*. Taxonomic notes are provided for plant entries that might be associated with additional local taxa (Chapter 5).

In addition to systematizing Hudson's botanical references, I also standardized his transcriptions of Northern Pomo plant names. Available published and archival materials regarding the Northern Pomo language (McLendon 1973; O'Connor 1990, 1992) were insufficient to permit updating Hudson's inconsistent transcriptions according to contemporary linguistic conventions for Northern Pomo. Accordingly, I reproduce native plant names as Hudson wrote them, if available. If Hudson wrote multiple versions of a single Northern Pomo plant name (for example, ***bu-ta' ba-ă***, ***bu-ta' ba-a***, and ***bu'-ta ba-a'*** for *Avena* spp.), I selected the most frequent or consistent form. It was not possible to determine whether these variations were due to transcription inconsistency, phonological variation, or lexical synonymy. When different native names were given for the same plant (for example, ***ca tai' ka-lĭ'*** and ***lau lau ka-di'*** for *Bromus carinatus*), I present all.

The resultant reconstruction of Potter Valley ethnobotany serves as the basis for my presentation in the chapters that follow. In the next chapter, I draw on these findings to discuss Potter Valley Pomo society and its historical relationship to the local landscape, giving special attention to the specific plant communities they utilized, the annual subsistence cycle, and traditional ecological knowledge and landscape management. In subsequent chapters, I discuss circumstances following the arrival of non-indigenous peoples in the region and systematically present the results of my ethnobotanical reconstructions by taxon and plant use category.

3. Cultural and Physical Landscapes

Pomoan Ethno-linguistic Groups

For over a century the term Pomo has been used by anthropologist and linguists to refer to socioculturally diverse indigenous peoples and their descendants from coastal regions of present-day Sonoma, Mendocino, and Lake Counties in Northern California who spoke (many still speak) seven distinct languages in the Pomoan family: Southern Pomo, Kashaya (Southwestern Pomo), Central Pomo, Northern Pomo, Eastern Pomo, Southeastern Pomo, and Northeastern Pomo (Halpern 1964; McLendon 1973; Oswalt 1964).

Before the arrival of non-indigenous settlers, the Northern Pomo population of about 5000 (Cook 1956) lived in communities within in an area extending along about 35 km of coast and reaching about 80 km inland. This was the northern-most Pomoan group, bordered to the south by the Central Pomo, to the east by the Eastern Pomo, and to the north by Yukian groups. Most Northern Pomo communities were located in the small valleys in the upper Russian River watershed. There were no permanent Northern Pomo settlements along the coast until the latter part of the nineteenth century (McLendon and Oswalt 1978).

Although these neighboring peoples shared many cultural and linguistic similarities, they had no single integrating political or social institutions, with the possible exception of certain ritualistic and trade activities (Barrett 1908a; Gifford and Kroeber 1937; McLendon and Oswalt 1978; Peri et al. 1985a). Additionally, no native word referred collectively to the entire set of peoples now called Pomo (Gifford and Kroeber 1937). The basic politically autonomous group was the local community or "tribelet," often consisting of several associated localized settlements or villages (Gifford and Kroeber 1937).

The manner in which these distinct and politically autonomous peoples came to be identified by a single term and thought of as a cultural unit involved a series of scholarly inaccuracies beginning in the 1850's. Pomo is an Anglicized version of two distinct Northern Pomo words (cf. McLendon and Oswalt 1978). The first, *Po'-mo* (following John Hudson's orthography), means "red magnesite mine" and refers specifically to the southernmost Pomoan village in Potter Valley, which controlled a nearby red magnesite (*po'*) mine and charged payment from members of other settlements for its use. The second word, *po'-ma*, is a designation for "those who live at" or "people" (cf. Kroeber 1925). In reference to the southernmost village in Potter Valley, for example, the two terms can be combined to designate "red magnesite mine people" (*Po'-mo po'-ma*). From Hudson's account, it appears that neither word has significance in any of the other six Pomoan languages. The native terms *Po'-mo* and *po'-ma*, each with its distinct meaning in Northern Pomo, appear to have come into general use at different times by non-indigenous peoples. In the nineteenth century local non-indigenous settlers used the term "Pomo" for residents of the southernmost Potter Valley village and "Poma" for the indigenous residents of Potter Valley. Subsequently, Stephen Powers (1872) popularized the use of "Pomo" for all of the peoples in the region who spoke related languages despite their sociocultural distinctiveness. This historical expansion of applicability of the word Pomo beyond a single Potter Valley settlement was accompanied by an anthropological tendency in the late 1800s and early 1900s to treat them as a socioculturally uniform tribe or ethnic group with a single language (e.g., Barrett 1905, 1908a; Dixon and Kroeber 1903, 1919; Gifford 1923; Hudson 1893; Kroeber 1911; Loeb 1926).

Potter Valley Pomo Settlements and Subsistence

According to a Potter Valley Pomo oral history account recorded by Hudson, the people first arrived in the region destitute at the headwaters of the Eel River (*Tce-dyu'*) from across mountains to the northeast (Figure 7). Fleeing from an enemy group (*Tou-maí-ya*) on the slopes of Mount Sanhedrin, they escaped by way of Tomki Creek (*Pǎ-bi-dǎ*) to the valleys of the Russian River, where they encountered small and agile men with "horrid" tattoos on their bodies and faces. These enemies were so cruel that the mythological being Coyote (*Du-wi'*) intervened by driving them away or turning them into beasts. The Russian River basin was then a busy travelling route and was occupied in its more distant stretches by at least two different indigenous peoples. After settling for some time in valleys near Clear Lake and Little Lake (*Bi-tam'kai*), small successive bands travelled up the well-worn Tomki Creek trail and headed eastward over a low divide. Following a stream down to its mouth at the warm, verdant, and secluded shores of Coyote Lake (*Du-wi ka'-mo*) in Potter Valley, they settled in peace and prospered in the valley's abundance.

According to Helen Carpenter (n.d.), there was "not a prettier nor more fertile valley any where in the mountains of the Coast Range." Located in the central portion of the North Coast Range, Potter Valley (elevation 275 to 400 m) is situated between a mountainous area with prominent peaks reaching about 2100 m to the east and a series of rolling hills to the west. From the valley flow the headwaters of the East Fork of the Russian River, which becomes a principal watershed in Sonoma County. The water table and deep alluvial soils of the valley floor suggest it was once a lake (Shelton 1986; G.L. Smith and Wheeler 1992; Watson and Pendleton 1916). Consistent with these scientific characterizations, Northern Pomo place names provide evidence of retained linguistic knowledge of very different local geomorphological conditions in the past, when Potter Valley contained a lake and surrounding mountainous areas were less eroded (Table 4).

Members of the Potter Valley community called themselves *Tcǎ ma-po'* ("persons from red earth") and neighboring groups called them *Ba-lo'kai*, which Hudson translated as "sprouting valley" and other scholars translated as "verdant valley" and "wild oat valley" (Kroeber 1925; Palmer 1880; Powers 1877). The Potter Valley Pomo population of up to 2500 spoke a

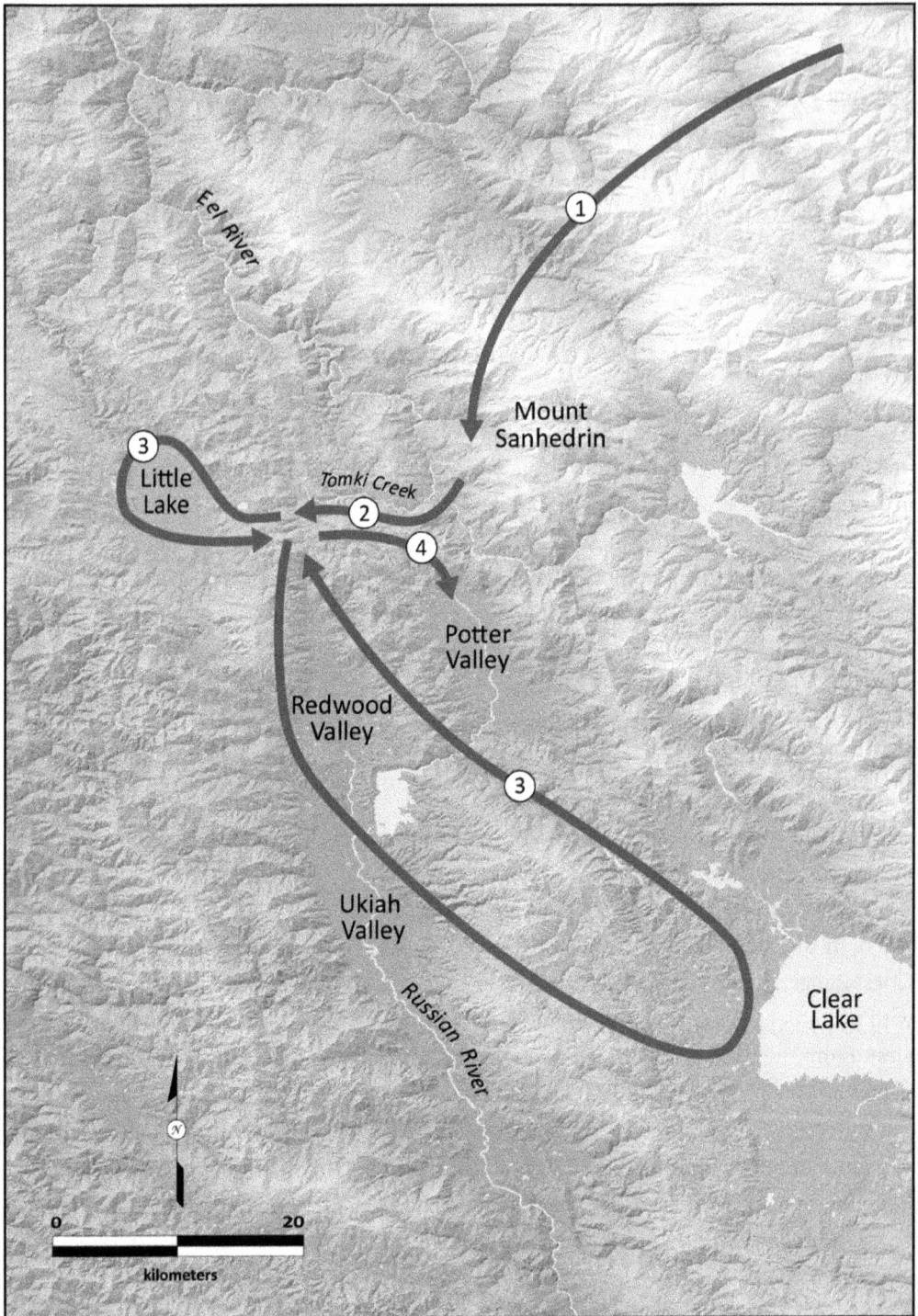

Figure 7. Migration routes to Potter Valley. Adapted from J. W. Hudson's unpublished account of Potter Valley Pomo oral history

Table 4. Northern Pomo place names indicating past geomorphological transformations. Adapted from J. W. Hudson's unpublished writings.

Northern Pomo place name	Translation	Current geomorphological condition	Location
Du-wi ka'-mo	"Coyote Lake"	Alluvial valley floor	Potter Valley
Ka'-mi-dal	"waters burst forth"	Calm riverway	Russian River at its exit from Ukiah Valley
Yo'-ca ko'-lo mai	"salmon spawning bed"	Valley "depression"	Coyote Valley
Da-no lok'-tăm	"mountain fell-in"	Gradual mountain pass	Between Cold Creek basin and Upper Blue Lake
Cu-nal do'-di mai	"boats built there"	Agricultural field	Lower Potter Valley

distinct dialect of Northern Pomo with slight variations between the forms spoken by residents of the valley's five politically independent main settlements (Figure 8).[‡] Located along the banks of the Russian River, each primary settlement had from 200 to 800 residents living in irregularly positioned thatched dwellings. The settlement *Ca-nĕl'* ("assembly chamber") had the only ceremonial house in the valley, which was shared by all Potter Valley Pomo. The other primary settlements were *Se-ĕl'-la* ("brush lodge"), *Se-e' dam* ("whitish thicket"), *Ka-lĕ'-sa-ma* ("tree bough lodge"), and *Po'-mo* ("red magnesite mine"). Additionally, each of these main villages had several smaller politically affiliated satellite settlements.

With access to enormously varied natural resources in the diverse botanical landscape of Potter Valley and neighboring lands (Figure 9), the Potter Valley Pomo subsisted substantially on local resources. In the late nineteenth century the alluvial valley floor (*kai'*) was dominated by grasslands interspersed with valley oak trees (*Quercus lobata*), suggesting a foothill woodland plant community (Shelton 1986). Also called valley oak woodlands, this type of vegetation type is widespread in Mendocino County foothills and valleys up to 900 m (Figure 10). Dominated by mature valley oak trees and other oak species with edible acorns (including *Quercus agrifolia*, *Q. chrysolepis*, and *Q. douglasii*), this type of vegetation also included such culturally important trees as California bay (*Umbellularia californica*), bigleaf maple (*Acer macrophyllum*), and Oregon ash (*Fraxinus latifolia*). Closely associated with these woodlands, riparian forests bordering the Russian River and smaller creeks (*bi da*) in Potter Valley provided diverse plant and animal resources (Figure 11). In addition to oaks, these forests contain such highly valued plants as bigleaf maple, Oregon ash, alders (*Alnus* spp.), Fremont's cottonwood (*Populus fremontii*), willow (*Salix* spp.), bulrushes (*Bolboschoenus* spp.), tule (*Schoenoplectus acutus* var. *occidentalis*),

The food sources along the Russian River were as great and as varied as in any section of California, and ample to support double the native population of 1850.

– John W. Hudson

[‡] Other sources identified just three primary settlements and made smaller population estimates (H. M. Carpenter 1899; Cook 1956; Kroeber 1925; Stewart 1943).

Figure 8. Indigenous village sites in Potter Valley and vicinity, 1908. Adapted from Barrett (1908a).

cattail (*Typha latifolia*), and sedges (*Carex* spp.). The dense riparian vegetation (**ca-pa'**) also provided access to abundant animal resources, being used by approximately 90% of the local woodland wildlife species (Allen-Diaz et al. 2007).

Varying microclimatically between north-facing slopes with moderate coastal influence to south-facing mountainsides with montane influence, vegetation cover in the landscape surrounding Potter Valley was highly varied. To the northeast and southeast, tall slopes (**ca-**

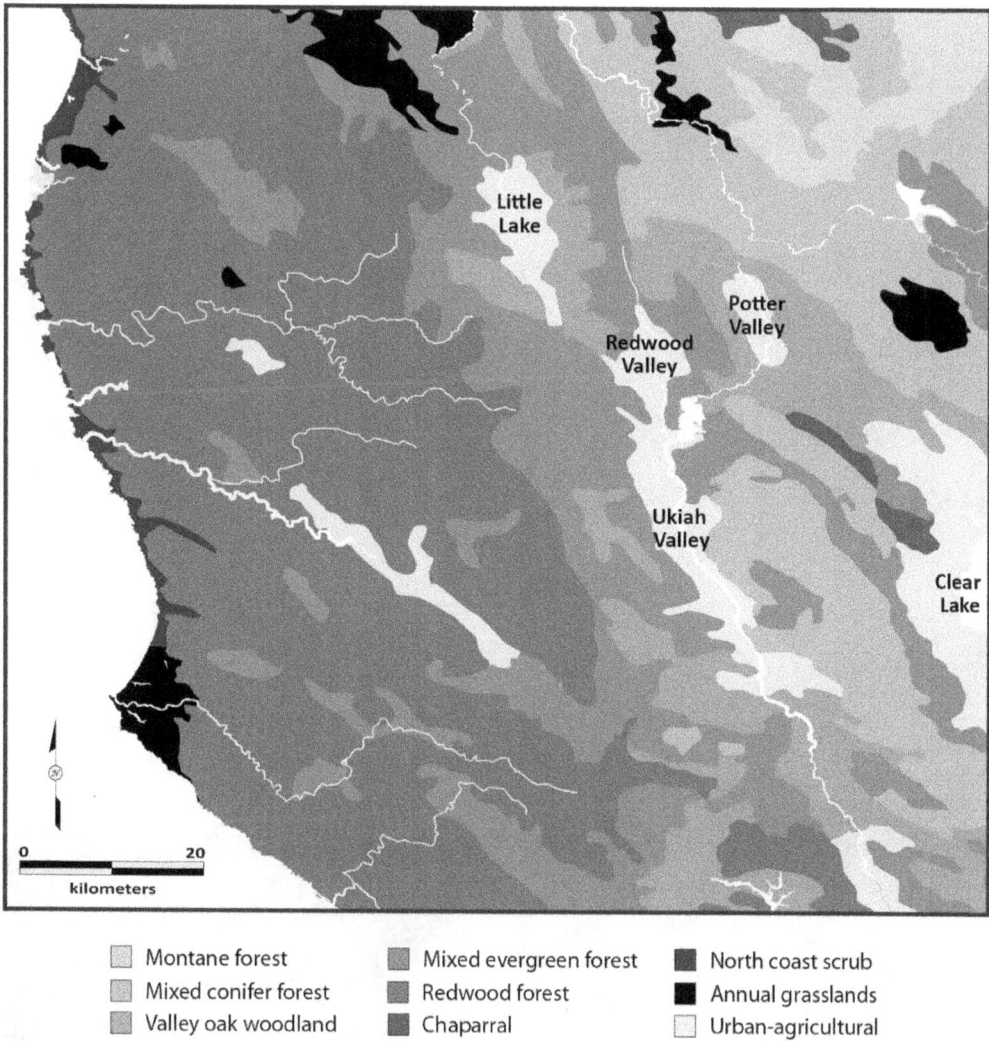

Figure 9. Approximate contemporary distributions of plant communities in lands historically frequented by the Potter Valley Pomo. Adapted from ICE MAPS (1997).

de'), ridges (*she de*), and mountains (*da-no'*) (600 to 900 m) supported chaparral vegetation (*hai-i-o'*) at lower elevations and mixed conifer forests at higher elevations (Figure 12). The Potter Valley Pomo preferred to avoid chaparral unless cleared by recent fire because they considered it to be the home of spirits and dangerous animals, such as mountain lions (*Felis concolor*). Nevertheless, many foods and materials were collected from such chaparral shrubs as chamise (*Adenostoma fasciculatum*), toyon (*Heteromeles arbutifolia*), California coffeeberry (*Frangula californica*), oaks (*Quercus* spp.), mountain mahoganies (*Cercocarpus* spp.), Klamath plum (*Prunus subcordata*), California lilacs (*Ceanothus* spp.), and manzanitas (*Arctostaphylos* spp.). In stark contrast to the dense chaparral, higher elevation mixed conifer

Figure 10. Foothill (valley oak) woodland, North Coast Range, California, 2012. Photograph by Chris K. Kjeldsen.

Figure 11. Riparian wetland, North Coast Range, California, 2008. Photograph by Chris K. Kjeldsen.

Figure 12. Mixed conifer succession, North Coast Range, California, 2012. Photograph by Chris K. Kjeldsen.

forests, also known as yellow pine forests, were typically open and patchy before fire suppression became widespread in California in the nineteenth century (Barbour and Minnich 2000). Among the mixed conifer trees used by the Potter Valley Pomo were ponderosa pine (*Pinus ponderosa*), sugar pine (*Pinus lambertiana*), white fir (*Abies concolor*), Douglas fir (*Pseudotsuga menziesii*), and black oak (*Quercus kelloggii*).

Hudson reported that in the late nineteenth century tanoak trees (*Notholithocarpus densiflorus*) were rare in the valley and their prized acorns were sought in the mountains to the west. The vegetation on these low hills (**bi cu' ta ko**) and mountains (reaching 450 m) includes mixed evergreen forests, which become more widespread towards the coast. Some of the dominant trees in these hills frequently used by the Potter Valley Pomo were Douglas fir, tanoak, canyon live oak (*Quercus chrysolepis*), madrone (*Arbutus menziesii*), and giant chinquapin (*Chrysolepis chrysophylla*).

With access to abundant local plant resources, the Potter Valley Pomo did not migrate seasonally to the coast as was typical of other Northern Pomo communities. Rather, small groups made brief collecting excursions to inland areas controlled by other Pomoan peoples and enemy groups and coastal portions of Pomoan and Miwok lands. Their inland travels included fishing trips to Clear Lake in the eastern portion of Pomoan lands and visits to other locations with mineral salt, magnesite, and obsidian deposits. Once dug from an inland mine along Stony Creek in present-day Colusa County, in the nineteenth century salt was collected with greater frequency at the ocean (Barrett 1952; Stewart 1943).

Experienced, well armed men only were chosen, for the salt was owned by hereditary enemies, the **Co ti'-ya** (Eastern natives) of ancient tradition, a **Wĭn-tun'** tribe. The trail from Potter Valley climbed eastward over Pine Mt., kept to ridges beyond Carrott Mt. where it joined the Keyan trail having the same objective; ran atop the water shed to Horse Mt. thence along Widow Craft ridge to Smiths and N.E., ascending toward Snow Mt. to a pass (near 3000 feet) called **Tsi-we ba-lai'-man** (Pass of Blood) near a source of Stony Creek. It was customary during a raid on the salt beds to descend the creek within a mile from the deposit, lie hid in the brush till near midnight, send spies to look for sentinels about the salt; and with favorable report all hands fell to work digging the lumps and crusts and filling their baskets, each load approximating half the weight of its carrier. About two hours was taken to finish and climb out of possible touch, but bows were kept strung and guards awatch till beyond the pass and on down grade homeward.

– John W. Hudson

During the summertime they visited the coast (**ka ma lal**) to collect seafood, seaweed, and other local resources (Stewart 1943). Planning the trips days in advance, every Potter Valley Pomo adult knew the dates of low tides, which were ideal collecting times (Hudson 1897). The walk to the stretch of coast in Northern Pomo territory took about two days, with the first night usually being spent at Orr's Springs (Loeb 1926). One of their other coastal destinations was Bodega Bay, to the south of Northern Pomo territory, where they acquired clamshells, especially Washington clam (*Saxidomus nuttallii*) and Pacific cockle (*Cardium corbis*). The Coast Miwok residents of Bodega Bay allowed Pomoan peoples to freely dig these shells (Loeb 1926), which they used to manufacture disk-shaped beads used as a trade currency ("wampum"). By 1893 their use as currency had been discontinued by all Pomoans except in Potter Valley (Hudson 1897). Whereas the 130 km journey from Potter Valley to Bodega Bay required only two days of travel, the return trip took approximately five days due to the burden of carrying baskets loaded with approximately 60 kg loads of shells, dried fish, and seaweed (Hudson 1897).

During their travels to the coast, the Potter Valley came into contact with numerous plant communities that do not occur in the immediate vicinity of Potter Valley and therefore provided access to an even greater variety of plant resources. For example, on seaward slopes beyond the mixed evergreen forests were redwood forests, closed-cone pine forests, coastal prairies, and freshwater marshes (**ka pa**). Located immediately along the coast were such varied plant communities as north coastal scrub, coastal strand, and salt marshes at the mouths of rivers. Plants from all of these plant communities were known and used by the Potter Valley Pomo even though they occur at greater distances from Potter Valley (see Chapter 5).

The manner in which the Potter Valley Pomo used and interacted with their local botanical landscape varied seasonally during the annual cycle, which was called "passing by" (*tci-mul*) in Northern Pomo. The first new moon after the appearance of the Pleiades constellation (*u-yi-mal' cu-we'*) in autumn marked the beginning of the annual cycle and was occasion for a feast (*ma-a' di-xa'-tcin hai'-tcil*) followed by a four-day festival (*ma a hai tcil*) to celebrate the abundance of the season. This moment also marked the transition between the semiannual seasons "good or plenteous moons" (*da ko-di'*) and "sleeping moons" (*si-mam' da*). Lasting from May to September, "good or plenteous moons" was the joyful and animated time which included the driest and hottest months of the year. In contrast, "sleeping moons" was a time of seclusion and lethargy due to heavy rainfall and cold temperatures that routinely fell below -10° C in the nineteenth century (Palmer 1880). The annual cycle was further divided into the four seasons "foods shaking off" (*ma-ă' tcă-ka*), "green earth" (*ka-tsa' ma*), "verdure complete" (*ka-tsa mĭ'*), and "smoke pall" (*sa-hă nĭm'*), each of which was accompanied by distinct plant resources and a particular set of associated subsistence activities.

Fall ("foods shaking off") was marked by the abundant availability of acorns and buckeyes. Acorns, which served as the primary caloric staple throughout the year, were harvested from oaks and other trees in the Fagaceae family, including giant chinquapin and tanoak. Buckeyes (*Aesculus californica*) were also an important staple food for the Potter Valley Pomo, especially in late winter when few other plant resources were available. Other important plant foods they collected in fall were California bay nuts, California hazelnuts (*Corylus cornuta* var. *californica*), some late-maturing fruits, as well as the first mushrooms of the season.

Between the fall harvest of nuts and fruits and the springtime flush of greens, winter ("green earth") was otherwise a time of restricted food supply. Nevertheless, stored acorns and late maturing buckeyes provided dietary security. As the Northern Pomo name suggests, the coldest part of winter in this portion of Northern California rapidly gives way to lush vegetative growth and a flourishing of available plant foods as spring approaches.

Tremendous diversity of fresh greens became available in springtime ("verdure complete"). The vegetative growth that is first apparent in wintertime reaches maturity in early spring before desiccating with the approach of summer. The availability of clovers (*Trifolium* spp.), which were symbolic of a large class of fresh greens available during this season, marked a dramatic increase in dietary diversity. As springtime vegetative growth slows, many grasses and forbs set seed, providing ample protein and fat rich foods that were often stored

> After a long trek from a hot valley, the cool salt air with fish, shell fish, sea weeds, game and berries as an incentive, made the sojourn on the coast a joyous labor.
>
> – John W. Hudson

The Indian at home had two meals daily, at sunrise and at sunset. But on a journey ate only when opportune. He was omnivorous in his tastes and usually moderate, though in spring he consumed enormous quantities of forage (*tso*).

Nature gave him a capacious digestive apparatus so he could feast or fast without injury.

No food was ever eaten hot, and a spoiled taint in meat was not objectionable.

It is good table manners to eat everything placed before one. If it is not eaten the surplus is carefully wrapped and carried home.

– John W. Hudson

for later use. Also of particular note, bulbs and corms in the Liliaceae and Themidaceae families, commonly called "Indian potatoes" in the nineteenth century, were an abundant seasonal source of energy in springtime.

Summer ("smoke pall") was also a time of diverse plant food availability in Potter Valley, as well as in the coastal and inland areas they visited during this season. In addition to some late maturing seeds and bulbs, summer was accompanied by the ripening of many edible fleshy fruits. A few of these important foods were manzanitas, strawberries (*Fragaria* spp.), gooseberries (*Ribes* spp.), elderberries (*Sambucus* spp.), California huckleberry (*Vaccinium ovatum*), and California wild grape (*Vitis californica*). With the addition of diverse fruits to the already varied diet of summer and early fall, a broad spectrum of foods was consumed in the months leading up to winter.

Plant Classification

The diversity of seasonal plant resources utilized by the Potter Valley Pomo is evident in a rich vocabulary related to plant parts (Table 5) and plant growth processes (Table 6). Deserving special note are the Northern Pomo words for "verdant growth" (*ba-lot'*) and "valley" (*kai'*), which combined to produce the name Hudson translated as "sprouting valley" (*Ba-lo'kai*), used by other Northern Pomo communities for Potter Valley.

The cultural importance of certain classes of plants is reflected in Hudson's linguistic evidence of eight major recurrent categories of plants used for food and other purposes (Table 7). The most general grouping is "branching plant or tree" (*ka-lï'*), associated explicitly or linguistically with diverse trees and smaller plants (Table 8). Many plant names contain this term, as in the case of California wild grape, which was called *bam-tu' ka-lï*. There are several clues as to how the plant category *ka-lï'* functions semantically. Kashaya (Southwestern) Pomo has a cognate term, *qʰale*, which functions at two different taxonomic ranks (Goodrich et al. 1996). As a "unique beginner," which distinguishes life forms at the most basic level (Berlin 1992),

Table 5. Northern Pomo terms for plant parts.

Native term	Plant part
ca pa	Leaves, bough, foliage
ce'-wa	Outer bark
di-san	Brittle limb
ha-a	Kernel
hai	Stick
kah ly'	Wood
ka-li ba ko	Stump
ka-li sha	Limb
ka-li sha se y	Dead tree brush
ka-li sil le	Tree "body"
ka-li u ba wo	Tree "bud"
ka-li yem	Root
ka-li' mi tol	Hollow tree
ka-li' pi-cul'	Treetop
ka-li' si-yan'	Inner bark
ka-li'ce	Tree root
ka-ta	Nut shell
lum	Thorns
ma-hu	Ground "sprouts"
mi-su	Tree trunk
mi-su'	Fallen log
pi-cu'	Apex of coniferous tree
ta la	Seed
tce-do'	Flower
tsi tol	Leaf
tsi-te'	Tree crotch or fork
tso-ol'	Sap or juice

Table 6. Northern Pomo terms for plant growth phases and processes.

Native term	Plant growth process
ba ka' ca man	Wilting of flowers
ba-de'-din	Growth
ba-lo' can	Leafing of annuals
ba-lo' tcin	Sprouting from the ground
ba-lot'	Verdant growth
ba-sat'	Sprouting
ba-si' ba-si'	Budding of trees
batsom	Secondary growth (also, young oak trees)
ca-pa kan	Regrowth of tree foliage
ka-li' ta-bo'	Defoliation
ma ba-lo' tcin	To become verdant
pu ca man	Blossoming
ui ba-wo'	Swelling of buds

q^hale means "plant kingdom." As a "life form" term, used to denote groups at an intermediate rank, it means "tree." Consequently, q^hale may be used to refer broadly to all plants or more narrowly to trees. The widespread appearance of the Northern Pomo term **ka-lǐ** in names for both trees and other plant forms suggests it was similarly used as a designation at both taxonomic ranks. Additionally, **ka-lǐ** was used to the distinguish stem portions of certain plants from their flowering, fruiting, and root portions. For example, the term for California wild grape (**bam-tu' ka-lǐ**) was used both for the whole plant and specifically its vine (stem) portions.

Table 7. Major Northern Pomo plant categories and examples of associated plants.

Category	Translation	Northern Pomo name	Translation	Scientific name
			Example of associated plant	
ba-ă	"seeds"	*bu-ta' ba-ă*	"bear seed"	*Avena* spp.
ba-kai'	"berries"	*du-mak' ba-kai'*	"cinnamon bear berry"	*Prunus virginiana*
bi-nic'	"nuts"	*ca-bă be-nic'*	—	*Corylus cornuta*
bu	"baked bulbs and corms"	*ba'-bă bu*	"grandfather's bulb"	*Brodiaea coronaria*
ka-lĭ'	"branching plant or tree"	*disă' kalĭ'*	"brittle tree"	*Aesculus californica*
ma-lu	"baked greens"	*ka-ai' ka-lĭ ma-lu*	"crow plant" + "baked greens"	*Lupinus bicolor*
tce	"mushroom"	*ka-li' tce e'*	"tree mushroom"	*Armillaria mellea*
tso'	"raw greens"	*tsi-wă' tsŏ*	"varied thrush clover"	*Asclepias* spp.

Table 8. Partial list of taxa associated with the native category "branching plant or tree" (*ka-lĭ'*).

Scientific Name	Common Name
Acer macrophyllum	Bigleaf maple
Adenostoma fasciculatum	Chamise
Aesculus californica	California buckeye
Apocynum cannabinum	Dogbane
Baccharis douglasii	Marsh baccharis
Baccharis salicifolia	Mule fat
Bolboschoenus robustus	Tuberous bulrush
Brassica nigra	Black mustard
Bromus carinatus	California brome
Calycadenia multiglandulosa	Sticky western rosinweed
Castilleja exserta	Owl's clover
Ceanothus spp.	Ceanothus
Ceanothus cuneatus	Wedgeleaf ceanothus
Cercis occidentalis	Buttonbush
Cercocarpus betuloides	Birchleaf mountain mahogany
Cercocarpus ledifolius	Curlleaf mountain mahogany
Chrysolepis chrysophylla	Giant chinquapin
Cornus glabrata	Brown dogwood
Cornus sericea	American dogwood
Crataegus gaylussacia	Suksdorf's hawthorn
Datisca glomerata	Durango root
Eriodictyon californicum	Yerba Santa
Eschscholzia californica	California poppy
Foeniculum vulgare	Fennel
Frangula purshiana	Cascara buckthorn
Fraxinus sp.	Ash
Hemizonia congesta	Hayfield tarweed
Hoita macrostachya	Leather root
Iris douglasiana	Douglas' iris
Iris macrosiphon	Bowltube iris
Iva axillaris	Poverty weed
Lupinus bicolor	Bicolor lupine
Lupinus formosus	Summer lupine
Lupinus nanus	Sky lupine
Madia sativa	Coast tarweed
Mentzelia sp.	Blazingstar
Mimulus aurantiacus	Bush monkeyflower
Navarretia squarrosa	Skunkbush
Nicotiana attenuate	Coyote tobacco
Nicotiana quadrivalvis	Indian tobacco

Table 8 continued.

Scientific Name	Common Name
Notholithocarpus densiflorus	Tanoak
Pinus contorta	Lodgepole pine
Pinus coulteri	Coulter pine
Pinus ponderosa	Ponderosa Pine
Pinus sabiniana	California foothill pine
Populus fremontii	Fremont's cottonwood
Pseudotsuga menziesii	Douglas fir
Quercus agrifolia	Coast live oak
Quercus chrysolepis	Canyon live oak
Quercus douglasii	Blue oak
Quercus dumosa	Nuttall's scrub oak
Quercus garryana	Oregon oak
Quercus kelloggii	California black oak
Quercus lobata	Valley oak
Rhus aromatica	Fragrant sumac
Ribes californicum	California gooseberry
Ribes divaricatum	Spreading gooseberry
Salix exigua	Sandbar willow
Salix gooddingii	Goodding's black willow
Salix laevigata	Red willow
Salix sitchensis	Sitka willow
Schoenoplectus acutus var. *occidentalis*	Common tule
Scrophularia californica	California figwort
Sequoia sempervirens	Coast redwood
Symphoricarpos mollis	Creeping snowberry
Taraxia ovata	Goldeneggs
Taxus brevifolia	Pacific yew
Torreya californica	California nutmeg
Unidentified (**can ka-li**)	—
Unidentified (**ka tsu ka-li**)	—
Unidentified (**lum ka-li**)	—
Verbascum blattaria	Moth mullein
Vitis californica	California wild grape

The other recurrent plant terms, which Hudson identified explicitly in his notes, function as utilization and spiritual categories designating more restricted classes of culturally important plants (Newmaster et al. 2006). In most cases, the native term refers to the principal plant part consumed and appears in the names of many of the associated plants. Seeds (**ba-ă**) were often parched for use in pinole. Many small fruits and berries (**ba-kai'**) and nuts (**bi-nic'**) were consumed fresh (Table 9). Diverse fresh greens and flowers (**tsŏ**) were eaten raw as what Hudson described as relishes, forage, lettuce, or condiments (Table 10). Other plants produced greens (**ma-lŭ**) that were baked or boiled before being eaten (Table 11). Many bulb and corm plants (**bu**) produced edible root vegetables (**ba tum bu**), which were usually prepared by baking or boiling. Some mushrooms (**tce**) were eaten, often being fried with lard on hot stones (Table 12). The "psychic" plants (**xa-nu'**), as Hudson called them, had unique spiritual qualities and were valued for good luck, protection, and curing (Table 13).

Table 9. Plants associated with the native category "berries" (*ba-kai'*).

Scientific Name	Common Name
Amelanchier alnifolia	Saskatoon serviceberry
Arbutus menziesii	Madrone
Arctostaphylos manzanita	Common manzanita
Carpobrotus chilensis	Sea fig
Crataegus gaylussacia	Suksdorf's hawthorn
Fragaria chiloensis	Mountain strawberry
Fragaria vesca	Woodland strawberry
Gaultheria shallon	Salal
Heteromeles arbutifolia	Toyon
Juniperus californica	California juniper
Prunus subcordata	Klamath plum
Prunus virginiana	Chokecherry
Ribes californicum	California gooseberry
Ribes divaricatum	Spreading gooseberry
Rosa californica	California wildrose
*Rosa pisocarpa**	Cluster rose
Rubus leucodermis	Western raspberry
Rubus parviflorus	Thimbleberry
Rubus spectabilis	Salmonberry
Rubus ursinus	California blackberry
Sambucus nigra ssp. *caerulea*	Blue elderberry
Solanum xanti	Purple nightshade
Vaccinium ovatum	California huckleberry
Vaccinium parvifolium	Red huckleberry
Vitis californica	California wild grape

Table 10. Plants associated with the native category "fresh greens" (*tso'*).

Scientific Name	Common Name
Amsinckia lycopsoides	Bugloss fiddleneck
Angelica californica	California angelica
Angelica tomentosa	Woolly angelica
Asclepias eriocarpa	Kotolo milkweed
Asclepias fascicularis	Mexican whorled milkweed
Geranium dissectum	Common wild geranium
Perideridia kelloggii	Kellogg's yampah
Plagiobothrys fulvus	Popcorn flower
Raphanus sativus	Wild radish
Sonchus asper	Prickly sowthistle
Taraxacum officinale	Common dandelion
Tauschia kelloggii	Kellogg's tauschia
Trifolium ciliolatum	Tree clover
Trifolium fucatum	Bull clover
Trifolium gracilentum	Graceful clover
Trifolium microdon	Valparaiso
Trifolium obtusiflorum	Clammy clover
Trifolium spp.	Clover
Trifolium variegatum	Variegated clover
Trifolium willdenovii	Tomcat clover
Trifolium wormskioldii	Cows clover

Table 11. Plants associated with the native category "baked greens" (*ma-lu*).

Scientific Name	Common Name
Chlorogalum pomeridianum	Soaproot
Lathyrus jepsonii	Delta peavine
Lomatium utriculatum	Common lomatium
Lupinus bicolor	Bicolor lupine
Nemophila menziesii	Menzies' baby blue eyes
Vicia americana	American vetch

Table 12. Plants associated with the native category "mushrooms" (*tce*).

Scientific Name	Common Name
Armillaria mellea	Honey mushroom
Leucoagaricus americanus	American parasol
Morchella sp.	Morel
Unidentified (*ba' ma-tci*)	—
Unidentified (*bu ta' tce e'*)	—
Unidentified (*stan'-tci*)	—
Unidentified (*ta tce e'*)	—
Unidentified (*tca la' tce e'*)	—
Unidentified (*to tol tce e'*)	—
Unidentified (*tsi tal' tce e'*)	—
Unidentified (*tso lom to*)	—

Table 13. Plants associated with the native category "psychic plants" (*xa-nu'*).

Scientific Name	Common Name
Adenocaulon bicolor	American trail plant
Angelica spp.	Angelica
Hoita macrostachya	Leather root
Lomatium utriculatum	Common lomatium
Osmorhiza sp.	Sweet cicely
Thalictrum fendleri	Fendler's meadowrue

Landscape Management

Many of the productive California landscapes described by chroniclers as pristine were in fact highly modified by human activities (Anderson 1993, 1999, 2005). Historical and linguistic evidence of Potter Valley Pomo plant knowledge suggests a close and dynamic relationship with the local landscape. Utilizing diverse seasonal plant resources in a varied phytogeographical setting, this historically populous community's reliance on non-domesticated local resources occurred in a highly domesticated landscape. With its population of up to 2500 individuals living in numerous indigenous settlements before the arrival of non-indigenous settlers, the approximately 26 km² floor of Potter Valley was an example of California's most humanized landscapes (Vale 2002). Although neither Hudson nor other early scholars of the Potter Valley Pomo dedicated much specific attention to landscape management practices, diverse lines of evidence suggests how their intensive use of the valley's resources served to improve the availability of desirable plants and animals.

Seasonal anthropogenic burning was likely the human activity that most significantly transformed the California vegetation and thereby improved access to desirable resources by reducing dense vegetation, accelerating the germination of certain taxa, stimulating the production of useful plant parts, expanding the coverage of plant assemblages with diverse food resources for humans and game animals, and reducing the destructiveness of periodic wildfires by controlling fuel loads (Anderson 1999, 2002, 2005; Bean and Lawton 1993; Lewis 1973, 2002; McCarthy 1993; Timbrook et al. 1993). Indigenous peoples in Northern California regularly burned numerous vegetation types, including grasslands, oak woodlands, chaparral, and montane forests (Anderson 2005; Bendix 2002; Lewis and Ferguson 1999) similar to those present in the Potter Valley vicinity. Neighboring indigenous communities in Redwood and Ukiah valleys burned the local vegetation in summer and autumn, thereby opening woodlands and improving gathering conditions (Kniffen 1939; Stewart 1943). Southern Pomo groups typically set fires in the summertime before the grasses and herbaceous plants became too dry (David W. Peri, personal communication, July 13, 2000).

Hudson's notes suggest that burning by the Potter Valley Pomo was common and had a significant impact on the composition and structure of local vegetation. As he documented, fires were set to collect grasshoppers and capture deer. Grassland were burned to drive grasshoppers into previously prepared trenches. Deer were trapped on open ridges during the summertime by driving them with fire into a series of fences converging in leeward direction toward snares. Typically set in chamise chaparral (*da-no' mine'*) and grassland transition zones, these chamise fires (*da-no' catan*) opened areas of impenetrable vegetation (*lai'-i*) and initiated rapid successional change (Figure 13).

Linguistic evidence suggests anthropogenic burning was common during the summer months. The Northern Pomo term for the summer season (*sa-hă nǐm'*) signifies "smoke pall," suggesting that skies thick with smoke were a characteristic feature of summertime. In my own research experience in a very different part of the world, the dry-season practice of hunting with fire among the Xavante of Central Brazil produces a dramatic but temporary atmospheric shift as fires set by multiple hunting parties at the end of the dry season produce a thick blanket of haze that lingers until first rains. At the risk of overstepping the limits of ethnographic analogy, my observations of anthropogenic burning in the fire-adapted cerrados of Brazil suggest the possibility that the summertime "smoke pall" evidenced in Northern Pomo vocabulary also resulted from cultural burning.

Using fire to collect grasshoppers and trap deer in foothill woodlands, grasslands, and chaparral would have resulted in increases in the abundance and accessibility of certain plant and animal resources. As elsewhere in California, indigenous burning in these particular plant communities reduced brushy vegetation to intermittent stands and thereby expanded the distribution of grasslands. The resultant open ecosystems contained greater abundance of many economically important plants and attracted deer and other grazing game animals (Anderson 2005; Lewis 1973). As elsewhere in North America (Weiser and Lepofsky 2009;

Figure 13. Chaparral in regrowth after fire, North Coast Range, California, 2011. Photograph by Chris K. Kjeldsen.

White 1980), early non-indigenous settlers were attracted to and took advantage of the land that had been previously cleared and managed by indigenous occupants. Early accounts describe the fire-dependent mosaic of plant communities that once existed in Potter Valley. As noted by Watson (1916:8):

> The first settlers found the valley parklike, with an open cover, including scattered trees of valley oak and small groves of various trees covering perhaps one-third of the area. They could plow many fields without the trouble of clearing.

Similarly, in the late nineteenth century Helen Carpenter (n.d.) wrote:

> The high ranges on every side are not heavily wooded, but have clusters of pines, oaks, and madronas with intervening chemissal and manzanita, and again open hillside thickly covered with a luxuriant growth of wild oats [...].

The Potter Valley Pomo also managed their plant resources and ecosystems by loosening the soil (tilling) and weeding. As with other Pomoan groups, these techniques encouraged vigorous plant growth (Allen and Brown 1972; Mason 1904; Peri 1985; Peri and Patterson

1979; Peri et al. 1982; Peri et al. 1985a; Theodoratus et al. 1975). Among the techniques Hudson documented for the Potter Valley Pomo is the use of digging sticks to uproot plant resources such as sedges and alkali bulrush (*Bolboschoenus maritimus*) rhizomes for basketry, edible bulbs and corms of liliaceous plants, and leather root (*Hoita macrostachya*) for cordage. For example, sedge plants were cultivated in three types of beds, each with distinct soil conditions and producing rhizomes of different colors and qualities. The soils in these beds were maintained by digging and hoeing (*ma pi-nan'*) and collected by an elaborate process of gentle loosening, lifting, and scooping with digging sticks and clamshells (Hudson 1893). Similar methods employed by other Pomoan peoples increase overall plant vigor by stimulating root formation, increasing soil aeration, improving drainage, and increasing moisture absorption (Allen and Brown 1972; Peri and Patterson 1979; Peri et al. 1982).

Ownership of resources is another important aspect of indigenous resource management systems (Fowler and Lepofsky 2011; Turner et al. 2005). Whereas red magnesite mines in Potter Valley were owned by local communities, certain plant resources were privately owned and controlled. Similarly to sedge beds, some proliferous oak trees, seed-producing grasslands, and ash trees (*Fraxinus* sp.) that hosted periodic outbreaks of edible caterpillars were owned by families and passed down between generations (Barrett 1936; Sentinel Archaeological Research 2007; Stewart 1943; Swezey 1978). These examples of long-term resource ownership, especially in this small but densely populated valley, likely reflect intensive use and management of local resources, similar to that described for other native California peoples.

Through the occupation of Potter Valley by non-indigenous settlers and the consequent dislocation of the Potter Valley Pomo in the mid-nineteenth century, evidence of these landscape management techniques quickly disappeared. In the following chapter, I discuss how these historical circumstances impacted the local indigenous peoples and introduce the Hudson-Carpenter family, who befriended them during this difficult transition and documented their lives and culture in intimate detail.

Table 14. Plants providing straight woody shoots used in basketry.

Scientific name	Common name	Application
Calycanthus occidentalis	Spicebush	Arrows
Cercis occidentalis	Redbud	Basketry weft elements
Cornus glabrata	Dogwood	Basketry warp elements
Corylus cornuta	California hazelnut	Basketry warp elements
Fraxinus sp.	Ash	Medicine
Quercus dumosa	Nuttall's scrub oak	Basketry warp elements
Quercus garryana	Oregon oak	Basketry warp elements
Quercus kelloggii	Kellogg's oak	Basketry warp elements
Quercus spp.	Oak	Basketry
Rhus aromatica	Fragrant sumac	Basketry warp elements
Salix exigua	Sandbar willow	Basketry warp elements
Salix spp.	Willow	Basketry
Unidentified (*ka tsu ka-li*)	—	Arrows

4. Historical Transitions and Encounters

John Hudson conducted his research at a complex and challenging time in Potter Valley Pomo history. Having experienced decades of brutal subjugation and been transformed through demographic disruption and geographical disarticulation following the arrival of non-indigenous settlers, they nevertheless maintained a rich living memory of the pre-settlement period. Hudson did not personally witness the initial decades of these changes, but developed a profound knowledge of them from his in-laws, who were among the early pioneer families in Potter Valley, and through his long-term associations and ethnographic research with members of the Potter Valley Pomo community. In this chapter, I explore the significance of these historical transformations for Potter Valley Pomo society and culture. After discussing events in the years immediately before and after their first encounters with non-indigenous people, I focus on how their enduring friendship with the Hudson-Carpenter family resulted in the accumulation of an incomparable set of ethnographic data, artifacts, and artistic representations related to the Northern Pomo from Potter Valley.

Due to its inland location, Potter Valley was not visited by the first non-indigenous people to arrive in the region by sea. Nevertheless, its indigenous residents potentially came into contact, directly or indirectly, with these people during collecting trips in the first decades of the nineteenth century. For example, they could have encountered Russians if they visited Bodega Bay in 1809 or 1812, years in which Alexandrovich Kuskov's hunting ships established contact with the Bodega Miwok, or at Fort Ross after 1812, when a permanent Russian settlement was established in the summertime home of the Kashaya Pomo (Thompson 1896). Nevertheless, soon thereafter the Potter Valley Pomo became victims to violent expeditions reaching their home settlements. The establishment of the Mexican Republic in 1822 was followed by the first broad invasion of northerly Pomoan lands by non-indigenous people. As the frequency of incursions increased in the 1820s and 1830s, permanent settlements were established near Clear Lake (Bean and Theodoratus 1978). According to Potter Valley Pomo oral history, Mexican parties raided their valley on multiple occasions to capture slaves, who were taken to work in mines in Siskiyou County (H. M. Carpenter n.d.). About this time the community was also likely impacted by epidemic diseases, such as the spread of cholera after an outbreak in 1837 at Fort Ross (Cook 1939). If infectious diseases reached Potter Valley, its population already may have been reduced before its first non-indigenous settlers arrived in 1850. If so, estimates by early observers that the pre-contact Potter Valley Pomo population was about 1000 (H. M. Carpenter 1899; Cook 1956; Stewart 1943) may have been gross underestimates. Consequently, Hudson's estimate of 2500 inhabitants in 1850 may be more accurate.

In 1850, the Potter Valley Pomo suffered a particularly devastating military assault in the aftermath of a massacre at Clear Lake, followed by a wholesale alteration in the character of life in the valley. This conflict began when two men, Andrew Kelsey and Charles Stone, beat, raped, and murdered their kidnapped Pomoan slaves (Bean and Theodoratus 1978). Several accounts of these events indicate that in the spring of 1849, Kelsey and Stone took a group of captive Pomo from the Clear Lake area on an expedition to the Sierra foothills (Barrett 1952; A. O. Carpenter and Millberry 1914; Forbes 1969; Heizer 1973). Being severely mistreated by their captors, all but one or two died of starvation (W. Benson 1981). Later that year, a distraught group of Pomoan men killed Stone and Kelsey in retaliation. Helen Carpenter (n.d.) provided a somewhat different version of these events, although her creative writing style suggests she may have reinterpreted the facts. According to her account, the killing of Kelsey and Stone occurred when they kidnapped "all the children they could lay their hands on" and shots were inadvertently fired amidst the confusion, killing the two men.

The deaths of Kelsey and Stone prompted a vicious campaign by the United States military against the Pomoans at Clear Lake and other groups that were not involved directly in the original conflict, including the Potter Valley Pomo. In her historical narrative, Helen Carpenter (n.d.) recounted the Potter Valley attack and its subsequent months of hardship. As she wrote, whereas other Pomoan communities to the south left their homes in anticipation of the military's campaign, the Potter Valley Pomo thought their valley to be too far from Clear Lake to warrant concern. However, the military contingent arrived in Potter Valley early one morning in 1850 and secured the entire settlement while its residents slept. Wakening to the sound of gunshots, everyone desperately attempted to escape into the hillside chaparral. Many adults were killed and so many children were immediately captured that the military did not pursue the others into the brush. As they left with these prisoners, they set fire to the recently constructed thatched houses. Within moments, all was reduced to ashes but the "charred remains of those ruthlessly murdered." Those who escaped into the hills returned to the village before nightfall to avoid dangerous chaparral animals and supernatural beings.

With their houses, stored foods, weapons, implements, and baskets destroyed, the Potter Valley Pomo were "reduced to such a state of poverty" as never before. According to Carpenter (n.d.), it took months for them to rebuild their homes and replenish their food reserves. Had conditions returned to normal after the massacre its memory might have eventually faded, as did Potter Valley recollections of previous Mexican slave raids. Instead, the massacre signaled the beginning of an accelerated period of encroachment by non-indigenous settlers. According to Carpenter, just as the Potter Valley Pomo were first regaining a sense of stability after the massacre, the valley's first pioneer William Potter arrived alone in the valley in search of livestock range. Finding the valley promising, he returned in 1852 with two companions, Thomas Potter and Mose C. Briggs, as well as cattle and horses (A. O. Carpenter and Millberry 1914; H. M. Carpenter 1893a, 1899). Relations between this first group of settlers and the native population were amicable and some Potter Valley Pomo willingly took employment with them. Potter and Briggs grazed their herds freely throughout the valley until other settlers began to arrive in 1856.

About this time, Mendocino County was gaining widespread recognition for its excellent agricultural potential. As a result, there began what Helen Carpenter (1899) described as an "exodus" of covered wagons crossing the Sierra Nevada to Mendocino. Among these wagons was the Carpenters', headed to California in 1857 filled with such unusual luggage as books, artwork, and musical instruments. Promptly after marrying in Kansas earlier that year, Aurelius and Helen Carpenter and their family began the long journey to Potter Valley, where they bought their first home in 1859. The Carpenters were unique in Mendocino County for their eccentricity and political progressiveness. Important figures in the early consolidation of Mendocino County and avid artists and performers for their own enjoyment, Aurelius and Helen took a keen interest in the local native peoples, whom they treated with respect uncharacteristic of the valley's other non-indigenous families. Through their friendship with the Potter Valley Pomo, especially members of the community *Po'-mo* near their home at the lower end of the valley, they came to know Potter Valley Pomo society in a very personal manner.

Aurelius Ormando Carpenter (1836-1919) was born in Vermont and moved to Kansas in the late 1850's, where, despite having little formal education, he worked with two of that state's earliest newspapers (K. Holmes 2006). In Potter Valley and later after moving with his family to Ukiah in 1969 he pursued interests in publishing, journalism, and photography, in addition to his ranching activities. Among his notable contributions, Aurelius assisted with the foundation of the Mendocino Herald in 1860, opened a photography studio in Ukiah in 1869, ran the Ukiah City Press after buying it in 1879, and published a history of Lake and Mendocino Counties in 1914 (A. O. Carpenter and Millberry 1914; K. Holmes 2006). He also served as assistant assessor and deputy collector for the U.S. Internal Revenue Department, board member for the County Board of Education, Deputy County Assessor, and Deputy County Recorder (K. Holmes 2006).

Aurelius's wife, Helen Carpenter (née McCowen; 1835-1917) was born in Ohio. Unlike many women of her time, she was well-educated, having attended a number of progressive schools, including a Quaker academy in Indiana (Crawford 2000). She was the first female teacher certified by Mendocino County, the first woman to sit on the Mendocino County Board of Education, and helped establish the Carnegie Library in Ukiah (Crawford 2000). She was also active in the women's rights movement, the local Presbyterian Church, the fraternal Order of the Eastern Star, and California's Rebekah Lodges (Crawford 2000). Additionally, Helen taught at a schoolhouse for Potter Valley Pomo children from the community *Po'-mo* and thereby came to care deeply about their society, lives, and wellbeing (Boynton 1989; Crawford 2000). A prolific writer, Helen wrote numerous articles, stories, and poems about Potter Valley Pomo mythology, history, and culture (1893a, b, 1899). Among her unpublished writings from the late nineteenth century is a historical novel about members of a Potter Valley Pomo family during the transformative decades following the Kelsey and Stone massacre (H. M. Carpenter n.d.). Although she adapted historical events for creative purposes, Helen's manuscript includes such richly detailed accounts of Potter Valley Pomo society based on years of personal observation that it also has value as an ethnographic document.

The Carpenters arrived in Potter Valley when agricultural use of the land was rapidly intensifying (Watson and Pendleton 1916). Whereas most local production had been for livestock and feed, in the late 1850s emphasis shifted to the commercial production of grains (principally wheat, oats, corn, and alfalfa), hops, prunes, and pears (Figure 14). By 1859 the entire valley was inhabited by settlers with legal land titles, thereby resulting in the total disappropriation of Potter Valley Pomo lands. Consequently, the valley's native residents were forced to live in impermanent rancherias on private property in exchange for providing cheap labor (Bean and Theodoratus 1978).

As the non-native population in Potter Valley grew, so did the injustices suffered by the Potter Valley Pomo. One important consequence of this growth was the circumscription of valuable landscape resources and the reduction of native oak woodlands by overgrazing and the intensification of grain agriculture. By the end of the 1850s, overgrazing had so stressed the local resources that native people were living in extreme poverty (H. M. Carpenter n.d.). By 1860, there was little available food to be collected or hunted and undernutrition led to rampant sickness and death (H. M. Carpenter in Shelton 1986). Also, slavery of native people became so commonplace that all but a few non-native households in Potter Valley

Figure 14. Agricultural field in Ukiah Valley, circa 1880s. Photograph by A. O. Carpenter. Original in the collections of Grace Hudson Museum, Ukiah, California.

had one to three indigenous child servants, many provided by a man known as Woodman, famous in Mendocino County for selling children he kidnapped after murdering their parents (H. M. Carpenter 1893b). Detesting the manner in which her non-indigenous neighbors treated the Potter Valley Pomo, Helen courageously published about the many injustices she witnessed (H. M. Carpenter 1893b, n.d.).

In 1865, the Department of Indian Affairs ordered all independent Pomoan individuals onto the Round Valley Reservation, established in 1858 at Covelo, about 55 km north of Potter Valley (California Indian Assistance Program 1994). Originally inhabited by the Yuki, many Pomoan people were also relocated there, including the Northern Pomo from Little Lake, Sherwood, and Potter valleys. In order to avoid relocation from their home, some Potter Valley Pomo fled into the mountains and others submitted themselves to legal guardianship by non-indigenous Potter Valley families (H. M. Carpenter 1893b). Despite providing an alternative to relocation, the guardianship arrangement often led to abuses. As Carpenter reported, typical methods guardians used to "correct" their Pomo wards were whippings with a picket fence and dragging by rope behind a horse. The Carpenters also signed papers to become guardians to 17 Potter Valley Pomo and thereby prevent their relocation to the Round Valley Reservation. However, unlike those guardians who sought to take advantage of their wards, the Carpenters used it as a mechanism to assist their indigenous friends in retaining their freedom.

By 1868 conditions had become so intolerable that most Potter Valley Pomo had left the valley, including about 600 who went to the Ukiah area (Hudson 1893). Several Potter Valley Pomo men and women formed private partnerships to purchase their own small parcels of land, while many others were forced to take up residence as guests in rancherias established by members of other Pomoan communities. In 1879 a group of men from Potter Valley orchestrated a purchase of land in Pinoleville, Ukiah Valley, by pooling their money and obtaining private loans (Bauer Jr. 2009; T. Benson 1991; Schneider 2010). Later, in 1892, another group from Potter Valley purchased a four hectare parcel at the south end of Potter Valley (Figure 15), which temporarily became home to people from Pomoan communities throughout the valley (Potter Valley Tribe 2010). Other rancherias established at this time by members of other Pomoan communities also received refugees from Potter Valley. These included Redwood Valley, Coyote Valley, Yokayo, and Guidivelle (T. Benson 1991; Kasch 1947; McLendon 1993; Sentinel Archaeological Research 2007; Smith-Ferri 2006). According to contemporary elders, life during this era was characterized by a great deal of mobility as people moved between rancherias and visited the coast in search of agricultural work and seasonal food resources (Potter Valley Tribe 2010; Sentinel Archaeological Research 2007).

Summarizing the wholesale transformation during the final decades of the nineteenth century of the Potter Valley Pomo from an autonomous indigenous community in an abundant local landscape to a dispersed population in a dismantled territory, Helen Carpenter (1893a: 153) wrote, using the word "wonderful" in the sense of astonishing:

Figure 15. Potter Valley Tribe cemetery, Potter Valley, 2011. Photograph by James R. Welch.

Thirty years have wrought a wonderful change. Where once the grizzly was wont to come and feed on clover, now stands the comfortable farmhouse and orchard. The home of the deer and jack-rabbit is converted into vineyards, and where once stood the native village of eight hundred or a thousand souls, not one casa remains.

"WHERE ONCE THE GRIZZLY FED ON CLOVER."

Figure 16. Grace Hudson illustration of Potter Valley, 1893. Illustration by Grace Carpenter Hudson. From Hudson (1893:155).

These changes were also observed by Aurelius and Helen's four children, including John Hudson's future wife, Grace (Figure 17). Born in Potter Valley, Grace Hudson (née Carpenter; 1865-1937) had close contact with the Potter Valley Pomo her entire life (Baird 1962). In her own evaluation, she came to understand the local native people by living among them since birth and building relationships with them based on mutual trust (Plover 1934). As a child, she developed a passionate interest in art, developing her talent on her own until she became an award-winning student at the San Francisco School of Design in 1880 (Boynton 1989; Lanson and Tetzlaff 2006). After a brief first marriage in San Francisco, she returned to Ukiah where, in 1889, she opened her own art studio to the public. Soon after returning, she met John Hudson and married him in 1890.

Although their careers and ambitions were distinct, together they cultivated a shared interest in native peoples. Their home in Ukiah served as Grace's studio and John's ethnographic repository and private museum. After their marriage, Grace gained increasing recognition for her paintings of the native people of Mendocino County, especially following two important events. In 1891, the Minneapolis Art Association, a leading institution at the time, purchased "National Thorn," a painting of a Pomoan in-

Five times *Cha-balla*'s people had been obliged to move, to accommodate the white man. This, together with the tightening of lines about them, caused so much dissatisfaction that some went away on a visit, and finding conditions more to their tastes, did not come back. Still others went with the intention of remaining, and their ranks had also been badly decimated by death. A few went to the Pomas of north *Be-lo-ki*, but the majority went to *Sho-de-ki* and *Yokaia*. When casas were rebuilt the last time, it was found that three were all that was necessary to accommodate the little band, now all that was left of the once happy village of 800 or 1,000 souls.

– Helen M. Carpenter

Figure 17. Aurelius and Helen Carpenter with family, circa 1873. Pictured from left to right are Helen, Louis Grant, Frank Leonard, May (standing), Grace and Aurelius. Photograph by A. O. Carpenter. Original in the collections of Grace Hudson Museum, Ukiah.

fant in a woven baby cradle basket (Boynton 1989). In 1893, her painting "Little Mendocino," also of a Pomoan child, was displayed to adoring crowds at the Mechanics Fair in San Francisco. By 1897, she had become extremely popular among art connoisseurs in San Francisco, who placed orders for her life-like paintings faster than she could paint them (Eames 1897). As demand rapidly increased from buyers in the United States and Europe, her paintings were acquired by many museums, including the Oakland Museum, the Los Angeles Museum of Art, and the National Gallery (Eversole 1979).

Grace's most popular paintings were of native infants in woven baby cradle baskets, and she became famous for capturing their "elusive, half-sad and yet winsome moods" (Baird 1962). She created her artistic representations with the same respect and insight that distinguished her mother's writings. Grace's desire to accurately represent the native people of Mendocino is evident in her statement (Plover 1934:11):

> My desire is that the world shall know them as I know them, and that before they entirely vanish. For they are vanishing. They are changing with a changing world. They have no longer the expression that they formerly had, nor are their garments distinctly their own.

In her paintings, Grace avoided depicting the historical changes she witnessed. Instead, she sought to convey circumstances as they were prior to the arrival of non-indigenous settlers. This choice was mirrored in her husband's timeless approach to ethnography, in which he sought to document Potter Valley Pomo culture in its "original" condition. In fact, Grace often adorned her models with John's ethnographic artifacts to improve the historical authenticity of her paintings.

Helen's husband, Dr. John Wilz Napier Hudson (1857-1936) was born in Nashville and followed his father's footsteps in becoming a medical doctor (Kaplan 1977). After graduating from the Medical College of Nashville and working at the University of Tennessee for several years, he practiced medicine as a homeopathic physician. It appears from early correspondence between Hudson and Gates P. Thruston, historian and ethnologist at the Tennessee Historical Society, that Hudson already had an interest in Native Americans as a young man. After moving to Ukiah in 1889 and marring Grace shortly thereafter, he took an immediate interest in the local native people. Although he continued to practice medicine sporadically in the 1890s, specializing in women's medicine and taking work for insurance companies, he gradually turned his attention to the ethnographic and linguistic study of the Northern Pomo from Potter Valley and other indigenous peoples.

Public recognition of John's ethnographic collections and Grace's paintings led to their home becoming "the first place of interest visited by tourists to Ukiah" (Eames 1897:387). By 1893, Hudson had amassed such an extensive basketry collection that he offered it for sale. Despite its quality and size, he was unsuccessful in finding a buyer with adequate financial resources. Hudson unsuccessfully sought a position with the Academy of Sciences in San Francisco in 1900 (McLendon 1993). Nevertheless, he closed his medical practice the following year so that he might dedicate himself exclusively to ethnography. He was then appointed to the California Ethnological Expedition of 1901, sponsored by the Field Colombian Museum of Chicago (Dorsey 1901). Remaining in this salaried position until 1905, he traveled throughout California, Nevada, and the Southwest conducting ethnographic investigations and acquiring objects of indigenous material culture.

In 1912, Grace and John built an architecturally unique home in Ukiah. Known as the Sun House, it became a "mecca for visiting ethnographers, linguists, collectors, explorers and others interested in Indians" (Kaplan 1977:48). It showcased John's continually expanding ethnographic collection, which eventually earned high praise from William H. Holmes of the American Bureau of Ethnology as the finest Pacific Coast Indian collection in America (James 1901). Similarly, Otis T. Mason, the first curator of ethnology at the Smithsonian Institution, described it as "the best scientific collection of basketry known to the writer from any people on earth" (Mason 1900:346).

Hudson's scientific interest in cultural documentation is evident in the thoroughness of his ethnographic collections, as it is in his extensive ethnobotanical notes. The historical circumstances that influenced his data collection, including the changing circumstances of life for the Potter Valley Pomo and the lasting friendships forged between them and the Carpenter-Hudson family, resulted in a body of ethnobotanical information containing immeasurable detail about this community at a very early time in Mendocino County history. In the following chapter, I present this cultural information about Potter Valley Pomo plants organized by contemporary scientific taxon and plant use category.

5. Potter Valley Pomo Plants

The extraordinary diversity of ethnobotanical knowledge among the Northern Pomo from Potter Valley, as documented by John Hudson and other observers in the late 1800s and early 1900s and reconstructed here, includes 261 plants, fungi, and algae (primary taxa). Ambiguities deriving from Hudson's imprecise botanical identifications and descriptions suggest that numerous other plants may also have been used, although they could not be identified precisely. Of these primary taxa, most were identifiable to species or subspecies, with the exceptions of 15 (5.7%) that could only be identified to genus and 22 (8.4%) to kingdom. The great majority are vascular plants (94.3%), while relatively few are fungi (4.6%) and algae (1.1%). Illustrating that Potter Valley Pomo plant knowledge was dynamic despite Hudson's goal to document this society as it was before being transformed in the decades following the arrival of non-indigenous settlers, his data contain ethnobotanical information for a substantial number of plants that are not native to California (8.0%) or could not be determined as to their native status due to insufficient botanical information (9.2%). Of the non-native taxa, all are naturalized locally except the South American monkey puzzle tree (*Araucaria araucana*), which was commonly planted in early Mendocino County gardens (Mabberley 1987).

Illustrative of the varied botanical landscapes the Potter Valley Pomo used, they had ethnobotanical knowledge of plants occurring in all of the plant communities in the vicinity of Potter Valley and many others that only occur near the coast or further inland (Table 15). Nevertheless, the greatest numbers of documented Potter Valley Pomo plants occur in nearby plant communities, such as foothill woodlands (57.4%), mixed conifer forests (53.5%), chaparral (47.4%), mixed evergreen forests (34.3%), and riparian wetlands (33.0%). These results suggest the Potter Valley Pomo were familiar with plants occurring in a large geographical area but retained most extensive knowledge of those available in their home valley.

Although plant resources have diverse applications and functions in indigenous societies, this variety is not always apparent in ethnobotanical accounts with limited scope or focus. It is also to be expected that Hudson did not document the complete range of cultural plant knowledge among the Potter Valley Pomo. Nevertheless, the exceptional topical breadth of ethnobotanical data contained in his notes conveys the pervasive significance of plants in numerous dimensions of Potter Valley Pomo subsistence, ethnomedicine, social life, and cultural expression (Table 16). For example, large numbers of plants were used for food and beverage (56.7%), food procurement and preparation (16.9%), and tools, containers, and fire making (13.4%). Among the food categories, salad foods available in spring stand out for having the greatest number of documented plant taxa (31.1% of the total number of taxa used for foods and beverages). Such diversity of fresh greens is unusual among indigenous peoples in North America, many of whom emphasize other classes of foods in their diets (Moerman 2010). Other food categories with the greatest frequencies of plant taxa illustrate

Table 15. Frequencies of taxa by plant community, in decreasing order.

Plant community	No. of primary taxa	Percent of total
Foothill woodland*	132	57.4%
Mixed conifer forest*	123	53.5%
Chaparral*	109	47.4%
Mixed evergreen forest*	79	34.3%
Riparian wetland*	76	33.0%
Red fir forest	61	26.5%
Redwood forest	42	18.3%
Northern oak woodland	33	14.3%
Northern coastal scrub	26	11.3%
Disturbed places*	26	11.3%
Closed-cone pine forest	22	9.6%
Coastal strand	17	7.4%
Coastal prairie	17	7.4%
Freshwater marsh	11	4.8%
Northern coast coniferous forest	8	3.5%
Coastal salt marsh	5	2.2%

Plant communities follow the CalFlora Database (2012), which is based on Munz and Keck (1973), Lum (1975), and Walker (1992). Percentages were calculated from a total of 230 primary taxa with botanical identifications sufficiently specific to permit association with at least one local plant community. Each plant may occur in more than one community. Asterisks (*) indicate plant communities in the immediate vicinity of Potter Valley.

Table 16. Frequencies of taxa by plant use category, in decreasing order.

Use	No. of primary taxa	Percent of total
Food and beverage	148	56.7%
Medicines and poisons	79	30.3%
Artistry and music	69	26.4%
Food procurement and preparation	44	16.9%
Tools, containers, and firemaking	35	13.4%
Legend, ceremony, and spirituality	34	13.0%
Clothing, fibers, and padding	25	9.6%
Gaming and competition	24	9.2%
Architecture, bedding, and matting	23	8.8%
Warfare and weapons	23	8.8%
Cleaning and disinfecting	11	4.2%
Transportation	10	3.8%
Trade, communication, and timekeeping	9	3.4%
Smoking, narcotics, and stimulants	8	3.1%
Grooming and fragrance	5	1.9%
Divination and doctoring	5	1.9%
Host plants	4	1.5%

the seasonal nature of the Potter Valley Pomo diet. Among these are seeds, underground foods, and cooked greens that became available in the spring, fruit foods collected in the summer, and breads and mushes made principally from the autumn harvest of acorns.

Demonstrating the importance of plants for aspects of Potter Valley Pomo life beyond material subsistence, several of the other domains with the highest frequencies of recorded plant taxa were medicines and poisons (30.3%), artistry and music (26.4%), and legend, ceremony, and spirituality (13.0%). The categories of medicines and remedies with the greatest frequencies of plant taxa illustrate the range of conditions addressed by Potter Valley Pomo ethnomedicine. Women's health, which was Hudson's specialty as a physician, was the category with the greatest number of plants, followed by first aid, laxatives, analgesics, gastrointestinal aids, and remedies used to treat sexually transmitted diseases. Additionally, the diversity of plants documented for use in basketry (44 taxa) is quite large, considering that just 29 taxa are documented elsewhere for all Pomoan groups, including the Northern Pomo (Moerman 1998, 2011).

In the remainder of this chapter, I present my reconstructed ethnobotany of the Northern Pomo from Potter Valley, organized by taxon and plant use. The first section, organized by scientific name, includes plants that were identifiable to species or genus from Hudson's data. The second section, organized by Northern Pomo plant name, includes plants that could not be identified precisely due to lack of information. Each entry includes the following information, if available or applicable: scientific names, Northern Pomo names, taxonomic notes, and plant use descriptions.

The scientific names included in the headers for each entry are the primary taxa that Hudson's data permitted identification with a high degree of certainty. Family or other classification information is included in parentheses after the scientific name. Some entries have two or more primary taxa because Hudson or the Potter Valley Pomo treated them as equivalent. Asterisks (*) indicate taxa not native to California. Following the scientific plant names in the header of each entry, I identify any applicable Northern Pomo plant names and their translations, reproduced as Hudson transcribed them. If Hudson documented slightly different versions of the same plant name, I present the most frequent or consistent version. Where Hudson documented more than one Northern Pomo name for a single plant, each is presented. Subsequently, I provide any applicable information about how I derived contemporary scientific names from Hudson's writings, including sources consulted. Where Hudson's scientific names were consistent with contemporary nomenclature, no additional information is provided. The remainder of each entry contains descriptions of Potter Valley Pomo plant knowledge and use organized by plant use category (Chapter 2). Unless otherwise cited, all data derived from Hudson's unpublished fieldnotes and writings. Many of the plant uses and preparations mentioned in these entries are described in greater detail in the following chapter.

Taxa by Scientific Name

Abies concolor (Gordon & Glend.) Lindl. ex Hildebr. (Pinaceae) · White fir

Taxonomic notes: Hudson referenced the common names "fir" and "white fir," but never the genus *Abies*. Although his use of "white fir" may be associated with *Abies concolor* with a high degree of certainty, "fir" may also refer to grand fir (*Abies grandis*), California red fir (*A. magnifica*), or Douglas fir (*Pseudotsuga menziesii*).

Adhesive: Pitch from fir and other conifers was used as an adhesive, generally being softened with heat before application. It was used for such applications as to secure string to fishing and fowling hooks.

Ceremony: Small beads of fir pitch were attached to one's hair to mourn a death. White fir poles were raised in front of the assembly house for Kuksu (*kuk'su*) ceremonies (cf. Barrett 1917a; Loeb 1926).

Divination and doctoring: Bear doctors wore ceremonial armor made from fir rods that was similar in construction to armor used in warfare.

Fire: The wood was used for fire drills.

Tool: Fir wood was used to manufacture diverse tools and utensils, including ladders.

War: Padded body armor used in warfare was assembled from approximately 1 cm fire-hardened fir rods.

Acer macrophyllum Pursh (Sapindaceae) · Bigleaf maple
Native name: *cǐm-mai' ka tǔ' ka-lǐ'*.

Taxonomic notes: At times, Hudson used just the genus name *Acer* or the common name "maple," both of which may also refer to vine maple (*Acer circinatum*).

Architecture: The plant was used in wattle, an architectural framework of wooden rods interlaced with grasses and reeds.

Basketry: The roots provided a strong light-colored weft fiber used in both twined and coiled baskets. Maple also provided long even warp rods used in one-rod coiled baskets.

Cooking: The leaves were used in underground ovens as moist insulation between the hot stones and cooking foods.

Gaming and competition: The shaft of one type of contest arrow was made from maple and other heavier woods.

Tool: Maple poles were used in the manufacture of a variety of tools. According to Helen Carpenter (n.d.), the leaves were also pinned together with small twigs to form pouches used to hold edible caterpillars.

Achillea millefolium L. (Asteraceae) · Yarrow
Native name: *kal' ma-ta* ("appearance of shell crushed").

Taxonomic notes: At times, Hudson used just the common name "yarrow."

Antidiarrheal: A fluid extract of the whole plant was given for summer diarrhea (*ka mal' ke lin*), an intense diarrhea in children associated with the heat of summer.

Burn dressing: The charred root was sprinkled on extensive burns.

Gastrointestinal aid: For nausea, the entire plant was boiled and the liquid sipped hourly. In some passages, Hudson specified that crushed shell was added during the boiling process, which may explain the native name.

Laxative: Hudson reported that the plant is a purgative, in apparent contradiction to his statement, mentioned above, that it was used to treat summer diarrhea.

Achyrachaena mollis Schauer (Asteraceae) · Blow-wives
Native name: *tě' ta-la* ("downy seed").
Seed food: The seeds were parched and ground into a meal (pinole).

Adenocaulon bicolor Hook. (Asteraceae) · American trail plant
Native name: *du wi ya-na.*
Spirituality: The plant was used to "anoint" gamblers, presumably for good luck. Considered one of the "psychic" *xa-nu'* plants, it was also used in a similar manner to angelica (*Angelica* spp.) as a ceremonial anointment to purify a dead body, preparing it for its future state.

Adenostoma fasciculatum Hook. & Arn. (Rosaceae) · Chamise
Native name: *ga-no' ka-lǐ'* ("mystery ash waste tree").
Taxonomic notes: At times, Hudson used just the genus name *Adenostoma* or the common names "chemissal" or "chamise."
Communication: A highly polished rod made from the wood was carried by messengers to other communities to announce the time and location of funerary cremations or other public events (cf. Barrett 1917a; Kroeber 1925). These invitation sticks were over 30 cm in length and about 2 cm in diameter, tapering towards the ends. Hudson explained that two cords were attached at one end of the rod. From the cords hung four small horizontal rods, spaced about 1 cm apart. To the end of the cords was attached a feather pendant identifying the host community. Once delivered, an invitation stick was hung from the center post of the assembly house in the invited community. Each of the four small rods represented one day preceding the event. The lowest rod was removed at sunset each evening until the last rod was removed the evening before the event.
Decoration: From this wood were fashioned hair pins used to secure hairnets. They were also used to pin ceremonial headgear (feather topknots) to hairnets and to secure other garments. The wood was only collected after fire had cleared the dense chaparral, leaving scorched and seasoned stalks. These stalks were fashioned into straight pins from approximately 25 to 50 cm long and 1 cm in diameter. They were pointed at both ends. Hudson commented that chamise wood is comparable to rose wood (*Rosa* spp.) in that it is extremely fine-grained and handsome. Such pins were often finely polished, etched with "totem signs," and tipped with bird feathers (cf. Loeb 1926).
Fire: The wooden rods were used as fire drill shafts.

Hunting: The standing vegetation was burned during the summer to drive deer into traps constructed on open ridges. As described by Hudson, when male and female deer separated for the season, the bucks tended to avoided thick vegetation because it would bruise their tender antlers. Thus preferring open areas with litter cover, they were difficult to stalk. Therefore, hunters constructed fences of intertwined poles converging leeward toward a series of snares. By setting fire to chamise brush on the windward side, they drove the deer inside and thereby easily dispatched them.

Adiantum jordanii Müll. Hal. (Pteridaceae) · California maidenhair fern

Taxonomic notes: In addition to using the full species epithet (written *Adiantum jordani*), Hudson sometimes used only the genus name *Adiantum*, which could also refer to five-fingered fern (*Adiantum aleuticum*).

Basketry: Hudson (1893) wrote that maidenhair fern was the most valued black weft used for basketry patterns, being much preferred to tule (*Schoenoplectus acutus* var. *occidentalis*) because it was less coarse and its black color was darker and more permanent. In his notes, however, he reported that alkali bulrush (*Bolboschoenus maritimus*) rhizomes provided the handsomest and most valued black basketry weft. The fibers of both plants were only used in ornamental baskets or baskets used for political and ceremonial purposes. These two sources of black fibers were also the most economically valuable of all basketry weft materials.

Decoration: Stem segments were used to enlarge pierced holes in earlobes and nose septa (cf. Barrett 1952).

Aesculus californica (Spach) Nutt. (Sapindaceae) · California buckeye

Native name: *disǎ' kalǐ* ("brittle tree").

Taxonomic notes: At times, Hudson erroneously used *Aesculus glabra* for the buckeye found in California, *A. californica* (Jepson Flora Project 2012b). In other instances he used the common name "buckeye."

Colorant: The charcoal was used as a black paint. In addition, it is likely that buckeye was a source of a charcoal powder used to produce the highly desirable and permanent black color of certain basketry weft fibers, such as alkali bulrush.

Fire: The wood was used for fire drills (Figure 18).

Gaming and competition: Staves of the wood were used in the "game without bickering" (*xa-dai*). Two or more women

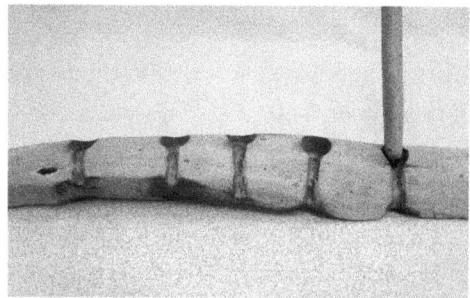

Figure 18. Fire drill apparatus made from buckeye. Photograph by Carlos E. A. Coimbra Jr., 2011. Accession no. 1438, in the collections of Grace Hudson Museum, Ukiah.

played the game on a woven mat spread between them. The staves, approximately 30 cm long, were flat on one side and rounded on the other. The rounded sides were etched with patterns.

Hunting: The branches were mounted as antlers on deer masks used for hunting camouflage.

Legend: In legends recorded by Helen Carpenter (n.d.), buckeyes and other important foods were given by mythological beings to feed the people. For example, in the legend "*La-moo* and *Ka-watth*," Gopher (*La-moo*) was transformed into acorns, buckeyes, and clover (*Trifolium* spp.) to feed the people abundantly forever.

Mush: Buckeyes were consumed in considerable quantities during late fall and winter (H. M. Carpenter n.d.; Chestnut 1902). While they produced a bland food, buckeyes were important because they could be collected from late fall through January, when there were few other plant foods available. According to Hudson, they stored reasonably well for future use. Helen Carpenter (n.d.) described their preparation in detail. They were first roasted in an underground oven for two to three hours (up to 10, according to Chestnut). They were then hulled, the bitter eye was removed, and the nut meats were mashed in a wooden bowl. The neurotoxin aesculin was removed through leaching the cooked mush or adding red earth (*ma-po'*) before cooking or baking.

Polish: The charcoal was used to polish the wooden surfaces of bowls, flutes, and blowing tubes. The surface of such objects was coated with crushed soaproot bulb (*Chlorogalum pomeridianum*) mixed with damp charcoal, often derived from California buckeye wood. This paste was rubbed into the surface with crushed green willow (*Salix* spp.).

Salt: Buckeye was used in processing sea salt for consumption. After grinding the raw salt in a stone mortar, it was mixed with powdered buckeye or manzanita (*Arctostaphylos* spp.) charcoal at a ratio of about 10 to one. This preparation may have prevented the salt from becoming too humid. In the post-settlement period, the salt mixture was made into hard cakes by drying in the sun or baking in an underground oven or directly in hot coals.

Tool: The wood was used to fashion diverse tools and instruments.

Agoseris spp. (Asteraceae) · **Mountain dandelion**

Agoseris apargioides (Less.) Greene · Woolly goat chicory

Agoseris grandiflora (Nutt.) Greene · Grand mountain dandelion

Native name: *i-tsa'* ("stubbed penis").

Taxonomic notes: Hudson used *Agoseris plebeja* (written *Agoseris plebia*), which corresponds with the contemporary species *A. grandiflora* (USDA and NRCS 2012). He also used *Agoseris gracilens* (written *Agoseris gracilenta*), which corresponds with the contemporary species *A. aurantiaca*, although this species has not been documented in Mendocino or Lake Counties (Abrams and Ferris 1960; Jepson Flora Project 2012b). In addition to specific references to the taxa listed above, Hudson also used the genus name *Agoseris* without further specification and *Agoseris* sp., based on botanist Alice Eastwood's 1928 determination, suggesting other local members of the genus may also have been used.

Salad food: The raw leaves were crushed and eaten with salt.

Allium spp. (Alliaceae) · Onion

Allium dichlamydeum Greene · Coastal onion

Native name: **ke-bai.**

Taxonomic notes: In addition to Hudson's citations identifying specifically *Allium dichlamydeum*, those mentioning the genus name *Allium* or the common name "wild onion," without further specification, are also treated here. These names likely refer to additional unspecified *Allium* taxa in the study area.

Legend: *Allium* is mentioned in one of the legends presented by Helen Carpenter (n.d.) as a gift from the mythological being Coyote (**Du-wi'**) for the people to eat.

Salad food: The leaves, stalks, and roots were eaten raw as a "relish." They were only available for collecting in early spring. Helen Carpenter (n.d.) described an incident where a group of children gave a handful of the fresh green plant to an older man, who thought it so pleasant a gift that he skipped lunch to tell them another story.

Allium bolanderi S. Watson (Alliaceae) · Bolander's onion

Native name: **ke-bai.**

Salad food: The stalks and roots were eaten raw.

Women's health: Mothers avoided eating *A. bolanderi* immediately after giving birth.

Alnus rhombifolia Nutt. (Betulaceae) · White alder

Native name: **ka-ci'-ti ka-li'.**

Taxonomic notes: Hudson used the abbreviated scientific name "*Alnus cal.*" (*Alnus californica*) for the contemporary species *A. rhombifolia* (Nuttall 1842). At times, he wrote only the common name "alder," which could also refer to gray alder (*A. incana*) or red alder (*A. rubra*).

Architecture: Alder shoots were used in constructing a framework for temporary shelters, probably of the same style described elsewhere as brush or thatched houses (Barrett 1916; Loeb 1926).

Basketry: According to Hudson (1893), alder had once been used for open-twined basketry, but was later replaced with willow.

Colorant: The bark was used to produce a red dye for leather root (*Hoita macrostachya*) and milkweed (*Asclepias* spp.) fibers, used in women's dance headbands. According to Chestnut (1902), this was accomplished by smoking the fibers over burning white alder wood.

Fire: Chestnut (1902) reported that most indigenous groups in Mendocino County used the soft wood as tinder for starting fires.

Legend: In the legend *"La-moo* and *Ka-watth,"* Coyote arranged 23 cm alder twigs, each with hawk wing feathers carefully tied to one end, side by side on the sweathouse floor (H. M. Carpenter n.d.). The legend does not indicate the significance of the sticks.

Medicine: Chestnut (1902) detailed a number of medicinal uses for alder that appear to have been widespread among the indigenous groups of Mendocino County, such as to produce perspiration, to purify the blood, and to treat diarrhea. In addition, he reported that skin burns were treated with dry rot from the decaying wood mixed with powdered arroyo willow bark (*Salix lasiolepis*).

Amelanchier alnifolia (Nutt.) Nutt. ex M. Roem. (Rosaceae) · Saskatoon serviceberry

Native name: *ba-tcau' ba-kai'*.

Taxonomic notes: Hudson occasionally used the common name "service berry," which might also refer to other local members of the genus.

Bow: Serviceberry wood was used to make resilient bows, being valued for its heavy, fine grained, strong, and elastic qualities.

Fruit food: Although Hudson did not specifically mention this plant as a food, Chestnut reported that the native people of Mendocino County occasionally ate the fresh fruit.

Hunting: The wood was used for foreshafts of war and big game arrows and small game arrows.

Amsinckia lycopsoides Lehm. (Boraginaceae) · Bugloss fiddleneck

Native name: *tcĭm-ma' tsŏ*.

Taxonomic notes: Hudson occasionally wrote only the genus *Amsinckia* or the name *Amsinckia* sp., the latter of which corresponds with a 1928 determination by botanist Alice Eastwood, suggesting that other local members of the genus may have been used.

Salad food: The plant was consumed as a raw green food, often accompanied by salt and bread.

Anemopsis californica (Nutt.) Hook. & Arn. (Saururaceae) · Yerba mansa

Native name: *mi cu' bu' ko ma*.

Taxonomic notes: Hudson used *Saururaceae californica*, properly represented as *Anemopsis californica* (Jepson Flora Project 2012b), which does not appear to exist in the study area and therefore leaves some doubt as to the identity of this plant.

Dermatological aid: The root was used for unspecified skin troubles.

Seed food: The parched seeds were used for pinole.

Angelica spp. (Apiaceae) · **Angelica**

Angelica californica Jeps. · California angelica

Angelica tomentosa S. Watson · Woolly angelica

Native name: ***ba tco' wă***.

Taxonomic notes: Hudson used the scientific name *Angelica tomentosa*. The former taxon *Angelica tomentosa* var. *californica* (Hickman 1993), located in the study area, now corresponds with the contemporary species *Angelica californica* (Jepson Flora Project 2012b). At times, Hudson used the name "angelica," which may also have referred to other local taxa in the genera *Angelica* and *Lomatium*.

Brush or broom: Among Hudson's collections at the Grace Hudson Museum and Sun House is a small baby brush made from angelica root fibers (Figure 19).

Cleaning agent: The root was used to sterilize, clean, and disinfect certain objects. Newly finished baskets were washed with angelica to purify them. Also, in preparation for ear piercing, a solution of the root was used to clean the earlobes and piercing instruments. It was also chewed and spit on deer hunting masks to cover fetid odors. Pieces of angelica root were also typically placed inside these masks.

Figure 19. Baby brush made from angelica root fiber with iris cordage. Photograph by James R. Welch, 2011. Collected by Dr. John W. Hudson, 1890. Accession no. 1336 in the collections of Grace Hudson Museum, Ukiah.

Decoration: Burnt angelica root was used as a black pigment for tattooing (cf. Barrett 1952; Chestnut 1902; Loeb 1926).

Divination and doctoring: Although Hudson did not explore the subject in great detail, angelica was valued for doctoring and other ceremonial and protective purposes (Chestnut 1902; Peri et al. 1982).

Hunting: Hunters chewed the root and cast the resulting quid into fire to produce a smoke that was believed to charm deer and thereby render them easier to kill.

Medicine: Although Hudson did not mention any specific medicinal used for angelica, evidence from Peri et al. (1982) and Chestnut (1902) suggests that it was widely used by Pomoan groups to treat problems such as headache, nightmares, sore eyes, colds, colic, fever, and inflammation of the nose and throat.

Salad food: In the springtime, fresh foliage was eaten in large quantities.

Spirituality: The plant was utilized to cleanse and remove odors from the body. The root was chewed and applied to the head and entire body above the waist. Hudson mentioned this use in two specific contexts. In the first, four days after childbirth a recent mother and father would purify themselves and expel "evils" with applications of masticated root. In the second, the plant juices were used ceremoniously to purify corpses.

*Anthemis sp. (Asteraceae) · Chamomile

Native name: *ta mi-sa'-tum* ("anus smarting").

Taxonomic notes: The association of this plant with the genus *Anthemis* is based on Hudson's use of the common name "dog fennel," which may potentially have also referred other local members of the genera *Anthemis* and *Chamaemelum*.

Abortifacient: Women took an infusion of the leaves and flowers to abort pregnancies.

Cathartic: Blue elderberry fiber (*Sambucus nigra* ssp. *caerulea*) was boiled with chamomile leaves to produce a liquid that was taken hot as a fast-acting cathartic.

Apocynum cannabinum L. (Apocynaceae) · Dogbane

Native name: *ma-ca' ka-li'*.

Taxonomic notes: At times, Hudson used only the common name "hemp" or simply *Apocynum*, which could also refer to bitter dogbane (*A. androsaemifolium*).

Basketry: The cordage was used for a variety of netted baskets, containers, and tumplines. For example, Hudson's artifact collections include elaborate wedding bags made with dogbane fiber and ornamented with clamshell disks and abalone beads (Figure 20).

Ceremony: Ropes made from dogbane and ornamented with goose or gull down were tied to ceremonial poles as flags. Additionally, heavy and highly ornamented woven belts, often made from bleached dogbane fiber, were exceptionally valuable possessions.

Clothing: Hairnets made from dogbane fiber were used to secure one's hair. Soft gowns made from dogbane fiber were worn by infants in conjunction with diapers and rigid rush (*Juncus* spp.) casings.

Cordage: Each of the many uses for dogbane was associated with its high quality fiber, which ranked above all other the Potter Valley Pomo plant fibers as the softest, strongest, and most durable material for cordage and rope. Stalks collected when beginning to mature produced a whitish fiber, whereas if collected after winter frosts, when dry and

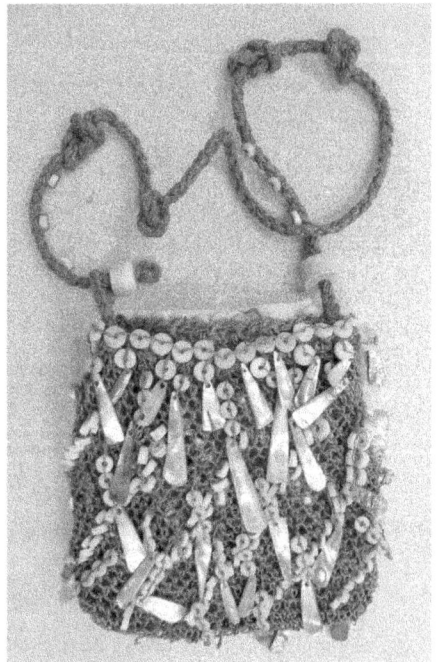

Figure 20. Dogbane wedding bag with shell beads. Photograph by James R. Welch, 2011. Accession no. 1764, in the collections of Grace Hudson Museum, Ukiah.

leafless, produced a deep red fiber. Bound in bundles and stored in a dry place until thoroughly seasoned, they could be used up to several years later. To prepare the fiber, the stalks were crushed between one's teeth. If not yet fully dry, they were first split open lengthwise and placed in the sun for about three days. The flaky exterior layer and the woody interior were cleaned from the fibers with one's fingers and the fiber was then scraped clean with one's teeth. The finished fibers were coiled, bundled, and stored until fully dry. To produce string or cordage, two strands of fiber were moistened with saliva and twisted on the knee. The finished string was stretched and smoothed by vigorously drawing it across one's lower teeth.

Decoration: Hairnets used by native doctors to support ceremonial headgear were often made with dogbane. In addition, war bonnets were constructed with an approximately 5 cm wide dogbane band supporting a row of upright eagle tail feathers. Some were sewn with down feathers or clamshell disks as decoration.

Fishing: Dogbane string was tied with fisherman's knots to make fishing nets shaped like grain sacks and to attach bone points to the prongs of double-pointed fish spears. These spears also employed dogbane check cords to secure the detachable barbs to the spear.

Gaming and competition: Wooden hoops bound with dogbane cordage were used in hoop games.

Hunting: Big game snares used to trap deer had small dogbane nets serving as triggering mechanisms when caught by a deer's antlers.

Packing or carrying: Pack nets and tumplines used to carry heavy loads were constructed with dogbane cordage.

Trade: Hanks of dogbane fiber were divided into small braided bundles with standard trade values from 10 to 19 clamshell disks.

Aralia californica S. Watson (Araliaceae)
· **Elkclover**

Native name: **kasi' zi tsŏ**.

Antihemorrhagic: An infusion of the plant was used for hemorrhaging in the lungs or stomach.

Medicine: A decoction of the root was highly valued for unspecified diseases of the lungs and stomach (Chestnut 1902).

Root food: The large roots were baked in underground ovens, presumably as food.

A basket so general in its use that an Indian woman was almost never seen away from her home without it. It was her pocket, her hand-bag, her truck. About 1900 they became rare and later disappeared. It was a handsome basket with a fine net-strap of native flax (*ma-ce'*) with wampum woven in a pattern on the head band.

– John W. Hudson

***Araucaria araucana* (Molina) K. Koch (Araucariaceae) · Monkey puzzle**

Taxonomic notes: This tree, a popular ornamental during the Victorian era, was brought to the United States from Chile (Mabberley 1987). Its presence in the study area is not documented in regional floras because it did not naturalize outside landscaped environments.

Nut food: The nut-like seeds were roasted and eaten.

***Arbutus menziesii* Pursh (Ericaceae) · Madrone**

Native name: *ka-bat'*.

Ceremony: Ceremonial batons were made from madrone wood. Resembling "a cross handled cane" and ornamented with eagle feathers affixed to the handle, these were used during nighttime sweathouse ceremonies, most likely associated with the Kuksu (*kuk'su*) ceremony described by Barrett (1917a).

Confection: Honey dew, a sweet clear sticky substance, was pleasurably licked or scraped from the underside of madrone leaves during the fall.

Fruit food: The berries were ground and toasted. Hudson reported the taste was insipid but could relieve one's hunger. The seeds and bark peelings were considered harmful.

Laxative: Honeydew from madrone leaves was considered a purgative.

***Arctostaphylos* spp. (Ericaceae) · Manzanita**

Arctostaphylos manzanita Parry · Common manzanita

Native name: *ka-ye'*.

Taxonomic notes: Although Hudson frequently used the name *Arctostaphylos manzanita*, he also used the common name "manzanita," evidently in reference to other unspecified local *Arctostaphylos* taxa.

Beverage: A sweet cider or tea was prepared by passing water through a meal made from the parched and dessicated ripe fruits using a fine mesh strainer. For additional sweetness, a small quantity of baked and macerated young green leaves and stems of autumn willowweed (*Epilobium brachycarpum*) were sometimes added.

Bread: Ripe fruits were lightly parched in hot ashes, rolled between the palms to separate the seeds, and baked into bread. Hudson is unclear as to whether autumn willowweed was added to the dough, as described above for manzanita tea.

Decoration: Awls made from the wood were used to pierce mature men's nose septa.

Fishing: Fish hooks were made from manzanita and other hardwoods. These straight double-pointed barbs had a groove in the middle, to which a length of string was tied and secured with pitch. Grasshoppers (order Orthoptera) were often used as bait.

Fowling: Hooks used to catch cranes, turkey vultures, and California condors were also made from manzanita. These were slightly larger than fish hooks and were not grooved in the middle.

<u>Fruit food</u>: Ripe manzanita fruits were eaten in moderation. They were collected in small utilitarian collecting baskets made especially for the purpose. The fruits stored well from season to season in elevated granaries. According to Hudson, eating excessive quantities of the seeds was dangerous for children because they could obstruct the colon. In about 1900, Hudson told Chestnut that he had seen at least five such fatalities in his medical career (Chestnut 1902). He described the symptoms as "cerebral," including opisthotonos, coma, and pinhole pupil. According to Helen Carpenter (n.d.), unripe manzanita berries were a food of last resort.

<u>Gaming and competition</u>: A shinny stick specimen in the collections of Grace Hudson Museum, used in game resembling hockey, was made from manzanita wood.

<u>Mush</u>: A mush food was made by boiling parched, seeded, and ground ripe fruits with water. Young green leaves and stems of autumn willowweed were baked and macerated for use as flavoring for the mush.

<u>Music</u>: Bullroarers ("thunder sticks") and split-stick clappers ("lightning sticks"), used in dance ceremonies, were made from manzanita and other woods (cf. Barrett 1952; Loeb 1926).

<u>STD remedy</u>: Manzanita was used as a remedy for advanced cases of an "obscene" disease. The seeds were ground in a medicine mortar with red paint and coyote dung and hair. The resulting substance was heated and applied topically over the patient's heart.

<u>Tool</u>: Split segments of manzanita wood were a preferred material for perforated arrow and drill shaft straighteners.

<u>Watercraft</u>: Paddles were made from manzanita, presumably for use in conjunction with tule balsas, which the Potter Valley Pomo used in open waters outside the valley.

Armillaria mellea **(Vahl) P. Kumm. (Fungi: Physalacriaceae) · Honey mushroom**
<u>Native name</u>: ***ka-li' tce e'*** ("tree mushroom").
<u>Fungus food</u>: Honey mushrooms were fried with tallow on flat heated stones or directly on coals.

Artemisia californica **Less. (Asteraceae) · California sagebrush**
<u>Native name</u>: ***ka am pi-lu'-lu'*** ("heart fluttering effect").
<u>Taxonomic notes</u>: Hudson often used the genus name *Artemisia* without further specification. California sagebrush (*A. californica*) was the only member of this genus specifically mentioned in his notes and writings, although its distribution is largely limited to coastal environments, such as coastal sage scrub and coastal strand plant communities, which do not occur in the immediate vicinity of Potter Valley. According to Chestnut (1902), the *Artemisia* taxon that was highly esteemed as a medicine by many Pomoan groups was *A. heterophylla*, now known as *A. douglasiana*, which is amply distributed in Potter Valley plant communities, such as mixed conifer forests, foothill woodlands,

chaparral, and riparian wetlands. Hudson's references to *"Artemisia"* may also have contemplated other local members of the genus.

Analgesic: Internal pain was treated with massage and the therapeutic application of warmth and moisture (fomentation) with *Artemisia,* probably in the manner described below for colic.

Antihemorrhagic: The leaves were placed in one's nostrils to treat nosebleed.

Asthma remedy: To treat asthmatic cough, a solution of the plant was poured on hot rocks and the vapor inhaled through a tube.

Ceremony: The foliage was used in sweat baths as an aromatic floor covering. Hudson reported that its excessive use caused "irregularity of the heart," presumably the effect referenced by the Northern Pomo name.

Cleaning agent: A decoction of the leaves was used as an antiseptic.

Counterirritant: A decoction of the leaves was used as a counter-irritant.

Decoration: The stalks were used to make men's ear sticks. Additionally, it was used to fashion men's nose sticks for home use.

Emollient: A decoction of the leaves was used as an emollient.

Febrifuge: A decoction of the leaves was used to reduce fevers.

Fragrance: A decoction of the leaves was used as a deodorant.

Gaming and competition: Counting rods used in women's stave games were made of wormwood. In addition, the shafts of arrows used in distance shooting competitions were often made from an *Artemisia* wood because it was considered lightweight yet rigid.

Gastrointestinal aid: The foliage was used with massage and fomentation to treat sharp abdominal pains. Additionally, it was used in conjunction with herbal steam baths to treat colic. The usual procedure involved preparing a steam bed made with a layer of fresh green leaves over hot stones. The most commonly used leaves were bush monkeyflower (*Mimulus aurantiacus*), which were often alternated with *Artemisia.* Hudson considered the effect to be penetrating and lasting.

Medicine: According to Chestnut (1902), *A. heterophylla* was the most highly valued medicinal plant among the indigenous peoples at Round Valley, being used to treat colic, colds, bronchitis, stomachache, headache, diarrhea, fever, sore eyes and dermatitis.

Panacea: *Artemisia* was considered a panacea, being used to treat many diseases.

Women's health: From adolescence to motherhood, women used *Artemisia* in numerous ways. After spending several days in seclusion after first menses and before returning to the community, young women were bathed in tepid water scented with *Artemisia* sprigs and soaproot (*Chlorogalum pomeridianum*). After expulsion of the afterbirth, mothers were bathed in the hip area with water strongly infused with *Artemisia.* The plant was also used to dress the newborn's navel. Additionally, a warm solution of sagebrush was used to cleanse, massage, and foment a mother's breasts to ensure abundant breast milk and to treat sore breasts.

Asclepias spp. (Apocynaceae) · Milkweed

Asclepias eriocarpa Benth. · Kotolo milkweed

Asclepias fascicularis Dcne. · Mexican whorled milkweed

Native names: **_du-wi cĭm'-ma_** ("coyote ears") and **_tsi-wǎ' tsŏ_** ("varied thrush clover").

Taxonomic notes: Hudson occasionally used the scientific name _Asclepias mexicana_ for the contemporary taxon _Asclepias fascicularis_ (USDA and NRCS 2012). He also used the common name "kotolo," widely used for _Asclepias eriocarpa_ (Calflora 2012; Chestnut 1902). Although he specified that two distinct taxa were used, his frequent use of the genus name _Asclepias_ without further specification suggests that other local taxa may have been used.

Clothing: Milkweed fiber was used to make soft baby gowns. A fine bird feather blanket worn only by the wives of prominent leaders consisted of four bands of red woodpecker scalp feathers woven into a mesh of milkweed fiber.

Cordage: The short glossy stalk fibers were an important source of fiber for string. Milkweed ranked fourth in strength among Potter Valley Pomo cordage fibers. The woodiness of the stalks was somewhat deteriorated after early winter frosts, such that the fiber could easily be collected. The cleaned fiber was much like cotton in appearance and strength.

Decoration: Clamshell disks and California quail crest feathers were interwoven with milkweed string to form forehead bands that were used in conjunction with hairnets. Women's ceremonial dance headbands also utilized milkweed fiber. Heavy ceremonial belts that ranked among the most valuable of Potter Valley Pomo possessions were also woven with milkweed fiber. According to Loeb (1926), this type of belt was a preferred wedding gift, being given by the groom's family to the bride's family.

Legend: In an unnamed legend recorded by Hudson, **Ce ta ta** gave his bride, Quail Woman, two milkweed blankets as wedding gifts. In another myth, Coyote (**_Du-wi'_**) mixed milkweed juice with clay in his attempts to create the first people.

Padding or toweling: Wrappings and swaddlings for newborns were made from shredded milkweed fiber.

Salad food: Green milkweed pods were eaten raw. The crushed leaves were also eaten raw with salt and California bay nut (_Umbellularia californica_) bread.

Snakebite remedy: Milkweed juice was used in conjunction with a tourniquet to extract snake poison.

Women's health: To stimulate lactation, a woman's breasts were scarified, applied with salted milkweed juice, and subsequently massaged.

*_Avena_ spp. (Poaceae) · Wild oats

*_Avena barbata_ Pott ex Link · Slender wild oats

*_Avena fatua_ L. · Common wild oats

Native name: **bu-ta' ba-ă** ("bear seed").

Taxonomic notes: Hudson cited *Avena barbata* and *Avena fatua* in a seemingly interchangeable manner. Although both were introduced to California from Europe, other sources indicate *A. fatua* was the most common *Avena* species in the Pomoan region (Chestnut 1902; Gifford 1967).

Architecture: Wild oats was used for house thatching.

Matting or bedding: Plain-twined woven mats were made with wild oat fiber.

Seed food: Abundant in the region, wild oat seeds were a substantial food source, being used for pinole. Hudson provided the following account of its arrival in the area, which is notable for the specificity with which it identifies the time, place, and circumstances of its first incorporation as food by the local indigenous population:

> 'Wild Oats', *Avena fatua*, first appeared on Corral Creek in Redwood Valley, at [the] camp site of three white men with horses, in the winter of 1840. The Indians feared the strange animals and the seed left by them spread rapidly into adjacent valleys and was named **bu-ta' ba-ă** (bear grain) because it 'crawled' when wetted. Its ground meal was tested on "some old squaws," who proved it safe by surviving. It subsequently came into common use. Some visitors from **Dol'-dam ke-ya** (a village in Ukiah Valley) took a sheaf of the plant home with them, but became suspicious and threw it away.

Wild oats became the preferred seed plant (**ba ă**) for pinole. In July, the seeds were collected with seed beaters and conical burden baskets. The chaff was removed by tossing about one liter of seeds with hot embers in a flexible disk-shaped basket. The wind was allowed to blow the chaff away. The seeds were then soaked for about three hours before being toasted with coals and ground in a stone mortar with a wooden pestle. The resulting flour was eaten dry or simmered in an equal volume of water to make cakes. A pinch of salt was used to preserve wild oat flour for long journeys.

Baccharis spp. (Asteraceae) · Broom

Baccharis glutinosa Pers. · Marsh baccharis

Baccharis salicifolia (Ruiz & Pav.) Pers. · Mule fat

Native names: **xăn xăn ka-lĭ'** and **ko-dĭm' mu-ca**.

Taxonomic notes: Hudson sometimes used the name *Baccharis douglasii* for the contemporary species *Baccharis glutinosa* (Jepson Flora Project 2012b), as well as *Baccharis viminea* for the contemporary species *B. salicifolia* (USDA and NRCS 2012).

Arrow: Collected when dry in autumn, broom was considered an arrow shaft wood of ordinary quality. It was the least desirable of the plants Hudson identified as arrow woods.

Balsamorhiza deltoidea Nutt. (Asteraceae) · Deltoid balsamroot

<u>Native name</u>: *ca lam' ba ă*.

<u>Seed food</u>: Mature seeds were winnowed and ground with mortar and pestle, presumably for pinole. It was considered a favorite food.

Beckmannia syzigachne (Steud.) Fernald (Poaceae) · American sloughgrass

<u>Native name</u>: *tce cim ka di*.

<u>Taxonomic notes</u>: Hudson used *Beckmannia erucaeformis* for the contemporary species *Beckmannia syzigachne* (USDA and NRCS 2012).

<u>Basketry</u>: The fiber was used as a basketry weft.

<u>Cordage</u>: The stalks were split, soaked, and twisted for string. It was considered very strong and convenient.

Bolboschoenus maritimus (L.) Palla (Cyperaceae) · Alkali bulrush

<u>Taxonomic notes</u>: Hudson referenced the species *Scirpus maritimus,* which corresponds with the contemporary taxon *Bolboschoenus maritimus* (Jepson Flora Project 2012b).

<u>Basketry</u>: Alkali bulrush rhizomes provided the most attractive and highly valued black basketry weft fiber with the possible exception of maidenhair fern, which was finer and had a more permanent black color. It ranked in value on par with such expensive trade items as salt and obsidian. According to Potter Valley Pomo custom, it was not used in plain-twined basketry. The rhizomes, found only in marshy soils fed by brackish waters in rare tidewater flats, were collected in autumn after the plants died back and often obtained by the Potter Valley Pomo through trade. Women collected the rhizomes with digging sticks, using their toes to follow each to the next plant. The freshly collected rhizomes were delivered to elderly women on the shore, who removed the rough coating by biting and chewing. The choicest rhizomes were about 45 cm in length and very narrow.

While still wet, the narrow rhizomes were split into even strips. This activity required experience because the fibers did not run parallel. First, the wider end was carefully split with an obsidian flake. With the smaller end secured between the toes and one of the strips at the wider end held with the teeth, other half of the wider end was gently pulled downward, thus splitting the rhizome lengthwise. The symmetry of the two strips was assured by bending the rhizome with the other hand ahead of the running split. Rhizomes strips were split again as many times as necessary to achieve the desired width. This procedure could be modified to divide each portion into thirds instead of halves and thereby economize material. The resulting strips had triangular cores that were scraped smoothed.

Natural rhizome fibers less than three years old were light tan in color and required dying to achieve a desirable black shade. Older rhizomes did not require dying, as they naturally achieved a deep black color in the fourth year of growth. The finished strips were made into coils of predetermined sizes for trade.

Legend: In Potter Valley Pomo mythology, Water Newt was guardian of the alkali bulrush rhizomes.

Bolboschoenus robustus (Pursh) Soják (Cyperaceae) · Tuberous bulrush
Native name: *ko-kal ka-li.*

Taxonomic notes: Hudson referred to *Scirpus robustus* and *Scirpus campestris,* the latter of which appears to have derived from *Scirpus robustus* var. *campestris* (Fernald 1900). Both taxa correspond with the contemporary species *Bolboschoenus robustus* (Jepson Flora Project 2012b).

Architecture: The stalks were used as a sturdy insulating thatch for houses.

Clothing: Stalk fibers were used to make soft and absorbent clothing for infants and the elderly. The stalks of male plants were considered the finest fiber material for this purpose.

Matting or bedding: Stalks were a preferred material for mattresses and mattings because they were flexible, resilient, and had a pleasant light color.

Salad food: The young shoots were eaten raw.

Watercraft: The stalks were used to make balsas, the primary Pomo mode of water transportation in open waters.

Brassica nigra (L.) W. D. J. Koch (Brassicaceae) · Black mustard
Native name: *tsi mu' duk ka-lî'.*

Taxonomic notes: In one instance, Hudson used only the common name "wild mustard," which could also refer to field mustard (*Brassica rapa).*

Cooked green: Black mustard greens were boiled and eaten.

Brodiaea spp. (Themidaceae) · Brodiaea
Brodiaea coronaria (Salisb.) Engl. · Harvest clusterlily
Brodiaea terrestris Kellogg · Dwarf clusterlily
Native name: *ba'-bǎ bu* ("grandfather's bulb").

Taxonomic notes: Hudson occasionally used *Hookera coronaria* for the contemporary species *Brodiaea coronaria* (Moerman 1998; Yanovsky 1936). He also cited *Brodiaea grandiflora,* an outdated species represented by two contemporary taxa in the study area, *B. coronaria* and *B. terrestris* (Munz and Keck 1973).

Bulb or corm food: The bulbs were baked in underground ovens and eaten. Chestnut (1902) specified that the bulbs gained a sweet flavor after roasting for an entire day.

Bromus carinatus Hook. & Arn. (Poaceae) · California brome
Native names: *ca tai' ka-lî'* and *lau lau ka-di'.*

Taxonomic notes: Hudson mentioned *Bromus carinatus* and *Bromus marginatus,* both of which are now included in *Bromus carinatus* (Jepson Flora Project 2012a).

Architecture: California brome was used for thatching.

Matting or bedding: The leaves were used for bedding (cf. Barrett 1916).

Seed food: Brome seeds were used for pinole.

Bromus diandrus Roth (Poaceae) · Ripgut

Native name: *ca tai' ka-di'.*

Taxonomic notes: Hudson used *Bromus maximus,* evidently based on botanist Alice Eastwood's determination, which corresponds with the contemporary taxon *Bromus diandrus* (USDA and NRCS 2012).

Architecture: Ripgut was used for thatching and in wattle, a framework of flexible rods intertwined with grasses and reeds.

Decoration: Hudson noted "ceremonial belt of novitiates (male)" in a page margin next to a reference to *B. diandrus* without additional information.

Calandrinia spp. (Montiaceae) · Redmaids

Calandrinia ciliata (Ruiz & Pav.) DC. · Fringed redmaids

Native name: *ba-lai' nu-căm* ("blood-like flower") and *ka tsi wa'.*

Taxonomic notes: Hudson used *Calandrinia menziesii* for the contemporary species *Calandrinia ciliate,* previously classified as *Calandrinia ciliata* var. *menziesii* (Jepson Flora Project 2012a; USDA and NRCS 2012). Elsewhere, based on Alice Eastwood's 1928 determination, he also used the name *Calandrinia insignis,* which is not found in the botanical literature for California, leaving its identity uncertain.

Disinfectant: The plant was used as an antiseptic for unspecified purposes.

First aid: A powder made from the dried plant was applied to persistent sores.

Insecticide: Fringed redmaids was used to treat head lice, although Hudson did not specify how it was prepared or administered.

Salad food: Leaves of the plant identified as *C. insignis* were eaten raw.

Stimulant: Hudson indicated that fringed redmaids was used as a stimulant, but did not elaborate further.

Calochortus spp. (Liliaceae) · Mariposa lily

Calochortus luteus Lindl. · Yellow mariposa
Calochortus superbus Purdy ex J. T. Howell · Yellow mariposa
Calochortus venustus Douglas ex Benth. · Butterfly mariposa

Native name: *bu-tum' bu.*

Taxonomic notes: Hudson's references to *Calochortus venustus* also included the contemporary taxa *Calochortus luteus* and *Calochortus superbus* (Jepson Flora Project 2012a).

The same Northern Pomo name is also associated with references to the genus *Calochortus* and the common name "mariposa lily" without further specification, suggesting that other local *Calochortus* were also used.

Bulb or corm food: The bulbs were baked in underground ovens and eaten.

Decoration: Helen Carpenter (n.d.) described an episode in which a group of young girls collected mariposa lily flowers before stealing "away to the most secluded spot they knew" to weave them into wreaths, which they placed on their heads while practicing dance steps. She explained that young girls used these flowers instead of feather decorations to practice dances before they were old enough to dance in public.

Calochortus amabilis Purdy (Liliaceae) · Golden globelily, Short lily

Native name: *bi-tĭt'*.

Taxonomic notes: Hudson's use of this scientific name corresponds with botanist Alice Eastwood's 1927 identification of a Hudson specimen labeled with the Northern Pomo name *b'tit bu*.

Bulb or corm food: The bulbs were baked in underground ovens and eaten.

Calochortus pulchellus (Benth.) Alph. Wood (Liliaceae) · Mount Diablo globelily

Native names: *bi-ce' bŭ* ("deer bulb").

Bulb or corm food: The bulbs were baked in underground ovens and eaten.

Calycadenia multiglandulosa DC. (Asteraceae) · Sticky western rosinweed

Native name: *ma-ko' ka-lĭ'*.

Taxonomic notes: Hudson occasionally used the common name "tarweed," but often distinguished between a white flowered type (*Calycadenia multiglandulosa*) and a yellow type, given as *Hemizonia luzaefolia* (see *Hemizonia congesta*).

Seed food: The late-maturing seeds were collected with seed beaters and prepared as pinole. These oily and strongly flavored seeds were used sparingly in seed meal.

Calycanthus occidentalis Hook. & Arn. (Calycanthaceae) · Spicebush, western sweetshrub

Arrow: The wood was used for arrow shafts, being ranked third in preference among Potter Valley Pomo plants used for this purpose.

Basketry: Both the wood and bark from young shoots were used as basketry weft materials (Chestnut 1902).

Calystegia sp. (Convolvulaceae) · False bindweed

Taxonomic notes: Hudson used the common name "morning-glory," which may refer to several local *Calystegia* species.

Hunting: *Calystegia* leaves were used to imitate the sound of a bleating fawn in order to attract deer of both sexes while hunting. According to Hudson, the sound was made by placing a soft leaf against the tongue and sucking.

Camassia spp. (Agavaceae) · Camas
Camassia quamash (Pursh) Greene · Large camas
Camassia leichtlinii (Baker) S. Watson · Common camas
Native name: ***bitĭtbu'***.

Taxonomic notes: Hudson used the name *Quamasia leichtlinti* for the contemporary species *Camassia quamash* and *C. leichtlinii* (Coville 1897).

Adhesive: Hudson made reference to a plant called ***bi ti*** with bulbs used to produce a glue for adhering sinew to the backs of bows for improved strength and resilience (cf. Pope 1923). The resemblance between the native names ***bi ti*** and ***bitĭtbu'*** suggest the identity of this plant may be large camas. The Northern Pomo name ***bitĭtbu'*** may be comprised of the plant name for camas (***bi ti***) and the word for bulb or corm (***bu***) or, literally, "camas bulb."

Bulb or corm food: Considered the largest and best tasting of the baked bulb foods, large camas was cooked in underground ovens and eaten. According to Chestnut (1902), the bulbs, harvested in June and July, were sometimes boiled.

Cardamine californica (Nutt.) Greene (Brassicaceae) · Milkmaids
Native name: ***Du-wi' tci tci'***.

Taxonomic notes: Hudson used *Dentaria californica* for the contemporary taxon *Cardamine californica* (Jepson Flora Project 2012b). He provided no information regarding its uses.

Carex spp. (Cyperaceae) · Sedge
Carex barbarae Dewey · Santa Barbara sedge
Carex mendocinensis Olney ex W. Boott · Mendocino sedge
Native name: ***ka-hum'***.

Taxonomic notes: According to Peri and Patterson (1976), inaccuracies regarding *Carex* taxonomy have persisted in the literature about Pomo basketry due to difficulties in identifying members of this genus. Although Hudson (1893) originally identified this important basketry fiber as *Carex mendocinoensis*, Chestnut (1902) published a correction identifying *C. barbarae*. Nevertheless, according to Hudson, multiple *Carex* taxa were employed for this purpose.

Basketry: Sedge rhizome fibers were highly valued in Pomo basketry as the finest light-colored weft. They were highly elastic, pliable, and of good tensile strength. Quality sedge beds were known and tended by weavers. Rhizome quality depended greatly on soil conditions, with wet soils, especially those near springs and waterways, being preferred. The Potter Valley Pomo distinguished three types of sedge beds. Boggy soils in rich wet lowlands produced the most desired rhizomes, used for fine stitching due to their flexibility and milky white color. Sandy soils produced the second most desirable rhizomes, producing somewhat angular and brittle fibers that yellowed with age. These were most appropriate for large, coarse vessels. Gravel beds produced the least desirable rhizomes, which were only suitable for open twining. According to Peri and Patterson (1976), the Southern Pomo also distinguished between three types of sedge beds, although these differed somewhat from those recognized by the Northern Pomo. For the Southern Pomo, "sand root beds" produce the whitest, straightest and longest rhizomes. Less desirable were rhizomes from "dirt root beds," due to their coloration, and "heavy clay beds," due to their shortness.

Peri et al. (1982) and Allen (1972) argued that rhizome collection was a formalized activity among the Pomoan peoples, involving cultivation practices that conditioned the soil and improved growth patterns (cf. Mason 1904; Sarris 1994). According to these sources, beds were visited periodically not only to collect rhizomes, but also to clean them of debris, weed, till, and replant. These custodial activities resulted in longer rhizomes that were minimally tangled and therefore easier to collect. According to Hudson, the Potter Valley Pomo collected the rhizomes in early spring. In contrast, Peri and collaborators reported that the Southern Pomo preferred to collect them from late summer to early autumn.

Both men and women collected rhizomes with digging sticks, although Hudson considered women to be more efficient because they did not stop at midday to rest and smoke. Once uncovered, a rhizome was grasped between the toes and gently lifted, to reveal the interconnected roots and the best direction to continue digging to reach adjacent plants. Two-year rhizomes were preferred because younger ones were shorter and older ones were coarser, more brittle and subject to darkening. Whereas women typically harvested about 20 rhizomes per day, men only collected about 10. Processing began at the collecting beds the following day, with care being taken to remove the rough exterior before the roots dried. Elder women often accomplished this without damaging the interior fibers by working them between their toothless gums (Hudson 1893). Cleaned rhizomes were then loaded into packing baskets and transported home. Several days later, the rhizomes were split lengthwise into three or four equal parts, depending on the fineness of the desired threads, and cleaned of the inner woody material. Finally, the fibers were bundled into rolls, each of which typically containing the fibers from two rhizomes (Figure 21).

Legend: According to a legend recorded by Hudson, Toad (**Bi-tcĭn'**) was the "patroness of the sewing art and of coil weaving" and the guardian of sedge rhizomes. She provided them to the people and taught them how to prepare the fibers and weave with them, thus transforming the previously imperfect Pomoan practice of weaving into a fine art.

Trade: A roll of split sedge rhizome fiber had a fixed trade value of about 100 clamshell disks (cf. Peri and Patterson 1976).

*Carpobrotus chilensis (Molina) N.E. Br. (Aizoaceae) · Sea fig

Native name: *ka'-hǎ ba-kai'*.

Taxonomic notes: Based on a 1928 determination by Alice Eastwood, Hudson used *Mesembryanthemum aequilaterus* (written *Mesembryanthemum aequilaterale*), which corresponds with the contemporary taxon *Carpobrotus chilensis* (Jepson Flora Project 2012a).

Figure 21. Rolls of sedge basketry fibers. Photograph by James R. Welch, 2011. In the collections of Grace Hudson Museum, Ukiah.

Fruit food: This plant produces a fine fruit that was sought by men while fishing on the coast during summer. It was sometimes sprinkled with salt water and dried in the sun. According to Hudson, the texture was similar to fig but lost its sweetness within a month.

Castilleja exserta (A. Heller) T. I. Chuang & Heckard (Orobanchaceae) · Owl's clover

Native name: *ba-wal' ka-lǐ'* ("eel plant").

Taxonomic notes: Hudson used *Orthocarpus purpurascens* (written *Orthocarpus purburascens*), which corresponds with the contemporary species *Castilleja exserta* (Jepson Flora Project 2012a).

Although he did not specify its uses, Hudson noted that owl's clover blooms announced the beginning of the Russian River eel run, presumably referring to the Pacific lamprey (*Lampetra tridentata*), which was eaten by the Northern Pomo (cf. Gifford 1967; Stewart 1943).

Ceanothus spp. (Rhamnaceae) · California lilac

Native names: *hai' i-ǒ'* ("thicket prickly") and *ba-kam' kǎ-lǐ'*.

Taxonomic notes: Hudson often used the genus name *Ceanothus*, and occasionally the common name "buckbrush," without further specification. These names could refer to a large number of local *Ceanothus* taxa.

Basketry: California lilac provided long, tough rods of even caliber used for warp in twined and one-rod coiled basketry.

Fire: The wood was used for fire drill shafts.

Fowling: The heartwood was used to fashion bird arrow points.

Tool: The wood was used for walking canes.

Ceanothus cuneatus Nutt. (Rhamnaceae) · Buckbrush

Native name: *ba-kam' kă-lĭ'*.

Tool: Buckbrush was used to fashion walking canes used by blind people and chiefs.

Ceanothus foliosus Parry (Rhamnaceae) · Wavyleaf ceanothus

Native name: *tsi-pul'* ("bluish").

Basketry: The plant was used for basketry warp elements, most likely with twining and one-rod coiling weaves.

Seed food: The seeds were eaten, presumably for pinole.

Cercis occidentalis Torr. ex A. Gray (Fabaceae) · California redbud

Native name: *mu-le' ka-li'* ("scorched tree").

Basketry: Redbud provided a thin but strong fiber of burnt sienna color that was used as weft in fine patterned basketry. The exterior layer of the straight shoots and twigs was collected in the fall when the color was brightest. Whole stems were softened by soaking for about an hour in hot water before removing the fibers with one's thumbnail. The strength of this fiber was improved by leaving a thin layer of interior wood adhered to the colored exterior layer. California redbud coils were hung from lodge ceilings for about a month to allow the smoke to season the fiber and enrich its color. Despite being highly desired as weft, it was considered difficult to work due to its brittleness and frequent knots. California redbud wood was also used as warp in coarse utilitarian baskets.

Colorant: Arrows, flutes, and game staves were often patterned by wrapping tightly with redbud bark before scorching the surface with fire. Removing these bark wrappings revealed a blackened negative pattern.

Cercocarpus spp. (Rosaceae) · Mountain mahogany

Cercocarpus betuloides Nutt. · Birchleaf mountain mahogany

Cercocarpus ledifolius Nutt. · Curlleaf mountain mahogany

Native names: *ha ma cŭ'* ("projecting lips") and *ma-cu ka-lĭ'*.

Taxonomic notes: At times, Hudson used only the genus name *Cercocarpus*. He also used *Cercocarpus parvifolius* (written *Cercocarpus parvifol*), which corresponds with the contemporary taxon *Cercocarpus betuloides* (Jepson 1936). In a few instances, he cited *Cornus parviflora* when, from the context, he appears to have meant *Cercocarpus parvifolius*.

Ceremony: Hudson reported that mountain mahogany batons ornamented with feathers were used to drive away the "devil."

Decoration: Armor fashioned from mountain mahogany rods was worn by bear doctors for ceremonial purposes. Similar to war armor, bear doctor armor consisted of approximately 1 cm wide dowels bound together with cordage made from iris (*Iris* spp.) or stinging nettle (*Urtica dioica*).

Fishing: The double points of fish spears used for salmon and steelhead were fashioned from mountain mahogany.

Gaming and competition: The wood was used for the foreshafts and conical heads of shorter-range contest arrows.

Hunting: Approximately 2.5 m spears used to stab trapped deer were made from the wood. These were sharpened at both ends and fire-hardened. Mountain mahogany was also highly desired for shafts and foreshafts of big game arrows.

Tool: Mountain mahogany was considered the toughest of woods, being highly valued for a variety of working tools such as pries, crowbars, picks, and canes. It was also a favorite wood for digging sticks, used to obtain roots and rhizomes. In addition, a perforated split section of the wood was used to polish and straighten certain implements, such as arrows and drills.

War: The wood was used to fashion fearsome club-ended stabbing spears, used in war. The Potter Valley Pomo also used mountain mahogany in constructing upper body armor, although this was more typical of northerly Yuki groups.

Chlorogalum pomeridianum (DC.) Kunth (Agavaceae) · Soaproot

Native name: *am' ka-li*.

Taxonomic notes: Hudson frequently used the genus name *Chlorogalum* or the common name "soap root," which could also refer to narrowleaf soap plant (*C. angustifolium*).

Adhesive: A liquid derived by baking the bulbs was used as glue for affixing feather fletching to arrows (Chestnut 1902). Glue used to affix sinew backing to bows was prepared by cooking soaproot bulbs with salmon skin and an unidentified plant (*bi ti*).

Brush or broom: The husks were used to make hair brushes and brushes used to collect scattered meal while grinding acorns (Figure 22).

Cleaning agent: Crushed mature bulbs were agitated with water for use as shampoo.

Colorant: When nearly dry, sun baked platters made from blue clay were decorated with a paint made from a red mineral pigment mixed with soaproot glue. According to Chestnut (1902), bows were permanently blackened and antiqued by applying the liquid from baked soaproot bulbs followed by an application of soot.

Cooked green: Young shoots were baked in ashes and eaten with meat. This food

Figure 22. Soaproot brush. Photograph by James R. Welch, 2011. Private collection, Ukiah.

was known to cause diarrhea if consumed in excess. Because the cooking process distorted the shoots into worm-like shapes, they were called "earth worm" (*bi-la'*).

Cooking: The moist leaves were used to line the interior of underground ovens.

Decoration: The dry husks were used as a soft lining for bear doctors' masks, especially when these were weighted down with hidden water bladders to imitate the sound of a bear's bowels. The husks were also shredded and used to line rod armor, used in war and in bear doctor ceremonial outfits.

Fishing: Fresh crushed bulbs were placed in streams to stupefy and thereby easily capture fish. Occasionally Durango root (*Datisca glomerata*) was added to assist the action of soaproot. Helen Carpenter (n.d.) described the use of soaproot for fishing. In her account, the brown husks were removed to expose the smooth bulb. Each bulb was vigorously rubbed, one at a time until sudsy, and dipped in the water in the middle of a large pool until the water became milky and the fish rose to the surface. The fish were then skimmed up with baskets. Carpenter explained that the quantity of soaproot used did not kill the fish, which soon revived if left in running water.

Insecticide: A strong solution of soaproot served as an insecticide, being used as a rinse for baskets to kill weevils.

Legend: In the legend "Poma Genesis," documented by Hudson, Coyote (*Du-wi'*) plastered split soaproot bulbs to the heads of the first man and woman before bringing them from the sweathouse into the daylight to fully dry and therefore complete their creation.

Polish: To prevent checkering, flutes and blowing tubes were polished by rubbing a mixture of crushed soaproot and damp buckeye charcoal into the surface with green willow leaves.

War: Shredded soaproot husks were sewn to the interior of rod armor as a soft lining and to provide an additional protective barrier against projectiles.

Women's health: Tender flower stalks were baked in ashes and used in an unspecified manner to induce or hasten menstrual flow. Also, attendants bathed young women at first menses in tepid water scented with sprigs of soaproot and wormwood or sagebrush.

Chrysolepis chrysophylla (Hook.) Hjelmq. (Fagaceae) · Giant chinquapin

Native name: *na-tol ka-li*.

Taxonomic notes: Hudson used *Castanopsis chrysophyla* for the contemporary species *Chrysolepis chrysophylla* (USDA and NRCS 2012).

Bread: Giant chinquapin acorn meal was leached or mixed with red earth (*ma-po'*) and baked into bread. Flour made from the parched seeds of such plants as California compassplant (*Wyethia* spp.), farewell to spring (*Clarkia amoena*), and common madia (*Madia elegans*) were often added to improve the flavor.

Mush: Leached acorn meal was also used to make mush, although giant chinquapin was the least preferred acorn for his purpose. Its poor flavor was often improved by adding parched seed flour (see above).

Clarkia amoena **(Lehm.) Nelson & MacBr. (Onagraceae) · Farewell to spring**
Native name: ***bi-mu' ba-ă.***

Taxonomic notes: Hudson used *Godetia lindleyii* for the contemporary species *Clarkia amoena*, which has erroneously appeared elsewhere as *Clarkia amoena* ssp. *lindleyi* (Best 1996; Jepson Flora Project 2012b).

Flavoring: The parched seed flour was the most popular seasoning for acorn mush and bread. It was especially appreciated for imparting a rich flavor to products made from less desirable types or grades of acorns. Inflorescences containing ripe seeds were dried in the sun before being beaten with a rod and crushed with mortar and pestle.

Claytonia perfoliata **Donn ex Willd. (Montiaceae) · Miner's lettuce**
Native names: ***ka mi-tol' mi-tol*** and ***ho mi-lik' pi-cum.***

Taxonomic notes: Hudson used *Montia perfoliata* for the contemporary taxon *Claytonia perfoliata* (USDA and NRCS 2012).

Salad food: The fresh leaves were eaten as lettuce.

Clinopodium douglasii **(Benth.) Kuntze (Lamiaceae) · Yerba buena**
Native name: ***ma ca kau'.***

Taxonomic notes: Hudson used *Micromeria chamissonis* for the contemporary species *Clinopodium douglasii* (Jepson Flora Project 2012a; USDA and NRCS 2012).

Beverage: The plant was used for tea.

Cornus **spp. (Cornaceae) · Dogwood**
Cornus glabrata Benth. · Brown dogwood
Cornus sericea L. · American dogwood
Native name: ***cu ta ka-lĭ'*** ("hornet tree").

Taxonomic notes: Hudson occasionally referenced *Cornus glabrata*, which he described as having red berries, red bark, and growing by streams. This description more closely fits *Cornus sericea*, creating some uncertainty as to his identification. He also used *Cornus californica* for the contemporary species *Cornus sericea* (Hrusa and Calflora 2001). In some passages, he used the genus name *Cornus* or the common name "dogwood" without further specification.

Architecture: The shoots were used to weave family granaries for storing acorns, buckeyes, and other foods for winter use (cf. Barrett 1916).

Arrow: The shoots were used for arrow shafts.

Basketry: Dogwood rods were used for weaving baby cradle baskets and other basketry requiring strength and delicacy. Constructed with U-shaped rods, cradles were considered very strong and resilient (cf. Barrett 1908b; Hudson 1893; Kroeber 1909; Purdy

1902). Dogwood also provided long, even, and sturdy rods that were used for warp in one-rod coiled and twined baskets.

Colorant: Patterns on the surface of arrows, flutes, and game staves were often created by wrapping with dogwood fibers, scorching with fire, and then removing the bark to reveal a darkened negative pattern.

Diuretic: A bark extraction, made by steeping in cold water for about 12 hours, was taken for urinary retention.

Fire: The wood was used for fire drills.

Fishing: Fish traps were woven from dogwood stalks.

Gaming and competition: The sticks were used to make rackets for a game that resembled lacrosse (Culin 1975).

Hunting: The wood was used for game bows.

Music: Hudson described the Potter Valley Pomo use of musical mouth bows made from light woods, such as dogwood, although Loeb later reported that these were only known among the Pomoan groups at Clear Lake (Loeb 1926).

STD remedy: The bark was steeped in cold water for about 12 hours and taken for quick relief of pain and acute inflammation associated with gonorrhea.

Tool: Blowing tubes used for woodworking consisted of a hollow section of elderberry stalk with a narrower tube insert, some 8 cm in length, made from dogwood or other hardwoods.

Corylus cornuta Marshall ssp. *californica* (A. DC.) E. Murray (Betulaceae) · California hazelnut

Native name: *ca-bă' be-nic'*.

Taxonomic notes: Hudson used *Corylus rostrata* for the contemporary taxon *Corylus cornuta* ssp. *californica* (Jepson Flora Project 2012b).

Basketry: California hazelnut was an important material for warp elements and black weft fibers used in twined and coiled basketry. According to Barrett (1908b), this use was acquired by the Northern Pomo from Athapascans groups to the north. For use as weft, hazelnut fibers were dyed black in wood ash, possibly in a similar manner to that described for tule.

Cordage: Hunters used California hazelnut as an impromptu binding to facilitate carrying large game animals (H. M. Carpenter n.d.).

Fishing: Conical fish traps were constructed from the stalks.

Nut food: The raw nuts were considered a delicacy.

Crataegus gaylussacia A. Heller (Rosaceae) · Suksdorf's hawthorn

Native name: *lum' ka-lĭ'* ("thorn plant").

Taxonomic notes: Hudson used *Crataegus rivularis* for the contemporary species *C. gaylussacia* (Jepson Flora Project 2012b; Jepson 1925; G. L. Smith and Wheeler 1992).

Fruit food: The fruits were eaten after ripening in autumn. Chestnut (1902) specified that they were occasionally eaten raw, but were more often boiled or roasted on coals.

Croton setiger Hook. (Euphorbiaceae) · Turkey mullein
Native name: *pcŭ koo*.

Taxonomic notes: Hudson referred to this plant as "turkey mullein" and *Eremocarpus setigerus*, which correspond with the contemporary taxon *Croton setiger* (Jepson Flora Project 2012b).

Fishing: Turkey mullein was used as a fish poison, although Hudson did not specify what part of the plant was used. Chestnut reported that other Pomoan groups used the crushed leaves (Chestnut 1902). Durango root was sometimes added to improve its action in large pools.

Flavoring: The plant was consumed as a condiment, although Hudson did not specify how it was prepared.

Cynoglossum grande Lehm. (Boraginaceae) · Hound's tongue
Native name: *du wi cim ma'*.

Taxonomic notes: Hudson's use of this scientific name corresponds with a determination in 1928 by botanist Alice Eastwood.

First aid: An infusion of the leaves was used to treat sores.

Datisca glomerata (C. Presl) Baill. (Datiscaceae) · Durango root
Native name: *hai tca-hă' ka-lĭ* ("wood acrid plant").

Emetic: About a teaspoon of a warm infusion of the root was used as a fast-acting emetic.

Fishing: The crushed leaves were used to stupefy fish in small pools. They were also used in large pools in conjunction with other fish poisons, such as soaproot and turkey mullein. Excessive quantities were considered to cause the fish to have a spoiled flavor and to be unhealthful. Chestnut (1902) reported that both leaves and roots were used.

Gastrointestinal aid: An infusion of the root was taken for stomach pains.

Laxative: A large dose of root infusion was taken as a purgative.

**Datura stramonium* L. (Solanaceae) · Jimsonweed
Native name: *ka-lum'*.

Taxonomic notes: Hudson referenced only the introduced species *Datura stramonium*. Native thorn apple (*D. wrightii*) also occurs in the area. Additionally, Hudson referenced another plant as "belladonna" (*lum ka-li*), a European plant that is not naturalized in the study area. The similarity between Hudson's transcriptions of the native names for "belladonna" and jimsonweed suggests the possibility that these are the same plant.

Divination and doctoring: A root decoction was taken by native doctors to bring about altered states of consciousness for purposes of divination, although Hudson reported such use was considered dangerous because it could occasionally result in death. Datura was also smoked as a means to achieve elevated psychological states.

Psychiatric aid: The female condition *tsil da-ko* ("clitoris desire"), described by Hudson as "sexual rage" and "nymphomania," was treated with an infusion of datura root.

> *Sa-ha' ka.* (smoke mystery) the smoking of leaves from such potent plants as Solanum, Stramonium and Nicotiana for their poisonous effect was not a vice, but a means to an elevated psychological state. Alcoholic intoxication was an ideal condition of mind, in which all evil vanishes and all good prevails.
>
> – John W. Hudson

Delphinium hesperium A. Gray (Ranunculaceae) · Foothill larkspur
Native name: *ke' ya da ko'.*

Taxonomic notes: Hudson referenced *Delphinium consolida*, which is a European species with blue or purple flowers that is not known to exist in the study area. Hudson's indication that the plant's corolla was used to produce a blue paint suggests *D. hesperium*, the common blue larkspur in the study area (cf. Chestnut 1902).

Colorant: Juice derived from the crushed corolla was applied with a feather as a blue paint for unspecified purposes.

Delphinium nudicaule Torrey & A. Gray (Ranunculaceae) · Red larkspur
Native name: *si ma yeno.*

Taxonomic notes: Hudson used both *Delphinium nudicaule* and *Delphinium cardinale* in reference to what he described as a forest plant occurring on high mountains. Although in 1928 Alice Eastwood provided Hudson with the determination *D. cardinale*, this is a chaparral plant that does not grow above about 1500 meters, and thus appears inconsistent with Hudson's description (Hickman 1993). Hudson's account is more consistent with the habitat of *D. nudicaule*, which grows on wooded rocky slopes to 2600 meters.

Gaming and competition: Competition sprinters sometimes spit masticated red larkspur on opponents to slow them down.

Narcotic: Powdered dried root could be blown in a person's face to cause drowsiness.

Dichelostemma capitatum (Benth.) Alph. Wood (Themidaceae) · Bluedicks
Native names: *ho bu* ("fire bulb") and *ti-le'.*

Taxonomic notes: Consistent with a specimen determination by Alice Eastwood in 1928, Hudson often used *Brodiaea capitata* for the contemporary species *Dichelostemma capitatum* (USDA and NRCS 2012).

Bread: Mush made from the bulbs was formed into cakes and baked in underground ovens.

Bulb or corm food: The bulbs were baked in underground ovens and eaten.

Dichelostemma congestum (Sm.) Kunth (Themidaceae) · Ookow

Native names: *bu las'* and *ti-le'*.

Taxonomic notes: In addition to using *Brodiaea congesta* for the contemporary species *Dichelostemma congestum* (USDA and NRCS 2012), Hudson also described an unidentified "long stem brodea," called *ho bu* in Northern Pomo.

Bread: The bulbs were made into mush and then baked into cakes.

Bulb or corm food: The bulbs were baked in underground ovens and eaten.

Dichelostemma ida-maia (Alph. Wood) Greene (Themidaceae) · Firecracker brodiaea

Native name: *tsim' bu* ("harmful bulb").

Taxonomic notes: Based on Alice Eastwood's 1928 determination, Hudson used *Brevoortia ida-maia* (written *Brevortia ida-maia*) for the contemporary species *Dichelostemma ida-maia* (USDA and NRCS 2012).

Poison: The bulbs were considered poisonous.

Dodecatheon hendersonii A. Gray (Primulaceae) · Shooting star

Native name: *ka tă o ba nă'*.

Taxonomic notes: Hudson's use of this scientific name was based on a 1928 determination by Alice Eastwood.

Analgesic: Toothache was relieved with the crushed roots. Alternatively, the leaves were combined with California bay oil and used for the same purpose.

Elymus elymoides (Raf.) Swezey (Poaceae) · Squirreltail

Native name: *mi-cu'-lu ko-ma'* ("lizard tail").

Taxonomic notes: Hudson used *Sitanion elymoides* for the contemporary species *Elymus elymoides* (USDA and NRCS 2012).

Seed food: The Potter Valley Pomo used the seeds for pinole, considering them second in quality for this purpose after wild oats.

Elymus triticoides Buckley (Poaceae) · Beardless wildrye

Native name: *tcu-sĭm' ba-ă'*.

Seed food: The seeds were used for pinole.

Epilobium brachycarpum C. Presl (Onagraceae) · **Autumn willowweed**

Native name: *mu cip*.

Taxonomic notes: Hudson used *Epilobium paniculatum* for the contemporary species *Epilobium brachycarpum* (Jepson Flora Project 2012b).

Beverage: The leaves and stems were baked, macerated, and added to manzanita cider for additional sweetness.

Bread: The baked and macerated leaves and stems may have been added to manzanita bread.

Flavoring: The leaves were added to buckeye mush to improve its flavor.

Equisetum hyemale L. (Equisetaceae) · **Scouringrush horsetail**

Native name: *cu-mai'*.

Taxonomic notes: Hudson frequently used only the genus name *Equisetum*, which could also refer to other local horsetails.

Basketry: Root stalks were infrequently used as black or dark brown basketry weft. The fibers were dyed to achieve a dark color, perhaps in a similar manner as described for tule. Horsetail was only used when preferable materials were unavailable.

Brush or broom: The roots were used to make hair combs. For this purpose, they were split into 15 cm filaments, which were folded in the middle and bound.

Cordage: The stiff, coarse root fibers, which ranked sixth among cordage fibers, were used to make rope.

Divination and doctoring: Chestnut (1902) reported that Potter Valley Pomo doctors revived patients with the explosive burning created by placing the hollow stems in fire.

Medicine: Horsetail was used as an unspecified medicine.

Polish: The surfaces of many implements were smoothed and polished with horsetail foliage and stems. The surface of clamshell disks was given an attractive shine by first rubbing with horsetail and then with buckskin. Similarly, horsetail was used to polish the surface of wooden smoking pipes and arrows.

Eriodictyon californicum (Hook. & Arn.) Torrey (Boraginaceae) · **Yerba santa**

Native name: *těk ka-lǐ'* ("sticky plant").

Cold remedy: From the leaves were prepared extracts and infusions used for coughs and bronchitis. The green leaves were also often chewed to treat coughs.

Medicine: According to Chestnut (1902), yerba santa was a most highly valued medicine among the native peoples of Mendocino County, being used "generally in the practice of medicine," suggesting it may have been considered a panacea. In addition to being used to treat colds, bronchitis, and coughs, it was also used for asthma, influenza, rheumatism, pulmonary tuberculosis ("consumption"), catarrh, fever, and to purify the blood. It was often administered externally as a wash or by smoking, chewing, or drinking the tea.

Smoking: Chestnut (1902) reported that the leaves were chewed as a substitute for tobacco (*Nicotiana* spp.).

Eriophyllum lanatum (Pursh) J. Forbes (Asteraceae) · **Common woollysunflower**
Native name: *ka-tsa' tsŏ*.
Hudson did not report any uses for this plant.

***Erodium cicutarium** (L.) L'Hér. ex Aiton (Geraniaceae) · **Redstem filaree**
Native name: *bi-dum' tci* ("storks bill").
Taxonomic notes: Hudson's use of this scientific name appears to have been based on a deter-
    mination by Alice Eastwood.
Salad food: The fresh leaves were eaten as salad.

Erythronium californicum Purdy (Liliaceae) · **California fawn lily**
Native name: *ka-si'-zi tsŏ*.
Taxonomic notes: Hudson referenced *Erythronium giganteum* (written *Erythronium gigan-
    tea*), which corresponds with the contemporary species *E. californicum* (Jepson Flora
    Project 2012b; The Plant List 2012).
Bulb or corm food: The bulbs were baked in underground ovens and eaten. According to
    Chestnut (1902), it was eaten sparingly.

Eschscholzia californica Cham. (Papaveraceae) · **California poppy**
Native name: *co ci-lĭn' ka-lĭ* ("milk drying-up plant").
Taxonomic notes: Hudson used only the genus name *Eschscholzia* (written *Escholzia*), among
    which *E. californica* is the most prevalent species in the study area. However, he may
    also have referred to other local poppies.
Analgesic: According to Chestnut (1902), the native peoples at the Round Valley Reservation
    used the fresh roots to treat toothache.
Antidiarrheal: After removing the flowers, the whole plant was boiled and the resulting liq-
    uid was used to treat diarrhea, especially in infants.
Women's health: Hudson reported that a nursing mother's milk was believed to be dimin-
    ished by the mere presence of California poppy plants nearby, with lactation ceasing
    altogether if a mother or her child touched the flowers.

***Festuca temulenta** (L.) Columbus & J.P. Sm. (Poaceae) · **Darnel ryegrass**
Native name: *ba-ă ko-ŏ'*.
Taxonomic notes: Hudson referred to this plant by the name *Lolium temulentum*, which
    corresponds with the contemporary species *Festuca temulenta* (Jepson Flora Project
    2012b).

Seed food: Hudson did not identify this plant's uses. Its seeds are known for their potential to cause poisoning (Jepson Flora Project 2012b), making it an unlikely food candidate.

Foeniculum vulgare Mill. (Apiaceae) · Fennel
Native name: *tcă-ha' ka-lĭ'*.
Salad food: The fresh leaves were eaten as salad.

Fragaria spp. (Rosaceae) · Strawberry
Fragaria chiloensis (L.) Mill. · Mountain strawberry
Fragaria vesca L. · Woodland strawberry
Native name: *ma da-kŏ'*.

Taxonomic notes: Hudson cited both *Fragaria chiloensis* and *Fragaria vesca*. However, he described *F. chiloensis* as growing near springs on hillsides and being consumed by mountain quail (*Oreortyx pictus*), which inhabit brushy mountain slopes and forest. This description does not accurately describe the coastal species *F. chiloensis*, but does fit the inland *F. vesca*. Hudson also used the outdated name *Fragaria californica* for *F. vesca* (USDA and NRCS 2012).

Fruit food: The sweet fresh fruit was eaten.

Frangula californica (Eschsch.) A. Gray (Rhamnaceae) · California coffeeberry
Native name: *ho mi-ta' si-yan*.

Taxonomic notes: Hudson referred to the contemporary species *Frangula californica* by the outdated name *Rhamnus californica* (Jepson Flora Project 2012b).

Laxative: At the first signs of labor, expectant mothers were given a laxative made from the bark.

Frangula purshiana (DC.) J. G. Cooper (Rhamnaceae) · Cascara buckthorn
Native name: *ho mi-tăk' ka-li'*.

Taxonomic notes: Hudson used the name *Rhamnus purshiana*, which corresponds with the contemporary species *Frangula purshiana* (Jepson Flora Project 2012b).

Gastrointestinal aid: A mixture of the inner bark was given in approximately 120 mL doses for upset stomach.

Laxative: Constipation was treated with an infusion prepared from the young inner bark or, alternatively, chewing pieces of the older bark. At the first signs of labor, expectant mothers were given a laxative made from the leaves.

Fraxinus sp. (Oleaceae) · Ash
Native name: *ma lăm' kalĭ'*.

Taxonomic notes: Hudson often used only the common name "ash," which may have referred to foothill ash (*Fraxinus dipetala*) or Oregon ash (*F. latifolia*). In other instances, he cited *Fraxinus velutina*, which is largely found south of the Transverse Ranges in Southern California, leaving some uncertainty as to its identity.

Basketry: The rims of hopper-mortar baskets were reinforced with loop of ash weft fibers. Also called milling or milling hopper baskets, these were bottomless baskets used to retain meal in the stone mortar while grinding with a stone pestle. They were placed atop the stone mortar and held in place by with one's legs, which rested across the basket's rim.

Cooking: A cylindrical pestle made of ash wood was used for crushing fruits, seeds, and nuts.

First aid: Bark from young ash shoots was added to threenerve goldenrod (*Solidago velutina*) to prepare an infusion for treating cuts and infected sores. A plaster also used to treat cuts and sores was prepared by mixing this infusion with a certain mud found on the east side of a mountain summit identified by Hudson as "Loftin," which was probably Laughlin Ridge, located about 11 km west of Potter Valley.

Fowling: Hardwood points for bird arrows were made from the wood.

Gaming and competition: Rackets made from the wood were use in a game resembling lacrosse.

Host plant: Edible caterpillars known in the ethnographic literature as army worms were occasionally collected in great quantities from ash trees (cf. Barrett 1936; Swezey 1978). Hudson described these caterpillars as about 6 cm long, smooth in texture, and dark in color with white and red dots on the back. They were gathered in May and June by digging trenches and building low mud barriers around the trunk of a tree in order to facilitate raking the caterpillars into baskets. Before being eaten, they were toasted with embers in a disk-shaped basket, roasted on a stone griddle, or baked in a hollow cow parsnip (*Heracleum maximum*) stalk. Hudson reported that they turned red when cooked. They could also be roasted, dried, and ground into flour.

Hunting: Deer were attracted by imitating the sound of a bleating fawn, produced by sucking on soft ash leaves held against the tongue.

Legend: In the legend "Poma Genesis" recorded by Hudson, the mythological being Coyote (**Du-wi'**) made the first people from mud and other ingredients packed on a framework of ash forks.

Leprosy treatment: A mixture of local mud, possibly from Laughlin Ridge, and an infusion of the bark from young shoots was heated and applied as a treatment for leprosy. To improve its effectiveness, the patient's nails were sometimes split before application.

Packing or carrying: Rudimentary firewood packs were constructed with a pair of ash forks slung on one's back with a tumpline. These were originally made from California wild grape vines (*Vitis californica*), but came to be made from ash and other woods in the late nineteenth century.

Smoking: Wooden smoking pipes, which Hudson argued postdated stone pipes, were shaped from a single section of ash wood. The pithy core was cleared to produce an air channel.

After rough shaping with an ember and blowing tube, decorative relief work and inlays were applied, followed by polishing.

Tool: A sharp pointed stick fashioned from ash wood was used to dig for worms. Also, blowing tubes, used in conjunction with embers in woodworking, consisted of a hollow section of elderberry stalk fitted with a narrower tube insert, about 8 cm in length, made from ash or other hardwoods. In addition, an axe-like implement was made by lashing a quartz or greenstone fragment to a short ash handle, some 5 cm in diameter. This tool was used with a lacerating motion to reduce old logs to firewood.

Watercraft: Used in conjunction with tule balsas while visiting locations with open waterways, paddles were constructed from oak blades (*Quercus* spp.) bound to approximately 1.5 m ash poles.

Fritillaria affinis (Schult. & Schult. f.) Sealy (Liliaceae) · Checker lily

Native name: ***bi-tit' bu***.

Taxonomic notes: Hudson used *Fritillaria mutica* for the contemporary species *Fritillaria affinis* (USDA and NRCS 2012).

Bread: The bulbs were made into mush, formed into cakes, and baked.

Bulb or corm food: The bulbs were baked in an underground oven or in the ashes of a fire and eaten.

Gaultheria shallon Pursh (Ericaceae) · Salal

Native name: ***la-ti'***.

Taxonomic notes: Hudson's use of this scientific name was based on a determination by botanist Alice Eastwood in 1928.

Fruit food: Hudson identified salal as a member of the native category "berries" (***ba-kai'***), suggesting the fruit was eaten.

**Geranium dissectum* L. (Geraniaceae) · Common wild geranium

Native name: ***si mǎ' da wai tsŏ***.

Taxonomic notes: Hudson's use of this scientific name is consistent with a 1928 determination by Alice Eastwood.

Salad food: Although Hudson provided no explicit information regarding its uses, he cited common wild geranium in association with tree clover (*Trifolium ciliolatum*), suggesting the two had the same native name and may have been used similarly as salad foods.

Helenium puberulum DC. (Asteraceae) · Rosilla

STD remedy: The whole plant was boiled for several hours to produce an extract consumed to treat venereal diseases. It was considered most effective for discharge caused by gonorrhea. Hudson reported that excessive quantities were toxic, producing violent head-aches, lethargy, and sphincter paralysis. Chestnut (1902) noted that this remedy was prepared by boiling three whole plants in approximately 3.5 liters of water, with three tablespoons being taken before meals for up to three days.

Hemizonia congesta DC. (Asteraceae) · Hayfield tarweed

Native names: *ma-ko' ba-a'* and *mu-tcă' ka-lĭ'*.

Taxonomic notes: Hudson used *Hemizonia luzulifolia* for the contemporary taxon *Hemizonia congesta* (USDA and NRCS 2012).

Seed food: The seeds, collected with woven seed beaters and used in pinole, were considered oily and flavorful.

Heracleum maximum W. Bartram (Apiaceae) · Cow parsnip

Native name: *pa co'*.

Taxonomic notes: Hudson used the terms *Heracleum* and *Heracleum lanatum*, the latter of which corresponds with the contemporary species *Heracleum maximum* (Jepson Flora Project 2012b).

Beverage: Juice from young peeled shoots was considered a treat.

Clothing: Soft baby gowns were made from the fibers.

Container: Tubular stalk sections, collected in autumn after drying, were used as bottles.

Cooking: The leaves were used as a moist lining in underground ovens. Army worm caterpil-lars were baked in the hollow stalks.

Host plant: Larvae found in cow parsnip flowers were consumed as a snack.

Salad food: Hudson reported that the flowers and seeds were eaten raw. Other sources also mention that the young leaves, collected in spring and early summer, were eaten (Chestnut 1902). The outer skin contains phototoxic chemicals, suggesting the leaves may have been peeled before being consumed (Kuhnlein and Turner 1986).

Snakebite remedy: For snakebite, a poultice prepared from the root was applied directly to the wound and an infusion of the peeled root was consumed. This remedy was consid-ered effective but dangerous.

Ulcer remedy: Chronic ulcer was treated with root infusion and poultice in the same manner as for snakebite.

Heteromeles arbutifolia (Lindl.) M. Roem. (Rosaceae) · Toyon

Native name: *bă tsa' tsă ba-kai'*.

Fruit food: A palatable food that stored well was prepared by toasting the fruits and removing the seeds.

Laxative: The toasted fruit was considered a mild laxative.

Hoita macrostachya (DC.) Rydb. (Fabaceae) · Leather root
Native name: *hai yăk' kalĭ.*

Taxonomic notes: At times, Hudson used *Psoralea macrostachya* (written *Psoralia macrostachya*), which corresponds with the contemporary species *Hoita macrostachya* (Jepson Flora Project 2012b). In other instances, he cited only the former genus name *Psoralea*, suggesting that other taxa may have been used.

Ceremony: Fastening laces made from leather root fiber were favored for ceremonial applications because they had a sweet odor.

Cordage: The stems were used to produce a gray fiber of moderate strength and smoothness. The root, collected with digging sticks, provided a tough and coarse rope fiber that ranked third in strength among Potter Valley Pomo cordage fibers. After removing the bark, root fibers were beaten with a mallet until dry. Finally, shredding and repeated washing served to remove the sap. This process produced a fiber with a lasting sweet odor. They were often dyed red, possibly through exposure to smoke from burning alder bark.

Hunting: Cordage made from one part root fiber and three parts stinging nettle was especially desirable for use in big game snares because of its sweet odor, presumably because it was effective in concealing human odors.

Spirituality: As one of the "psychic" *xa-nu'* plants, leather root was considered to have spiritual qualities.

Iris spp. (Iridaceae) · Iris
Iris douglasiana Herb. · Douglas iris
Iris macrosiphon Torr. · Bowltube iris
Native name: *tsi-lĭm' ka-lĭ'.*

Taxonomic notes: In some instances, Hudson used *Iris californica* (written *Iris cal.*, based on a determination by Alice Eastwood) for the contemporary species *Iris macrosiphon* (USDA and NRCS 2012). Having specified that three types of iris were used by the Northern Pomo, Hudson's references to the common name "iris" suggest the possibility that other local members of the genus were used.

Colorant: The flowers were crushed in hot water and used as body paint.

Cooking: Iris leaves were used as a moist lining in underground ovens.

Cordage: A single strand of iris fiber was derived from each leaf edge. The mature leaves were gathered in May and shredded with an awl or nail. After a few weeks they were buried in damp soil and subsequently rubbed between the palms to remove debris. Perhaps because this was a very labor intensive process, iris was substantially been replaced by dogbane in the nineteenth century. The fiber had a rough texture, but was valued for adding strength and structure to rope. It ranked above all other cordage fibers in strength.

Diuretic: A fluid extract of the plant was used as a diuretic.

Gaming and competition: The netted loops of ball rackets were made with coarse iris string mesh.

Hunting: The cordage was used in big game snares.

War: Rod armor, used by bear doctors and occasionally for war, was stitched with iris cordage.

Iva axillaris Pursh (Asteraceae) · Poverty weed
Native names: ***tsi-tă' ta-la*** ("birdseed") and ***ca-m tca ka-li*** ("birdseed").

Seed food: The seeds were roasted and ground for food, presumably for pinole.

Juncus spp. (Juncaceae) · Rush
Juncus effusus L. · Common rush

Juncus exiguus (Fernald & Wiegand) Lint ex Snogerup & Zika · Klamath rush

Juncus laccatus Zika · Shiny rush

Native name: ***tca-ba'***.

Taxonomic notes: Hudson referenced both the genus *Juncus* and the species *Juncus effusus*. The former taxa *Juncus effusus* var. *exiguous* and *Juncus effusus* var. *gracilis* (Hickman 1993), both located in the study area, were subsequently changed to *Juncus exiguous* and *Juncus laccatus*, respectively (Jepson Flora Project 2012b). His use of the term *Juncus*, with no further specification, suggests that other local taxa may have been used.

Basketry: Chestnut (1902) reported that the stems were the first material children used when learning to weave baskets at the Round Valley Reservation. The same author also noted that rush was occasionally used in wicker seed beaters.

Brush or broom: Hair combs were made from the plant.

Ceremony: Female dancers held small bunches of shredded rush in loops over the middle fingers of each hand, waving them rhythmically while dancing.

Clothing: Wisps of rush, bound at one end, were spread over one's head as a sun shade. The fibers were used to prepare soft baby wrappings, swaddlings, and gowns. For this purpose, mature flower stalks were shredded with a bone awl, cleaned, and hung to dry.

Cooking: Mats woven from rush were used to line the inside of sand basins while leaching acorns and buckeyes.

Decoration: Ornamental caps were woven from rush.

Fishing: Chestnut (1902) described a fish trap in Hudson's collection at the Smithsonian Institute that was made exclusively of rush stems.

Gaming and competition: Wooden play dolls were dressed with soft skirts made from rush fiber.

Matting or bedding: Rush was woven to produce mats.

Padding or toweling: Common rush fiber was used as a soft and absorbent cushion in conjunction with children's clothing.

Trade: Green flower stalks of diverse diameters were used as an axle to support clamshell disks during the smoothing process. A stalk was strung with about 18 cm of roughly chipped and perforated disk-shaped beads and then rolled with the hands sideways on a stone slab to remove the rough edges.

Women's health: Menstruating women used the fiber as soft padding.

Juniperus californica Carriere (Cupressaceae) · California juniper
Native name: *tsi-pu' ka-li*.

Basketry: Ideal basketry weft fibers were obtained from the roots of California juniper and other conifers. These were dug from late autumn through winter, cut into sections about 1 m long and baked in underground ovens for about 24 hours, until they easily split into thin tapes. This weft had an attractive buff color and was valued for its strength and pliability.

Confection: The ripe fruits were toasted or baked and ground to create a sweet confection that stored well.

War: Juniper was a preferred wood for war bows.

Lathyrus jepsonii Greene (Fabaceae) · Tule pea
Native name: *ca-bu' ma-lŭ'*.

Taxonomic notes: Hudson used *Lathyrus watsonii* for the contemporary taxon *Lathyrus jepsonii* (USDA and NRCS 2012).

Cooked green: The leaves were baked in underground ovens and eaten with toasted California bay nuts. Chestnut (1902) specified that at Round Valley, the plant was picked early in the season when it was just about 8 cm tall, cooked and eaten.

Lathyrus vestitus Nutt. (Fabaceae) · Pacific peavine
Native names: *ma-bi hě'* ("the climbing vine").

Taxonomic notes: In addition to explicitly citing *Lathyrus vestitus*, Hudson also used the common name "wild pea," which may have referred to other local taxa.

Salad food: The fresh green beans were eaten.

Leucoagaricus americanus (Peck) Vellinga (Fungi: Agaricaceae) · American parasol
Native name: *kom tce e'*.

Taxonomic notes: Hudson used the name *Lepiota Americana*, which corresponds to the contemporary taxon *Leucoagaricus americanus* (Vellinga 2000). He also specified that it grows under evergreen trees. This species is, though, exceedingly rare in Northern California (Arora 1986), leading to uncertainty as to the identity of this fungus.

Fungus food: The mushroom was fried in tallow on a hot stone slab or directly on coals.

Lomatium utriculatum (Nutt. ex Torr. & A. Gray) J. M. Coult. & Rose (Apiaceae) · Common lomatium

Native name: *ca-bu' ma-lu'*.

Taxonomic notes: Hudson used *Cogswellia utriculata,* based on a determination by botanist Alice Eastwood in 1928, and *Peucedanum utriculatum* (written *Peucedanum utriculata*) for the contemporary species *Lomatium utriculatum* (Jepson 1936; Moerman 1998; The Plant List 2012). He also occasionally referred to *L. utriculatum* as "angelica."

Cooked green: Leaves, flowers, or entire young plants were baked or steamed in underground ovens and eaten with game meat and breads made from acorns or California bay nuts.

Fishing: The plant was applied to one's hands, arms, and spears for luck while fishing.

Spirituality: Common lomatium was used as an anointment with spiritual qualities (*xa*).

Lupinus spp. (Fabaceae) · Lupine

Lupinus bicolor Lindl. · Bicolor lupine

Lupinus formosus Greene · Western lupine

Native names: *ka-ai' ka-lĭ* ("crow plant") and *tsi tu' ka-lĭ'*.

Taxonomic notes: Hudson used *Lupinus micranthus* for the contemporary species *Lupinus bicolor* (Jepson Flora Project 2012a; USDA and NRCS 2012). In a letter dated 1928, Alice Eastwood identified *Lupinus formosus* from Hudson's botanical specimens. Elsewhere, he used the genus name *Lupinus* without further specification, suggesting the possibility that other members of the genus were used. Additionally, Chestnut (1902) identified *L. affinis* (as *Lupinus carnosulus*) as a common shrub throughout the Round Valley area that was used in a manner consistent with Hudson's notes.

Cooked green: The whole plant, except the roots, was baked or roasted and eaten (cf. Chestnut 1902).

Salad food: The young leaves were eaten raw.

Lupinus nanus Benth. (Fabaceae) · Sky lupine

Native names: *ka-ai' ka-lĭ* ("crow plant") and *du we' ka-lĭ'* ("coyote night").

Taxonomic notes: Hudson's use of this scientific name was consistent with a determination in 1928 by Alice Eastwood.

Salad food: The young leaves were eaten raw.

Macrocystis pyrifera (L.) C. Ag. (Chromalveolata: Laminariaceae) · Giant kelp

Native name: *pcu nŭm' ma*.

Sea vegetable: Moist giant kelp, collected during trips to the coast, was eaten raw.

***Madia elegans* D. Don (Asteraceae) · Common madia**
Native names: *ko-o' ba-a* and *ca-sĭl' ba-ă*.
Taxonomic notes: Hudson used *Madia densifolia,* a synonym for *Madia elegans* var. *densiflora* (The Plant List 2012), which corresponds with the contemporary species *Madia elegans* (Jepson Flora Project 2012b).
Flavoring: Small quantities of the seeds were used to flavor mush and bread made from poorer grades of acorns. They were considered rich and fattening.
Seed food: The seeds were ground and eaten with salt, presumably as pinole.
Women's health: Mothers avoided eating common madia soon after giving birth.

***Madia sativa* Molina (Asteraceae) · Coast tarweed**
Native name: *ka-la ka-lĭ'* ("ankle joint").
Flavoring: Small quantities of the seeds were used to impart a rich flavor to acorn mush and bread.
Seed food: The seeds were ground and eaten with salt, presumably as pinole.

***Marah* sp. (Cucurbitaceae) · Man-root**
Native name: *ma-bi hĕ'* ("the climbing vine").
Taxonomic notes: Hudson only used the genus name *Echinocystis,* without further specification, for the contemporary genus *Marah* (Hitchcock et al. 1959). The specific identification of this plant is unclear.
Eye medicine: Ripe seeds were strung as a necklace and used in an unspecified manner to prevent eye infection.
Medicine: According to Chestnut (1902), native people at Round Valley used the seeds and roots of this poisonous plant to treat a variety of illnesses, including rheumatism and urinary disorders.
STD remedy: For gonorrhea, the seeds were ground and boiled. About 30 mL of the resulting fluid was taken three times per day.

***Marrubium vulgare* L. (Lamiaceae) · Horehound**
Native name: *ka tcăn'.*
Taxonomic notes: Hudson used only the common name "hoarhound."
Hudson identified no information regarding its uses.

***Matricaria discoidea* DC. (Asteraceae) · Pineapple weed**
Native name: *cĭ-ba' mi-tsă tum* ("body benumb").
Women's health: An unspecified preparation of the flowers was taken to ease painful menstruation or stimulate absent menstruation.

Mentzelia sp. (Loasaceae) · Blazingstar

Native name: *tĕk' ka-lĭ* ("cling plant").

Taxonomic notes: Hudson used only the genus name *Mentzelia,* making it unclear which local taxon was used.

Gastrointestinal aid: An infusion of the flowers was used for biliousness.

Microseris laciniata (Hook.) Sch. Bip. (Asteraceae) · Cutleaf silverpuffs

Native name: *ka mac ba-ti'-la* ("piquant").

Taxonomic notes: Hudson used *Scorzonella procer* and *Scorzonella maxima* for the contemporary species *Microseris laciniata* (Best 1996; Moerman 1998).

Bread: The baked root mush was formed into disk-shaped cakes and dried in the sun.

Mush: The roots were baked in an underground oven and prepared into mush.

Salad food: The roots, leaves, and buds were consumed raw with bread. It was considered to have a pungent flavor.

Mimulus aurantiacus Curtis (Phrymaceae) · Bush monkeyflower, sticky monkeyflower

Native name: *kan kan ka-lĭ'.*

Taxonomic notes: Hudson used *Diplacus glutinosus* for the contemporary species *Mimulus aurantiacus* (Jepson Flora Project 2012a; USDA and NRCS 2012).

Analgesic: Internal pain was treated with massage and herbal fomentation with bush monkeyflower.

Gastrointestinal aid: Colic was treated by laying the patient on a steam bed consisting of layers of fresh bush monkeyflower leaves on hot stones. Monkeyflower was sometimes alternated with sagebrush or wormwood. According to Hudson, this treatment had a "penetrating and lasting effect."

Women's health: The herbal steam treatment was also used for sore breasts.

Morchella sp. (Fungi: Morchellaceae) · Morel

Native name: *pi-ko' tci.*

Taxonomic notes: Hudson cited *Morchella crassipes,* now known as *Morchella esculenta,* which is unlikely to occur in the study area (Arora 1986), thus leaving some uncertainty as to his determination.

Confection: The raw mushrooms were considered a sweet confection.

Navarretia squarrosa (Eschsch.) Hook. & Arn. (Polemoniaceae) · Skunkweed

Native name: *sĭl lĕt' ka-lĭ'.*

Antirheumatic: The fresh plant was rubbed on patients to treat rheumatism.

Nemophila menziesii Hook. & Arn. (Boraginaceae) · Menzies' baby blue eyes

Native name: *ca kal' ma lŭ'.*

Taxonomic notes: Consistent with a determination by Alice Eastwood in 1928, Hudson used *Nemophila insignis* for the contemporary species *N. menziesii* (Munz and Keck 1973).

Cooked green: Although Hudson did not document this plant's uses, the Northern Pomo name indicates that the above-ground parts may have been baked and eaten as green (*ma-lu*).

Nicotiana spp. (Solanaceae) · Tobacco

Nicotiana attenuata Torr. ex S. Watson · Coyote tobacco

Nicotiana quadrivalvis Pursh · Indian tobacco

Native name: *sa-hǎ' ka-lĭ.*

Taxonomic notes: Hudson used *Nicotiana bigelovii* (written *Nicotiana biglovii*) for the contemporary species *Nicotiana quadrivalvis* (Jepson Flora Project 2012b). In addition to mentioning *Nicotiana attenuate* specifically, he also specified that several types of *Nicotiana* were used, although the others were not identified.

Legend: In the legend "Poma Genesis," documented by Hudson, Coyote (***Du-wi'***) and Wolf (***Tsi-me'-wu***) smoked tobacco while discussing "important matters of the world's creation."

Smoking: The mildest smoking tobacco was produced from leaves that dried naturally on the plant. These were collected and quickly cured in the sun. Stronger tobacco was made from mature green leaves. These were picked, dried in the sun, rolled, and cured in the shade. The strongest and most infrequently made tobacco was prepared by harvesting the entire stalk, which was hung whole to cure in the shade. Hudson reported that all men smoked both for pleasure and ceremony, carrying their tobacco in bags made from tanned squirrel or fawn skin (Figure 23). It was used to reach an "elevated psychological state." Upon smelling new tobacco or lighting his pipe, a smoker would invoke or thank Coyote (***Du-wi'***), who gave tobacco to the people. Although smokers inhaled deeply, they never displayed what Hudson recognized to be the symptoms of nicotine addiction.

Figure 23. Ash smoking pipes and bag of tobacco. Photograph by Carlos E. A. Coimbra Jr., 2011. Accession nos. 1345, 1386, and 1426, in the collections of Grace Hudson Museum, Ukiah.

Notholithocarpus densiflorus (Hook. & Arn.) Manos, C.H. Cannon, & S. Oh (Fagaceae) · **Tanoak**

Native name: ***bi-du ka-li***.

Taxonomic notes: Hudson used *Quercus densiflorus* (written *Quercus densiflora*) as well as the common name "tanoak" for the contemporary species *Notholithocarpus densiflorus* (Jepson Flora Project 2012b).

Bread: The large tanoak acorns were the most desired of all the Potter Valley Pomo acorns. They were also the least accessible in Potter Valley because they tended to grow to the west in areas with more coastal influence. The nut meat was more easily ground to a fine meal than other acorns and had lower tannin levels that could be completely neutralized with red earth (***ma-po'***) without leaching.

Mush: Tanoak acorns were also preferred for mush above all the other acorns because they required less cooking time and resulted in a light-colored and savory product. Tanoak acorn meal was closely watched during leaching to prevent the loss of desirable oils.

Nuphar polysepala Engelm. (Nymphaeaceae) · **Western yellow pond-lily**

Native name: ***ku-la' ka-lï'***.

Taxonomic notes: Hudson wrote *Nymphaea polysepala* for the taxon currently classified as *Nuphar polysepala* (Jepson Flora Project 2012a; USDA and NRCS 2012).

Salad food: The tender shoots were eaten fresh.

Oenanthe sarmentosa C. Presl ex DC. (Apiaceae) · **Water parsley**

Native name: ***du wi' ba tco'*** wă.

Salad food: The sour stems, leaves, and seeds were eaten raw by hunters and travelers.

Osmorhiza sp. (Apiaceae) · **Sweetcicely**

Native name: ***du wi ya' na***.

Taxonomic notes: Hudson used only the genus name *Osmorhiza*, based on a 1928 determination by Alice Eastwood, which could refer to any of numerous local members of the genus.

Legend: In the legend "Poma Genesis," Coyote (***Du-wi'***) chewed sweetcicely root while waiting for the first people to come to life. He then fell asleep and was overtaken with dreams.

Psychiatric aid: The root was used in treating mental disorders.

Spirituality: As one of the "psychic" ***xa-nu'*** plants, it was used as an anointment for success in fighting, gambling, and hunting large game animals.

Pedicularis densiflora Hook. (Orobanchaceae) · **Indian warrior**

Taxonomic notes: Hudson used this scientific name (written *Pedicularis densiflorus*) based on a 1928 determination by Alice Eastwood.

Confection: The nectar, sucked directly from the flowers, was a favored delicacy.

Perideridia kelloggii (A. Gray) Mathias (Apiaceae) · **Kellogg's yampah**

Native names: *ca bu'-tă* and *pcû buta' tsŏ.*

Taxonomic notes: Evidently based on a determination by Alice Eastwood, Hudson used *Carum kelloggii* (written alternatively as *Carem kelloggii*), which corresponds with the contemporary species *Perideridia kelloggii* (Moerman 1998; The Plant List 2012). In some instances he used the common name "anise" for the same plant.

Bread: According to Chestnut (1902), the tubers and roots were prepared in the same manner as acorn bread.

Brush or broom: Hair combs or brushes were made from split root stalk sections, which were hardened by exposure to fire.

Insecticide: Dry ashes or an extract of the plant were applied to living spaces to eliminate fleas.

Root food: The roots were roasted and eaten.

Salad food: The fresh plant tops were eaten as a salad food. Chestnut (1902) noted that the raw foliage has a sweet taste.

Seed food: The seeds were eaten, being used to add flavor pinole made from other types of seeds (cf. Chestnut 1902).

Snakebite remedy: A poultice of the plant was used to treat snakebite.

Phalaris angusta Nees ex Trin. (Poaceae) · **Timothy canarygrass**

Native name: *mi cu to ko ma* ("lizard tail").

Architecture: The grass was used to thatch temporary shelters constructed while travelling.

Matting or bedding: The grass was used for bedding in temporary shelters.

Phoradendron villosum (Viscaceae) · **American mistletoe**

Native name: *tsai ma-atc* ("jay's grub bag").

Taxonomic notes: Hudson referenced European mistletoe (as *Viscum album*), which is not known from Mendocino or Lake Counties, although it has a very restricted distribution in Sonoma County (Hawksworth and Scharpf 2007). Chestnut cited *Phoradendron flavescens* for the contemporary species *Phoradendron villosum,* which is widely distributed in the study area (Chestnut 1902; Jepson Flora Project 2012b).

Abortifacient: Expectant mothers wishing to abort a fetus consumed an infusion of the plant. Similar applications have been documented in other Pomoan communities (Aginsky 1939).

Analgesic: Chestnut (1902) documented that the native peoples of Mendocino chewed the leaves as a toothache remedy.

Fishing: Hudson reported that the roots were used as clubs for killing large fish.

Picea sitchensis (Bong.) Carrière (Pinaceae) · Sitka spruce

Basketry: An ideal basketry weft fiber was obtained from the roots of Sitka spruce and other conifers.

Pinus spp. (Pinaceae) · Pine

Taxonomic notes: Hudson evidently used the name *Pinus* without further specification for many members of this genus, leaving uncertainty as to which taxa were used. These instances are treated here.

Adhesive: Tree pitch from a variety of conifers, including the pines, was heated for use as a general purpose adhesive.

Basketry: Ideal basketry weft fibers were obtained from the roots.

Ceremony: The wood was used for ceremonial poles raised during festivals. Sweet pine exudate was placed in miniature clay conical burden baskets and given to girls upon reaching puberty and to brides.

Colorant: The pitch was used to fill decorative depressions on the exterior of elderberry flutes (Barrett 1952).

Hunting: Hunters charmed deer by chewing angelica root and pine seeds to form a quid, which was cast into the fire to produce smoke.

Nut food: Nuts meats were cracked, parched, and kneaded into cakes, which were eaten with salt.

Timekeeping: Most settlements had a timekeeping device called a "shadow pole" (*pa-cit' hai*), which was often made from a straight, smooth pine sapling about 3.5 to 6 m in height. A short wooden cross-bar lashed to its tip, such that it cast a shadow that could be used to ascertain the time of day.

Pinus contorta Loudon (Pinaceae) · Lodgepole pine

Native name: *ba-ko ka-li* ("fine root").

Basketry: Although Hudson did not mention lodgepole pine being used in basketry, its native name suggests that it may have been used in the same manner as other conifers as a fine weft fiber.

Pinus coulteri D. Don (Pinaceae) · Coulter pine

Native name: *ko-ti' ka-li'*.

Basketry: Ideal basketry weft fibers were obtained from the roots.

Pinus lambertiana Douglas (Pinaceae) · Sugar pine
Native name: *cuye' ka-lĭ'*.
Basketry: Excellent quality basketry weft fibers were obtained from the roots.
Confection: The sweet tree sap was considered a rare delicacy.
Laxative: The condensed pitch was taken as a laxative.
Nut food: The nuts were eaten.

Pinus ponderosa Douglas ex Lawson & C. Lawson (Pinaceae) · Ponderosa Pine
Native name: *tcom' ka-lĭ'* ("in grove pine").
Adhesive: The tree pitch was heated and used as an adhesive.
Basketry: Fine basketry weft fibers were obtained from the roots.

Pinus sabiniana D. Don (Pinaceae) · California foothill pine
Native name: *ko-ti' ka-lĭ'*.
Basketry: Basketry weft fibers were obtained from the roots. According to Chestnut (1902), these were not as pliable as sedge fibers and were thus only employed for more simple basketry weaves.
Nut food: The edible nuts were removed by opening the cones with heat. They were then cracked, parched, and kneaded into cakes, which were eaten with salt.

Plagiobothrys fulvus (Hook. & Arn.) I. M. Johnst. (Boraginaceae) · Popcorn flower
Native name: *tu wĕl'-lĭ tso*.
Taxonomic notes: Although in 1928 Alice Eastwood provided Hudson with a termination only to the genus *Plagiobothrys*, Hudson referred to the scientific name *Plagiobothrys campestris*, which corresponds with the contemporary taxon *Plagiobothrys fulvus* (Jepson Flora Project 2012a; USDA and NRCS 2012).
Colorant: The flowers were used to produce a red stain.
Salad food: The fresh leaves were eaten. According to Chestnut (1902), the flowers were also eaten.
Seed food: The seeds were prepared as pinole.

Plantago major L. (Plantaginaceae) · Common plantain
Native name: *ma-yu' ta-lă'* ("dove seed").
Taxonomic notes: At times, Hudson used "lamb's tongue," which may also have referred to other members of the *Plantago* genus.
Flavoring: Unspecified parts of the plant were consumed as a condiment.
Food: Unspecified parts of the plant were eaten.

Platystemon californicus Benth. (Papaveraceae) · **California creamcups**

Native name: ***ma'-hu*** ("ground sprouts").

Taxonomic notes: Hudson's use of this scientific name corresponds with a 1928 determination by Alice Eastwood.

Salad food: The plant was eaten as a lettuce.

Polygala californica Nutt. (Polygalaceae) · **California milkwort**

Native name: ***ma tcu-pǐl'***.

Antihemorrhagic: The whole plant was boiled for about two hours and the resulting liquid was consumed to treat pulmonary or stomach hemorrhaging. The first dose was administered to revive the patient and continued use was expected to bring about a cure.

Populus fremontii S. Watson (Salicaceae) · **Fremont's cottonwood**

Native name: ***ta la ta lau ka-li***.

Taxonomic notes: At times, Hudson used only the common name "cottonwood," which may also have referred to black cottonwood (*Populus balsamifera*).

Gaming and competition: Wooden dolls were made from the wood.

Music: Large foot drums, suspended by ropes towards the back of the assembly house, were made from cottonwood. In addition, the wood was used for bullroarers ("thunder sticks") used in a ceremonial contexts.

Pediatric aid: The inner bark was used to make a thread used to tie a child's umbilicus several centimeters from the body before it was cut and dressed.

Porphyra sp. (Eukaryota: Bangiaceae) · **Nori**

Native name: ***to-nok*** ("goiter unknown").

Taxonomic notes: Although Hudson usually used the common names "leaf kelp" or "sea weed," the Northern Pomo name ***to-nok*** closely resembles other Pomoan names for *Porphyra* species. For example, the Central Pomo name ***tō'nō*** referred to *P. perforata* and the Little Lake Pomo name ***to-ne'*** referred to *P. lanceolata* (Barrett 1952; Chestnut 1902).

Sea vegetable: Nori was dried in the sun for storage and prepared for eating by frying in animal fat.

Prunus subcordata Benth. (Rosaceae) · **Klamath plum, Sierra plum**

Native name: ***tsai ba-ka' ta-la***.

Taxonomic notes: Although Hudson cited *Prunus subcordata*, he described it variously as having either blue or red fruits, leaving some uncertainty as to the taxon referenced.

Fruit food: The fruits were eaten fresh or after drying in the sun.

***Prunus virginiana* L. (Rosaceae) · Chokecherry**
Native name: *du-măk'* ("cinnamon bear").
Basketry: The plant was used as basketry material in an unspecified manner.
Fruit food: The fruits, which ripened in autumn, were a favorite food.

***Pseudognaphalium californicum* (DC.) Anderb. (Asteraceae) · Ladies' tobacco**
Native name: *ka-ti we'-no*.
Taxonomic notes: Hudson referred to this plant as *Gnaphalium californicum*, which corresponds with the current species *Pseudognaphalium californicum* (Jepson Flora Project 2012b).
First aid: The leaves were bruised and applied to sores and wounds.

***Pseudotsuga menziesii* (Mirb.) Franco (Pinaceae) · Douglas fir**
Native names: *ka'-we* ("gum") and *ka-wa' ka-lĭ* ("gum tree").
Taxonomic notes: Hudson used the common name "spruce" for *P. menziesii*. At times, he also used only "fir," which may also have referred to members of the genus *Abies*.
Adhesive: The tree pitch was heated and used as an adhesive for such applications as attaching a stone point to a drill shaft and affixing stone axe heads to handles. The gum was also used to mold finger grips at the base of arrows.
Basketry: High quality basketry weft fibers were obtained from the roots.
Beverage: According to Chestnut (1902), most of the native peoples in Mendocino County used the fresh leaves as a coffee substitute.
Confection: The young needles were consumed as a sweet snack.
Decoration: Mourners expressed their grief by singeing the hair before adhering pitch from Douglas fir and other conifers mixed with wood ash.
Fishing: Two-pronged fish spears made from Douglas fir saplings were used for salmon and steelhead.
Fragrance: Hunters and warriors prepared themselves by standing over smoldering Douglas fir leaves, possibly to conceal their odor.
Nut food: The nuts may have been consumed.
Polish: Animal sinew was applied with Douglas fir pitch to protect the mouth end of blowing tubes and flutes. The pitch was also used as a varnish to protect arrow decorations and the sinew bindings securing feather fletching.
Salad food: The young buds were eaten as a fresh food.

***Pteridium aquilinum* (L.) Kuhn (Dennstaedtiaceae) · Bracken fern**
Native name: *bis*.
Basketry: The roots provided a basketry weft material of poor quality that was sometimes used in plain twining. It was considered an undesirable material because it lacked

a smooth surface, could not be produced in flat tapes of even width, and tended to stain adjacent light colored weft fibers. The most desirable roots were close to 45 cm in length, less than 2 mm in diameter, and characterized by longitudinal striations and shades of tan. The coloration of this material varied according to its stage of growth and soil conditions. Before use, the pitch was removed by washing and scraping repeatedly or laborious chewing, the latter technique usually being accomplished by elderly women. Because the natural color of these fibers was considered insufficiently dark for basketry patterns, they were often dyed black. However, the resulting color was considered impermanent.

Quercus spp. (Fagaceae) · Oak

<u>Taxonomic notes</u>: Hudson's references to the common name oak, which evidently referred to multiple unspecified members of the genus, are treated in this entry.

<u>Architecture</u>: Storage granaries were woven with oak shoots. Also, assembly houses were constructed with six oak posts arranged around a center post.

<u>Basketry</u>: Needles, often made from a splint of oak wood, were used in basketry. These were split on one edge to accept the thread. The wood was sometimes also used as a dense and moderately pliable warp material for coarse utilitarian baskets. Wicker seed beaters, used to collect seeds from grassland plants, were made with young oak shoots. The 25 cm handles consisted of bundles of 12 or more narrow shoots bound along half their length with a slender willow twig. A 25 cm hoop was attached to this bundle at its midpoint. The free ends of the bundled shoots were then spread evenly, in a fan-like arrangement, to the edge of the loop and were bound to it with slender willow twigs. The interior of the loop was closed by weaving the fanned handle sprouts with wickerwork or twining.

<u>Bread</u>: Acorns were used to bake bread.

<u>Colorant</u>: Charcoal derived from oak galls was used as a black paint and as a hair dye. According to Chestnut (1902), a black dye was prepared by mixing the light-green juice from fresh galls with rusty iron nails. Immediately upon contact with iron, the juice turned black. In addition, one of the methods used to dye light-colored weft fibers black involved burying them with crushed acorn shells.

<u>Container</u>: Woody gnarls found on the trunks were used to make durable and lightweight vessels of diverse sizes (Figure 24). These were detached from the trunk by cutting and hammering. They were shaped by burning in a controlled manner with blowing tubes and then scraped smooth.

Figure 24. Grace Hudson illustration of small wooden grinding bowl. From Carpenter (1893b:155).

Cooking: The leaves were used as a moist lining inside underground ovens. According to Chestnut (1902), the wood was a preferred fuel for baking and parching seeds because it burns slowly.

Decoration: Bear doctors wore masks woven with sturdy oak rods in a coarse weave. To the front of women's ceremonial dance headbands were affixed 5 cm projecting oak rods, which were wound with milkweed fiber that had been stained red with alder bark and ornamented with clamshell disks.

Fire: According to Chestnut (1902), dry powdered oak leaves were used as tinder for starting fires.

Fishing: Fish hooks were made from oak. Also, conical and tubular fish traps were woven from the second-year shoots.

Fowling: Hooks used to catch large birds and the hardwood points of bird arrows were fashioned from oak.

Gaming and competition: Oak sticks were used to make rackets for a game that resembled lacrosse (cf. Culin 1975). Game balls were also made from oak knots.

Hair treatment: A solution made from oak gall charcoal was applied to the hair as a black dye and to promote hair growth. Green oak gall juice was mixed with water and applied to invigorate the hair.

Host plant: Mildew found on old acorns was used to produce a bluish paint that was used to decorate arrows. Lichens collected from oak trees were used for items such as clothing, pads, and cushions. Oak trees were also the primary host for American mistletoe, used for fishing and in medicine.

Insecticide: Oak galls were used to treat lice.

Legend: In some of the legends documented by Helen Carpenter (n.d.), mythological beings gave acorns and other important items to the people so they might be fed. In the legend "Poma Genesis," documented by Hudson, Coyote (**Du-wi'**) gave the recently created first men acorn mush to eat and oak galls to "cleanse & darken" themselves. He gave the recently created first women the "best" acorns, as well as digging sticks, stone pestles, wild lettuces, medicines, bulb and corm foods, and red earth (**ma-po'**). In other legends, Coyote made secret trips in an acorn shell boat in order to steal acorns from the great and fruitful land across the ocean from which he originated.

Medicine: Oak galls were used as a medicine of unspecified qualities.

Mush: Acorns were used for mush.

Music: Strings of acorn shells were used as instruments. Hudson explained that one end was held in the mouth while the other was rapidly spun to produce musical notes. According to other sources, these strings were made with whole acorns (Barrett 1952; Loeb 1926). Additionally, bullroarers and split-stick clappers were made from oak wood.

Packing or carrying: Simple firewood packing baskets were made from oak branches. Also, men used coarsely woven conical pack baskets made from oak shoots to carry heavy loads, such as firewood, buckeyes, and fish. Another type of conical carrying basket, used to transport salt from mines located in inland enemy territories, was constructed from a mesh of oak withes reinforced with hoops and closed with chain fern (*Woodwardia fimbriata*) fronds. Hung from the head with a leather tumpline, this construction also served as a protective barrier against enemy arrows.

Tool: Wood was split with mallets made from oak in conjunction with antler wedges. These mallets were also used to pound leather root fibers. Oak wood was used to make scrapers, cooking dippers, and arrow straighteners. Heavy oak rams, wielded by several people, were used to crush logs into smaller pieces. Oak mortars, also called mealing blocks, were commonly used for food processing in the nineteenth century. Stone axe handles were cut from secondary growth stalks.

Watercraft: Spade-like paddles, used in conjunction with tule balsas while visiting locations with open waterways, were fashioned from oak wood.

Quercus agrifolia Née (Fagaceae) · Coast live oak

Native name: *ca-tcam ka-li*.

Taxonomic notes: Hudson often used the common name "live oak," suggesting the possibility that other taxa were used.

Architecture: Helen Carpenter (n.d.) noted that during difficult times one Potter Valley Pomo family used a hollow live oak tree trunk as a summertime home that provided adequate protection from light rains.

Bread: The acorns produced light-colored bread that was valued for being sweet and delicate, despite being especially laborious to prepare. The nuts were covered with a tightly adhering skin that was removed with difficulty by rubbing between the palms. They were also slow to grind because they adhered to stone pestles. Nevertheless, they had only small quantities of tannins that could be easily removed by soaking and straining through a loosely woven basket. During this process the runoff water was watched to ensure that the desired oils did not escape.

Mush: Coast live oak mush was light-colored and sweet. Although it ranked sixth in preference among Potter Valley Pomo acorns used for mush, it grew at some distance, produced a sparse crop, and was difficult to prepare.

Tool: The dense wood was used for a variety of tools and implements.

Quercus chrysolepis Liebm. (Fagaceae) · Canyon live oak

Native names: *kĭ-că'* and *ki-ca ka-li*.

Taxonomic notes: Hudson frequently used the common name "live oak."

Bread: The acorns were used to bake bread.

Mush: Canyon live oak ranked seventh in preference among acorns used for mush.

***Quercus douglasii* Hook. & Arn. (Fagaceae) · Blue oak**
Native names: *kă-kul'* and *ka-kul ka-li*.
Bread: The acorns were used to bake bread.
Mush: Blue oak acorns ranked third in preference among acorns used for mush.

***Quercus dumosa* Nutt. (Fagaceae) · Nuttall's scrub oak**
Native name: *ba-tsam ka-li*.
Bread: The acorns were used to bake bread.
Fishing: Conical fish traps were constructed from the second-year shoots.
Mush: The acorns were used for mush, but were only ranked ninth in preference. Being considered lean and acrid, they were used as an emergency food.

***Quercus garryana* Hook. (Fagaceae) · Oregon oak**
Native names: *bi-yu'* and *bi-yu ka-li*.
Bread: The acorns were used to bake bread.
Fishing: Conical fish traps were constructed from the second-year shoots.
Mush: Oregon oak ranked fourth in preference among acorns used for mush.

***Quercus kelloggii* Newb. (Fagaceae) · California black oak**
Native names: *nu-ci'* and *nu-ci ka-li*.
Bread: The acorns were used to make bread. For this purpose, the tannins were typically removed with an extract of red earth (*ma-po'*) rather than by leaching.
Colorant: Alkali bulrush fiber was dyed black by soaking for a day in a mixture of water, powdered charcoal, and crushed California black oak and blue elderberry leaves.
Container: The woody trunk gnarls were hollowed and shaped into vessels of various sizes.
Fishing: Conical fish traps were constructed with second-year shoots.
Mush: California black oak produced a mild mush of excellent quality, being ranked second in preference among the acorns.
Packing or carrying: Forked branches were used as a pack to carry firewood.

***Quercus lobata* Née (Fagaceae) · Valley oak, California white oak**
Native names: *tsi-pă'* and *tsi-pa' ka-lĭ*.
Bread: Grinding dried valley oak acorns was considered difficult because they have a particularly coarse texture. Bread was made either by leaching or by adding red earth. It was called "cold cake" (*ka-sil'-li*) if prepared by leaching. Inadequate leaching produced bitter bread. The leached meal was kneaded and baked on a rock slab to produce a flavorless and lumpy cream colored bread that was often used to soak up gravies. "Water fetid bread" (*ka-to' tcu-ni*) was made by finely crushing the acorns on wooden mortars and

adding red earth (***ma-po'***) prior to baking. The resulting loaf was black and glutinous. In Hudson's evaluation it tasted similar to cornbread.

Mush: At one time, the local California white oak trees produced acorns in far greater quantities than were required by the local population. However, because it was bitter and tough it was considered of average quality, ranking fifth in preference among acorns used for mush.

Ramalina menziesii Tayl. (Fungi: Ramalinaceae) · Lace lichen

Native names: ***ku-tcĭ'*** ("matted") and ***ka-lĭ ku-tcĭ'*** ("tree matted").

Taxonomic notes: At times, Hudson used just the common names "Spanish moss," "tree moss," or "lichen." From the context it is apparent that he used "tree moss" for this epiphytic lichen.

Clothing: Diapers, worn in conjunction with other baby clothing, were made from lace lichen that was thoroughly beaten, cleansed, and dried. Children were also seated on cushions of absorbent lichen when laced in baby cradles.

Gaming and competition: The lichen was used to stuff game balls.

Matting or bedding: Lace lichen was used as a bedding material.

Padding or toweling: During childbirth, a female assistant kneeled on the floor with her feet spread wide. She filled the space between her thighs with a cushion of lace lichen covered with greased buckskin to receive the infant. After childbirth, she wiped the infant with lichen towels before passing him or her to the mother and her maternal representative.

Women's health: After expulsion of the afterbirth and a subsequent bath, mothers received a napkin made of beaten and cleaned lace lichen. Menstruating women used napkins, cushions, and towels made from the same material.

Ranunculus californicus Benth. (Ranunculaceae) · California buttercup

Native name: ***tce-dŏ ba ă*** ("glade flower").

Taxonomic notes: In some instances, Hudson used only the genus name *Ranunculus* or the common name "buttercup," suggesting that other local members of the genus may have been used.

Seed food: The seeds were toasted, ground, and consumed as food, presumably in pinole.

Ranunculus canus Benth. (Ranunculaceae) · Great valley buttercup

Native name: ***du-wi tco pi-cum***.

Hudson did not provide information regarding this plant's uses.

Ranunculus occidentalis Nutt. (Ranunculaceae) · Western buttercup

Native name: ***ta-la'*** ("tick").

Taxonomic notes: At times, Hudson used *Ranunculus eisenii* for the contemporary species *Ranunculus occidentalis* (USDA and NRCS 2012). In other instances, he used only the genus name *Ranunculus* or the common name "buttercup."

Seed food: The seeds were consumed. Chestnut (1902) documented that the seeds, gathered in great quantities in May, were used alone or with other seeds for pinole.

Ranunculus orthorhynchus Hook. (Ranunculaceae) · Bloomer's buttercup
Native name: *ka mi tol' mi tol.*

Taxonomic notes: Consistent with a determination by botanist Alice Eastwood in 1928, Hudson used *Ranunculus bloomerii* for the contemporary species *Ranunculus orthorhynchus* (USDA and NRCS 2012).

Eye Medicine: The fresh leaves were warmed and applied to relieve eye inflammations.

Raphanus sativus L. (Brassicaceae) · Wild radish
Native name: *di-tsa' tso.*

Cooked green: The fresh leaves were simmered in water for about a half hour and eaten.

Salad food: The foliage was eaten fresh and the green pods were consumed as a relish. A food for infants was prepared by crushing or grinding the ripe pods to a fine powder and mixing with warm water.

Rhamnus spp. (Rhamnaceae) · Redberry
Rhamnus crocea Nutt. · Redberry
Rhamnus ilicifolia Kellogg · Hollyleaf redberry

Taxonomic notes: Hudson used the scientific name *Rhamnus crocea*. The former taxon *Rhamnus crocea* ssp. *ilicifolia* (Hickman 1993) corresponds with the species *Rhamnus ilicifolia* (Jepson Flora Project 2012b).

Hunting: The wood was used to make foreshafts for big game or war arrows.

Rhus aromatica Aiton (Anacardiaceae) · Fragrant sumac
Native name: *bu' yam kali'.*

Taxonomic notes: At times, Hudson used only the genus name *Rhus*. He also used *Rhus canadensis trilobata* and *Rhus trilobata canadensis* for the contemporary species *Rhus aromatica* (IPNI 2012; Jepson Flora Project 2012b).

Basketry: The plant provided a long and resilient rod of even caliber that was infrequently used for warp elements in one-rod coiling and plain twining. It was also highly valued as one of three primary sources of red-colored weft fibers used in fine patterned basketry. Contradicting Hudson's evidence, Loeb (1926) claimed that the use of fragrant sumac as weft was restricted to Southern California.

Cathartic: The seeds were consumed as a cathartic.

<u>Fishing</u>: Conical fish traps were fashioned from the stalks.

<u>Gastrointestinal aid</u>: The seeds were eaten for dyspepsia and indigestion.

Ribes californicum Hook. & Arn. (Grossulariaceae) · California gooseberry

<u>Native name</u>: *lum ba-kai'* ("prickly berry").

<u>Fruit food</u>: The ripe fruit was considered a delicacy and eaten raw in substantial quantities. The bristles on the fruit were singed off with fire and the rind was not swallowed.

Ribes divaricatum Douglas (Grossulariaceae) · Spreading gooseberry

<u>Native name</u>: *hai ǒ' ka-lǐ'*.

<u>Fruit food</u>: The ripe fruit was considered a rare and luxurious snack.

Rosa spp. (Rosaceae) · Rose

Rosa californica Cham. & Schldl. · California wildrose

Rosa pisocarpa A. Gray · Cluster rose

<u>Native name</u>: *ka' ba-kai'* ("waterberry").

<u>Taxonomic notes</u>: Hudson often used the genus *Rosa* or the common name "rose" without further specification, which suggests he may have referred to other local members of this genus.

<u>Arrow</u>: The stalks were used for arrows.

<u>Fruit food</u>: The late season fruit was eaten freely when other fruits were not available. The seeds and skin were not swallowed. Toasting increased their sweetness.

<u>Gaming and competition</u>: Cluster rose rods were used as shafts for short-range contest arrows.

<u>Hunting</u>: The wood was used to make foreshafts for big game and war arrows.

Rubus leucodermis Douglas ex Torr. & A. Gray (Rosaceae) · Western raspberry

<u>Native name</u>: *cǐn-na' da-bo'-li ba-kai'*.

<u>Fruit food</u>: The fresh berries were eaten.

Rubus parviflorus Nutt. (Rosaceae) · Thimbleberry

<u>Native names</u>: *cǐn-na da-bo' ma* and *da-to'-la ba-kai'*.

<u>Fruit food</u>: The fresh berries were eaten.

Rubus spectabilis Pursh (Rosaceae) · Salmonberry

<u>Native names</u>: *ti'-ta hai* and *ti'-ta hai ba-kai'*.

<u>Taxonomic notes</u>: Hudson's use of this scientific name corresponds with a 1928 determination by Alice Eastwood.

<u>Fruit food</u>: The fresh berries were eaten.

Rubus ursinus Cham. & Schldl. (Rosaceae) · California blackberry
Native name: *ti'-ti mi ba-kai'*.
Taxonomic notes: Hudson used *Rubus vitifolius* for the contemporary species *Rubus ursinus* (Jepson Flora Project 2012b).
Fruit food: The fruit was eaten fresh in large quantities and dried for winter storage.

Rumex sp. (Polygonaceae) · Dock
Native name: *mu si-pal'*.
Taxonomic notes: Instances in which Hudson referenced the genus *Rumex* or the common name "dock" without further specification are included in this entry. Such citations may suggest that unspecified local members of this genus were used.
Antidiarrheal: An infusion of the mature seeds was taken for diarrhea.
Cooked green: The young leaves were baked or fried with animal fat.
Seed food: The seeds were toasted and ground for use in pinole.

*Rumex crispus L. (Polygonaceae) · Curly dock
Native name: *ka si pal' pa*.
Antidiarrheal: An infusion of the mature seeds was used for diarrhea.
Seed food: The seeds were used for pinole.

Salix spp. (Salicaceae) · Willow
Native name: *ci-kau'*.
Taxonomic notes: Instances in which Hudson used only the genus name *Salix* or the common name "willow" are included in this entry. The specific taxa referenced are unknown.
Architecture: The plant was used to thatch the exterior of temporary shelters.
Basketry: The shoots provided dense woody splints of moderate pliability, good strength and length, and even caliber, which were used as warp in twined, coiled, and wicker basketry. The roots of most taxa provided an abundant but poor quality weft fiber for basketry. It was considered weak, brittle, and of an undesirable gray or straw color that darkened with age. One-year old roots were preferred as weft and were prepared in the same manner as sedge weft. The fibers were dyed black in wood ash. In addition to its use as warp and weft, willow provided slender twigs used to bind the handles of seed beaters. According to Hudson (1893), in the nineteenth century willow replaced alder as the most common material for open-twined acorn collecting baskets.
Clothing: Women's formal skirts were made from willow bark fringe.
Colorant: The charcoal was used to make a black paint. The ash was used to blacken light-colored basketry weft fibers. One technique involved evenly painting the fibers with willow charcoal paste, followed by burial in a moist earthen pit, covered with willow ash, for about 80 hours.

Fishing: Willow was used in preparing fish nets and traps. Nets were held open with an arching willow rod. Willow pegs were driven into stream beds during low waters to form a weir to direct fish into a trap, also made from willow.

Gaming and competition: Willow staves were used in the "game without bickering." Also, 2.5 m willow lances were used to pierce wooden rings in the "hoop mystery" game.

Music: Mouth bows were made from willow wood.

Polish: To prevent checkering on flutes and blowing tubes, the exterior surfaces were polished by rubbing with green willow leaves and a mixture of crushed soaproot and damp buckeye charcoal.

Trade: Roughly chipped and perforated clamshell disks were strung on willow shoots and smoothed by rolling them against stone slabs (Hudson 1897).

Salix exigua Nutt. (Salicaceae) · Sandbar willow
Native name: *băm kalĭ'*.

Taxonomic notes: Hudson used *Salix sesselifolia hindsiana* and *Salix hindsiana* for the contemporary species *Salix exigua* (Jepson Flora Project 2012b).

Basketry: The ivory-colored shoots were a principal basketry warp material, used for all twining and coiling weaves. Two year-old growth was gathered in early summer before boring pests appeared in autumn and destroyed the product. The branches were immediately scraped bare, bound in sheaves, and allowed to season. Although Barrett (1908b) indicated that the different willow species were all valued equally, Hudson documented that sandbar willow rods were exceptionally tough yet pliant and lightweight, and could be obtained in long sections with even taper and free of knots (cf. Chestnut 1902). It was also used in coarse utilitarian baskets to bind the handles of seed beaters and in baby cradles.

War: The wood was used for war arrows.

Salix gooddingii C. R. Ball (Salicaceae) · Goodding's black willow
Native name: *ma-lo' ma-lo ka-lĭ'*.

Taxonomic notes: Hudson used *Salix nigra* for the contemporary species *Salix gooddingii* (Munz and Keck 1973).

Basketry: The root fibers were considered the best type of willow for use as basketry weft. The shoots were also used as warp in all types of basketry.

Clothing: Rain coats were made with the shredded inner-bark fiber. This was stripped from the tree with an obsidian knife or stone axe, shredded with a bone awl, and bound with string made of the same fiber. When nearly dry, the garment was rubbed thoroughly with grease to improve its softness and to promote resistance to moisture. Rain aprons or skirts were made in the same manner and worn to protect the lower body.

Cordage: When split, twisted, and greased, the fibers became both pliable and somewhat resilient, although they ranked below all other plant fibers in terms of strength.

Matting or bedding: The fibers were woven into mats.

Salix laevigata Bebb (Salicaceae) · Red willow
Native name: *ci-kŏ' ka-lĭ'*.
Basketry: The roots were used as a low quality tan-colored weft fiber. In addition, the shoots were used as a basketry warp material.

Salix lasiolepis Benth. (Salicaceae) · Arroyo willow
Native name: *ci ko' yem*.
Basketry: The root fibers were considered a weft material of reasonably good quality, yet inferior in color and strength to other materials. The young shoots were also used as warp in twined and coiled basketry. According to Chestnut (1902), this was the most commonly used basketry willow in the region.
Clothing: Chestnut (1902) reported that prior to the late nineteenth century the inner bark was used to make a skirt-like garment.
Cordage: The inner bark fiber was used to make rope (Chestnut 1902).
Panacea: According to Chestnut (1902), the bark was widely used by all indigenous groups in the region as a panacea and for such ailments as itches, chills, fever, and diarrhea.

Salix sitchensis Sanson ex Bong. (Salicaceae) · Sitka willow
Native names: *ca-kŏ' ka-lĭ'* and *bom' ka-lĭ'*.
Arrow: The wood was used for arrows.
Basketry: The shoots were used as a basketry warp material.

Sambucus nigra L. ssp. *caerulea* (Raf.) Bolli (Adoxaceae) · Blue elderberry
Native names: *ke-tĕ'*, *ke-te' ba-kai'*, and *ke-te' kalĭ'*.
Taxonomic notes: Hudson used the names *Sambucus glauca* and *Sambucus nigra* for the contemporary taxon *Sambucus nigra* ssp. *caerulea* (Jepson Flora Project 2012a; USDA and NRCS 2012). He also used the genus name *Sambucus* and the common name "elder," which may also refer to red elderberry (*S. racemosa*).
Cathartic: The bark was boiled with chamomile leaves for use as a fast-acting cathartic.
Colorant: Light-colored weft fibers were dyed black by soaking for one day in a mixture of water, powdered charcoal, and crushed elderberry leaves.
Decoration: Men's ear sticks were made from 8 cm sections of the wood, with the pith removed and the exterior surface polished.
Fiber: The fiber was utilized for unspecified purposes.
Fire: Fire drill shafts were fashioned from the wood.
Fruit food: The ripe fruit was eaten fresh or dried. The juice was also pressed from the berries and consumed with one's index finger.

Gastrointestinal aid: The dried flowers were taken for stomach troubles (Chestnut 1902).

Music: Flutes and whistles were made from hollowed elderberry sections (Figure 25). The flutes were decorated with a "Robin's signature" pattern. The legendary being Robin invented the great flute to charm worms out of the ground. They were used by hereditary Kuksu (*kuk'su*) doctors. Ceremonial split-stick clappers ("lightning sticks") were also made from elderberry.

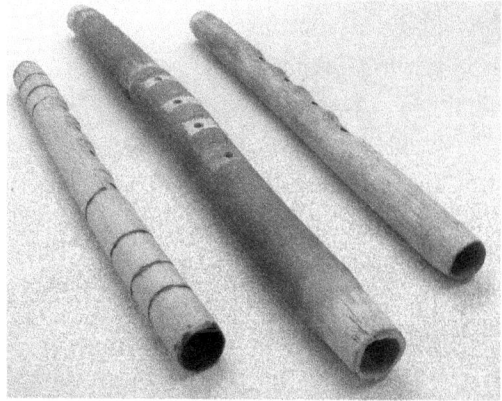

Figure 25. Elderberry flutes. Photograph by James R. Welch, 2011. Accession nos. 1398, 1399, and 1743, in the collections of Grace Hudson Museum, Ukiah.

Tool: The wood was used for blowing tubes, used with embers for woodworking, and as clamps to secure clamshell and magnesite disk beads while drilling.

Sanicula tuberosa Torr. (Apiaceae) · Tuberous sanicle

Native name: *ke-e' pu.*

Febrifuge: The tuberous roots were grated and eaten raw to treat fever (*du ci*).

Fragrance: The plant was used as a deodorant.

Root food: According to Hudson, the baked roots were consumed but considered of poor quality. However, Chestnut (1902) reported that they had a delicate flavor and were among the finest of the bulbs and root foods.

Schoenoplectus acutus (Muhl. ex Bigelow) Á. Löve & D. Löve var. occidentalis (S. Watson) S. G. Sm. (Cyperaceae) · Common tule

Native name: *ba-tco' ka-lĭ.*

Taxonomic notes: In addition the common name "tule," Hudson referenced *Scirpus acutis* and *Scirpus lacustris,* both of which now correspond with *Schoenoplectus acutus* var. *occidentalis* (Jepson Flora Project 2012b; S. G. Smith 1995). In some instances, Hudson's lack of specificity could suggest that other local tules or bulrushes were used. Although he attributed its use primarily to Pomoan groups in the vicinity of Clear Lake, it also appeared in his notes regarding the Northern Pomo from Potter Valley. Stewart (1943) noted that the Potter Valley Pomo obtained this plant at Clear Lake.

Architecture: The stalks and leaves were used as house thatch. It was considered an excellent insulator with good architectural structure. This thatch was also used in constructing subsurface chambers, which were long, narrow residential spaces used by the elderly women of a family. Such chambers were covered with thatch near the entrance steps.

Basketry: The rhizomes produced an attractive black weft fiber for basketry.

Clothing: The insulating and absorbent stalk fibers were used to weave clothing for the elderly and infants. The shredded stalks were also used to make a loose sleeveless outer garment (Figure 26), women's dress skirts, and raincoats that were tossed over the shoulders.

Cooking: Rush mats were used to line the inside of sand leaching pits to keep acorn and buckeye meal clean. Also while leaching, loose rushes were placed under the pouring water to distribute it evenly across the meal.

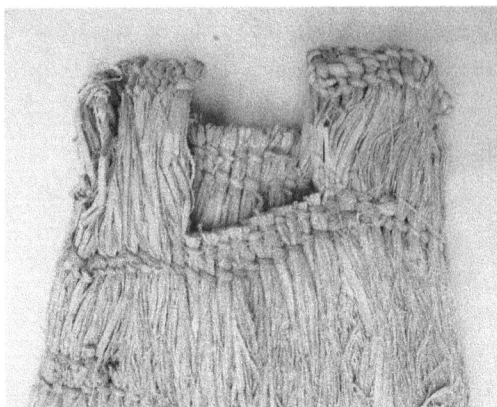

Figure 26. Child's sleeveless tule garment. Photograph by James R. Welch, 2011. Accession no. 1715, in the collections of Grace Hudson Museum, Ukiah.

Gaming and competition: "Hoop shooting" was an archery contest with a target consisting of a plain-woven tule mat with a 2.5 cm ring at the center. Juggling games involved keeping one or more 8 cm balls, made of tightly wrapped tule fiber, in the air by striking them with the hands.

For the purposes of competition, the usual balsa design was modified for racing boats. Such racing balsas were long and narrow in shape and were more tightly bound. Hudson reported that they could reach speeds of about 10 kilometers per hour (a "six mile gait").

Matting or bedding: Partially dried stalks were collected in autumn and used to make plain-woven mats. Essential components of every home, they were used as platters, bedding, rugs, and carpeting. In addition, a rare and expensive tule mat covered with woodpecker scalps was spread as a seat for political dignitaries or for use on ceremonial occasions.

Padding or toweling: The partially dried plant material was plain-woven into mats used as baby swaddlings.

Salad food: The light-colored tender young shoots were eaten raw, being especially appreciated by thirsty fishermen.

Watercraft: Tule balsas were the primary mode of water transportation among the Pomoan groups and were used by the Potter Valley Pomo for fishing in open waters, such as during visits to Clear Lake. Hudson reported that these buoyant vessels remained impervious to water for one or two seasons. The abundantly available mature stalks were collected when turning gray in autumn. Balsa construction involved bundling tule stalks into five rolls approximately 3 m in length, which were firmly lashed together to form a prow, a keel, and a cavity in the middle for the operator.

Women's health: Menstruating women often used soft padding made from stalk fibers as an absorbent pad or belt.

Scrophularia californica Cham. & Schldl. (Scrophulariaceae) · California figwort

Native name: *tca ha kalĭ* ("boils plant").

Disinfectant: The leaves were bruised for use as a strong poultice for boils, deep infected sores, and ulcers. The macerated roots were also used for the same purpose after the leaves had fallen in the autumn.

Sequoia sempervirens (D. Don) Endl. (Cupressaceae) · Coast redwood

Native name: *kasil' ka-lĭ'*.

Architecture: Where the redwood lumber industry operated in the late nineteenth and early twentieth centuries, such as the coastal areas visited seasonally by the Potter Valley Pomo, discarded slabs of redwood bark were used to construct conical shelters (*hai-tca*). Whereas Hudson's notes suggest that the Northern Pomo use of this construction style was a recent innovation, other sources suggest it was an early construction style of the coastal Pomoan groups (Barrett 1916; Loeb 1926).

Clothing: The bark was used to make raincoats.

Legend: Hudson mentioned a "mysterious woman" in Northern Pomo legend who lived in a hollow coast redwood tree, captured naughty children, and ate hunters.

Watercraft: The wood was used to manufacture dugout canoes, although these would not have been used in the small streams and rivers in Potter Valley. The practice was adopted in the mid-1850s, when government expedition dugouts fell into the hands of local Pomoans and were subsequently copied.

Solanum xanti A. Gray (Solanaceae) · Purple nightshade

Native names: *ma-yus' ma-yus'* and *tsi mu' duk*.

Fruit food: The ripe berries were eaten raw and were considered to promote the appetite and sound sleep.

Solidago velutina DC. (Asteraceae) · Threenerve goldenrod

Native name: *ce-ko'-dŏ cĭm-mă'* ("hares' ears").

Taxonomic notes: Hudson used *Solidago californica* (written *Salidago cal.*) for the contemporary species *Solidago velutina* (Jepson Flora Project 2012b).

First aid: An infusion made from goldenrod and ash bark was applied directly to cuts and infected sores. Alternatively, it was mixed with a particular local mud, probably from Laughlin Ridge, and applied hot to cuts and sores.

Leprosy treatment: The mud mixture described above was also used for leprosy.

*Sonchus asper (L.) Hill (Asteraceae) · **Prickly sowthistle**

Native name: *ca-kos' tso*.

Taxonomic notes: Hudson's use of the name *Sonchus asper* was based on a 1928 determination by botanist Alice Eastwood.

Cooked green: The plant was cooked and eaten.

Root food: The roots were eaten raw.

Salad food: The sour young leaves, buds, and green seeds were eaten raw with salt.

Symphoricarpos mollis Nutt. (Caprifoliaceae) · **Snowberry**

Native name: *ba-kal' ka-lǐ'* ("brush plant").

Taxonomic notes: At times, Hudson used *Symphoricarpos racemosus* for the contemporary species *Symphoricarpos mollis* (Jepson Flora Project 2012b; Munz and Keck 1973). He also referenced *Symphoricarpos setigerus*, which does not appear in the botanical literature and may have resulted from confusion with *Croton setiger* (previously *Eremocarpus setigerus*).

Decoration: Men's ear sticks were made from the wood.

Smoking: The wood was used for pipe stems.

Tool: The branches were used as brooms. In addition, straight rods were polished and used for drills.

*Taraxacum officinale F. H. Wigg. (Asteraceae) · **Common dandelion**

Native name: *di-tsa' tsŏ*.

Laxative: The greens were boiled and eaten to move the bowels. The leaves were also given to expectant mothers as a laxative upon first symptoms of labor.

Salad food: The fresh plant parts were eaten.

Taraxia ovata (Nutt.) Small (Onagraceae) · **Goldeneggs**

Native name: *kai-yăn' ka-lǐ*.

Taxonomic notes: Based on a determination by Alice Eastwood in 1928, Hudson used *Oenothera ovata* for the contemporary taxon *Taraxia ovata* (Jepson Flora Project 2012b).

Bulb or corm food: The bulbs were baked in underground ovens and eaten in small quantities.

Emetic: The fresh root was considered a strong emetic.

Tauschia kelloggii (A. Gray) J. F. Macbr. (Apiaceae) · **Kellogg's umbrellawort**

Native name: *ba tco' wǎ*.

Taxonomic notes: Based on a 1928 determination by Alice Eastwood, Hudson used *Drudeophyton kelloggii*. The genus *Drudeophytum* was changed to *Oreonana* (Munz and Keck 1973), suggesting that this plant in fact pertains to the closely related genus *Tauschia*.

Salad food: The raw stems were eaten in large quantities. Hudson reported that it had "an odor that announced the coming of an Indian."

Taxus brevifolia **Nutt. (Taxaceae) · Pacific yew**
Native names: *yun' ka-lǐ* and *be-nish ka-lǐ'*.
Arrow: The wood was used for arrows.
Bow: Pacific yew provided the most highly valued bow wood in Mendocino County (cf. Chestnut 1902).
Tool: The wood was used for numerous wooden implements and tools.

Thalictrum fendleri **Engelm. ex A. Gray (Ranunculaceae) · Fendler's meadowrue**
Native name: *du wi' ba tco'* wǎ ("coyote angelica").
Taxonomic notes: Consistent with a determination by Alice Eastwood in 1928, Hudson sometimes used only the genus name *Thalictrum* (written *Thallictrum*). Elsewhere, he used *Thalictrum polycarpum* (written *Thallictrum polyca.*) for the contemporary species *Thalictrum fendleri* (Jepson Flora Project 2012b).
Emetic: The seeds were boiled and taken hot as an emetic.
Laxative: The seeds were boiled and taken hot as a purgative.
Spirituality: This is one of the Potter Valley Pomo "psychic" *xa-nu'* plants with spiritual properties. An infusion of the root was used as an ointment for funeral attendants.
STD remedy: An infusion prepared from the roots was used to treat gonorrhea.

Torreya californica **Torr. (Taxaceae) · California nutmeg**
Native name: *kě-bi' ka-lǐ'*.
Basketry: High quality basketry weft fibers were obtained from the roots.
Bow: The wood was used for to make fine bows.
Nut food: The ripe nuts were buried in moist earth for about a month to remove the bitterness. Eaten raw, they were considered oily and flavorful. The nuts were also cooked in ashes. According to Chestnut (1902), the whole roasted nuts tasted like peanuts.
Poison: The powdered bark was used by sorcerers (*ka-tan'*) as a poison causing irritation, pain, and blindness. It was sprinkled on a victim's eyelids and skin in the sweathouse, where men were often sleepy and perspiring.

Toxicodendron diversilobum **(Torr. & A. Gray) Greene (Anacardiaceae) · Poison oak**
Native name: *mi tu' yo ho*.
Basketry: The stems were used as a basketry warp material (cf. Chestnut 1902).
Colorant: The fresh juice, which turns black upon exposure to the air, was used as a dye for basketry and other materials (Hudson in Chestnut 1902:364–365). It produced some of the deepest black weft fibers used in Pomoan basketry.

Divination and doctoring: Sucking doctors used poison oak wood to fashion objects used in curing. Four painted pegs made of this material were planted in the ground at a patient's feet, serving to dissipate a disease or poison. Medicine bows and arrows, also made from poison oak, were painted with four red bands signifying the four "earth men" associated with the cardinal directions. The doctors used the medicine bows and arrows to drive the affliction towards the patient's feet, where it was dissipated by the pegs. These paraphernalia were made new for each treatment and destroyed by the doctor's assistant at the end of each curing session.

First aid: A poultice of the plant was used to treat boils.

Medicine: Hudson indicated that it used as a medicine for unspecified ailments. Chestnut (1902) reported that its primary medicinal use at Round Valley was to treat hand warts. After cutting off a wart, poison oak juice was applied repeatedly for one or two days.

Toxicoscordion spp. (Melanthiaceae) · Death camas

Toxicoscordion fontanum (Eastw.) Zomlefer & Judd · Marsh zigadenus
Toxicoscordion micranthum (Eastw.) A. Heller · Small flowered star lily
Toxicoscordion venenosum (S. Watson) Rydb.· Death camas

Native name: *tsim' bu* ("harmful bulb").

Taxonomic notes: Hudson used *Zigadenus micranthus* and *Zigadenus venenosus* for the taxa now classified as *Toxicoscordion micranthum* and *Toxicoscordion venenosum,* respectively. The former taxon *Zigadenus micranthus* var. *fontanus* (Hickman 1993), also located in the study area, is now known as *Toxicoscordion fontanum* (Jepson Flora Project 2012b). At times, Hudson used only the genus name *Zigadenus,* suggesting that other members of the genus may have been contemplated.

Analgesic: According to Chestnut (1902), the bulb was cooked, mashed, and bound for about 12 hours as a poultice to reduce the pain associated with strains and bruises.

Antirheumatic: Chestnut (1902) also reported that death camas was widely used for rheumatism. The fresh bulb was mashed and applied to painful joints twice a day for about a month.

First aid: The bulb was cooked, mashed, and bound as a poultice for a half day to treat boils (Chestnut 1902).

Poison: The plant was generally avoided due to its poisonous qualities.

Tragopogon porrifolius L. (Asteraceae) · Purple salsify

Native name: *ka mac ba ti' la* ("piquant").

Taxonomic notes: Hudson used this scientific name based on a determination by Alice Eastwood in 1928. Occasionally, use erroneously wrote *Tragopogon parvifolius.*

Root food: The roots were eaten raw.

Salad food: The leaves, eaten raw, had what Hudson considered a "strong peculiar flavor."

Trichostema lanceolatum Benth. (Lamiaceae) · Vinegarweed

Native name: *mi-cǐm' mi-ce'-u* ("smell-smell").

Febrifuge: A liquid extract of the whole dried plant was taken for fevers.

Fragrance: Hunters applied the chewed leaves or a tea made from the leaves externally to the body as a deodorant. These substances were also applied to hunting weapons to mask human odors.

Seed food: The ground seeds were consumed, perhaps as pinole.

Trifolium spp. (Fabaceae) · Clover

Taxonomic notes: Treated in this entry are instances in which Hudson cited only the genus *Trifolium* or the common name "clover."

Matting or bedding: According to Helen Carpenter (n.d.), clover fields were frequent settings for "love affairs."

Salad food: The green plant parts were eaten fresh. Most taxa were collected for this purpose before flowering.

Trifolium ciliolatum Benth. (Fabaceae) · Tree clover

Native name: *ka-lǐ' tsǒ* ("tree clover").

Taxonomic notes: Consistent with a determination by Alice Eastwood in 1928, Hudson identified this species by name (written *Trifolium ciliatum*).

Salad food: Fresh plant parts were eaten as a salad food.

Trifolium fucatum Lindl. (Fabaceae) · Bull clover

Native name: *bo-hǒ' tso*.

Taxonomic notes: At times, Hudson used *Trifolium virescens*, presumably for the taxon *Trifolium fucatum* var. *virescens*, which corresponds with the contemporary species *Trifolium fucatum* (Jepson Flora Project 2012b; Moerman 1998).

Salad food: The whole plant, often crushed and salted, was eaten fresh. Considered to have a sweet flavor, it was a favorite among the clovers (cf. Chestnut 1902). Unlike many of the other clovers, this plant was often eaten when the plant was in flower.

Trifolium gracilentum Torr. & A. Gray (Fabaceae) · Graceful clover

Native name: *tcu-pǐl' tsǒ*.

Salad food: The leaves and stems were eaten fresh, often with California bay nut bread.

Trifolium microdon Hook. & Arn. (Fabaceae) · Valparaiso

Native name: *pa-a' ma tsǒ*.

Taxonomic notes: Hudson's use of this scientific name is consistent with a determination by Alice Eastwood in 1928.

Salad food: The peppery-flavored plant was eaten fresh.

Trifolium obtusiflorum Hook. (Fabaceae) · Clammy clover
Native name: *ke tsu luk tsŏ*.
Salad food: The plant was eaten fresh, although according to Chestnut (1902) it has an acid-tasting exudate that was usually washed off first.

Trifolium variegatum Nutt. (Fabaceae) · Variegated clover
Native names: *bu-tǎ' tso* ("bear forage") and *ka-bo' tsŏ*.
Taxonomic notes: Hudson's use of the name *Trifolium variegatum* follows a 1928 determination by Alice Eastwood.
Cooked green: The fresh plant was boiled and eaten.
Salad food: The foliage was a favorite salad food, often eaten in large quantities with salt.

Trifolium willdenovii Spreng. (Fabaceae) · Tomcat clover
Native name: *tcu-pĭl' tsŏ*.
Taxonomic notes: Based on a 1928 determination by Alice Eastwood, Hudson used *Trifolium tridentatum* for the contemporary species *Trifolium willdenovii* (Jepson Flora Project 2012b).
Salad food: The fresh leaves and stems were eaten with California bay nut bread.

Trifolium wormskioldii Lehm. (Fabaceae) · Cows clover
Native name: *bu-ta' tso* ("bear forage").
Salad food: The plant was eaten fresh. According to Chestnut (1902), this was the only clover taxa that was customarily collected and eaten into late June.

Triteleia hyacinthina (Lindl.) Greene (Themidaceae) · White brodiaea
Native name: *pa-a' bu'*.
Taxonomic notes: Hudson used *Hesperoscordum lacteum* for *Brodiaea hyacinthine* (Jepson 1909; Moerman 1998), which corresponds with the contemporary species *Triteleia hyacinthine* (Jepson Flora Project 2012b).
Bulb or corm food: Chestnut (1902) reported that the bulbs were eaten raw or cooked, noting that it grew abundantly in the coastal valleys of Mendocino County.
Women's health: Mothers avoided eating this plant soon after giving birth because doing so was believed to cause child diarrhea.

Triteleia laxa Benth. (Themidaceae) · Ithuriel's spear
Native name: *bu-tum' bu*.

Taxonomic notes: Following a determination by Alice Eastwood in 1928, Hudson used *Bro-diaea laxa* for the contemporary species *Triteleia laxa* (USDA and NRCS 2012).

Bulb or corm food: The baked or roasted corms were eaten.

Triteleia peduncularis Lindl. (Themidaceae) · Long-rayed brodiaea

Bulb or corm food: According to Chestnut (1902), the bulbs were occasionally eaten by all Pomoan peoples.

Typha latifolia L. (Typhaceae) · Common cattail

Native name: *hal*.

Taxonomic notes: At times, Hudson used only the genus name *Typha*, which may have referred to other local members of the genus.

Architecture: Cattail was a usual material for awnings or sun shades (cf. Barrett 1916).

Bread: The ground seeds were baked into bread.

Clothing: Shredded and cleaned fibers from the dry mature stalks were a preferred material for clothing, wraps, diapers, and belts. Considered soft, flexible, and insulating, they were ideal for baby gowns and women's skirts. Also, rain cloaks, skirts, hoods, and leggings were woven from shredded fibers collected from partially dry male plants. A coating of deer tallow made them water resistant.

Matting or bedding: Slit female stalks were considered the best material for woven mats and bedding. The leaves were also used for this purpose.

Root food: The fleshy rootstalk and base were eaten raw. Their high water content made them refreshing snacks.

Salad food: The male sprouts, young stalks, and buds were eaten raw.

Women's health: Menstruating women used soft cattail padding as a belt or napkin.

Umbellularia californica (Hook. & Arn.) Nutt. (Lauraceae) · California bay

Native name: *bi-he'*.

Analgesic: Headache was treated with shooting star leaves mixed with California bay oil.

Bread: The nuts were gathered in large quantities in late autumn and stored in granaries for later use. They were used to bake bread that was considered a pleasant deviation from the usual monotonous winter diet of acorns. They were first roasted in hot ashes and embers to expel the volatile oils and render them more friable. They were then cracked and ground. Although they were usually only removed from granaries and cooked as needed, the addition of salt after cooking served as a preservative. The resultant oily meal was shaped into small loaves and cooked by repeatedly dipping a heated hardwood stick or stone pestle into the meal, grilling on a heated stone slab, or heating under a flaming bundle of sticks. The resulting bread was solid, crumbly, and dark in color. Often softened by reheating and eaten with salt, it made an ideal travelling ration and added flavor to salad foods and acorn mush or bread.

Ceremony: Hunters and warriors perfumed themselves over the smoldering leaves.

Cleaning agent: The leaves were heated over flames and rubbed on hunting masks made from deer pelts to disinfectant fetid parts.

Colorant: Scorched but not burned nut meats were used as black face and eyebrow paint.

Decoration: The leaves were used to make wreaths worn on the head and around the waist.

Flavoring: The leaves were added to buckeye mush to improve its flavor.

Fruit food: The flesh of ripe fruits was eaten.

Gaming and competition: Balls used in a game that resembled lacrosse were made from the woody knots.

Legend: In the legend "The Creation of the People of *Sho*," recorded by Helen Carpenter (n.d.), a cluster of California bay shrubs situated beside a lake was home to the "animals of the earth."

Nut food: The roasted, cracked, and salted nuts were eaten in small quantities.

Tool: The wood was used to make a variety of tools and implements.

Urtica dioica L. (Urticaceae) · **Stinging nettle**

Native name: *ka mi-to' mi-to* ("by water very stinging").

Taxonomic notes: At times, Hudson used *Urtica californica* and *Urtica lyallii* (written *Urtica loyalii*) for the contemporary species *U. dioica* (USDA and NRCS 2012).

Clothing: Women's hairnets were made from the fiber.

Cordage: The stalks, collected after they died back in the fall, were crushed, cleaned, and twisted for string. Considered a fine light-colored fiber with an attractive silky luster, it ranked fifth in strength among the cordage fibers.

Hunting: Cordage made with one part leather root fiber and three parts nettle fiber was especially valued for use in big game snares because it had a sweet odor.

STD remedy: Mature roots were macerated and boiled to make a pleasantly tasting infusion that was freely taken for gonorrhea. According to Hudson, this use was introduced by the Spanish in the eighteenth century.

War: The cordage was used in the construction of rod armor used by bear doctors and infrequently for war.

Vaccinium ovatum Pursh (Ericaceae) · **California huckleberry**

Native name: *pi'-ni' ba-kai'*.

Taxonomic notes: At times, Hudson referenced only the common name "huckleberry." In other instances, he used *Vaccinium oviflorum* and *Vaccinium ovifolia*, names that closely resemble the contemporary species *Vaccinium ovatum*, which is abundant in the region (Jepson Flora Project 2012b). Although Hudson's names *Vaccinium oviflorum* and *Vaccinium ovifolia* also resemble *Vaccinium ovalifolium*, this species does not occur in the study area (USDA and NRCS 2012).

Fruit food: The fresh or sundried berries were eaten in "enormous" quantities. Hudson reported that weapons were carried during the harvest because bears were equally fond of huckleberries.

Vaccinium parvifolium Sm. (Ericaceae) · Red huckleberry
Native name: *ci cam' ti*.

Fruit food: Hudson did not explicitly say the berries were eaten. However, he did include it in a list of plants belonging to the native category "berries" (*ba-kai'*).

**Verbascum blattaria* L. (Scrophulariaceae) · Moth mullein
Native name: *hai tca-ha' ka-li'*.

Fishing: Hudson recorded in a single passage that moth mullein was used as a fish poison. However, this statement is of questionable reliability because it is not corroborated elsewhere in his data or in the ethnobotanical literature. This entry may have resulted from confusion with turkey mullein.

Vicia americana Willd. (Fabaceae) · American vetch
Native names: *ca wa' kă ma-lu* and *ma-lu' tsŏ*.

Taxonomic notes: At times, consistent with a 1928 determination by Alice Eastwood, Hudson used only the genus name *Vicia*, which may also have referred to other local members of this genus.

Cooked green: The plant was harvested when in flower and baked in underground ovens. It was typically eaten with salt and bread foods.

Vitis californica Benth. (Vitaceae) · California wild grape
Native names: *bam-tu' ka-lĭ'* and *ci-yĭn' ka-lĭ'*.

Taxonomic notes: At times, Hudson used only the common name "wild grape."

Basketry: The stems were used for warp elements in coarse utilitarian baskets. It provided dense, woody splints of moderate pliability. Root fibers were infrequently used as weft in coarse basketry.

Colorant: Decorative patterns were made on the surfaces of arrows, flutes, and game staves by wrapping them with wild grape bark and scorching with fire to blacken the uncovered surfaces.

Cooking: Minnows were cooked for about an hour between layers of the green leaves in steaming beds. These were constructed by placing the leaves between two layers of hot cobbles.

Cordage: Split sections of the green vine or smaller runners were used for bindings, lashings, or ties. These were heated by slowly passing them through fire to facilitate splitting. The resulting fiber, considered pliable and strong, was used to lash the structural poles of permanent dome-shaped residences, to bind stone axe heads to handles, as well as for cables, stays, swings, and bridges. The roots were also used as rope.

Fruit food: The fresh fruits were collected in large quantities and enthusiastically eaten. Hudson reported that the Potter Valley Pome failed to recognize that obstruction of the colon by the seeds was a major cause of child mortality. Considered a delicacy, the fresh fruit juice was pressed into vessels and consumed by dipping and licking one's index finger.

Legend: In the legend "Poma Genesis," documented by Hudson, Coyote (**Du-wi'**) added wild grape exudate to the clay mixture employed in his third unsuccessful attempt to create the first people.

Packing or carrying: Rudimentary firewood packs were made with the vines.

Smoking: Dry grape vine material was used to make cigarettes.

Watercraft: Flexible lengths of stem were used to bind tule balsas.

Woodwardia fimbriata Sm. (Blechnaceae) · Chain fern
Native name: *le-bi'*.

Matting or bedding: The foliage was used for tablecloths and mattresses.

Packing or carrying: The fronds were used to close the mesh of a particular style of conical basket used to carry salt from inland mines in enemy territory. Used in this manner, they provided additional protection against arrows.

Wyethia angustifolia (DC.) Nutt. (Asteraceae) · California compassplant
Native name: *ca-lam'*.

Taxonomic notes: Hudson's use of this scientific name was consistent with a 1928 determination by Alice Eastwood. In one instance, Hudson referenced only the genus name *Wyethia*, which could have also referred to other local members of the genus.

Flavoring: Small quantities of the seeds were toasted, ground and used to flavor mush and bread made from poorer grades of acorns. The crushed dried flowers may also have been used for flavoring.

Salad food: The fresh peeled stems were eaten.

Wyethia glabra A. Gray (Asteraceae) · Coast Range mulesears
Native name: *ca pa' la*.

Taxonomic notes: Hudson used *Wyethia glabra* following a 1928 determination by Alice Eastwood.

Emetic: An infusion of the root was used as an emetic.

First aid: An infusion of the root was used to treat sores.

Yabea microcarpa **(Hook. & Arn.) Koso-Pol. (Apiaceae) · California hedge parsley**
Native name: **dima kai yĕm'**.
Taxonomic notes: Based on a 1928 determination by Alice Eastwood, Hudson used *Caucalis microcarpa* for the contemporary species *Yabea microcarpa* (Jepson Flora Project 2012b).
Salad food: The crushed fresh leaves were eaten with salt.

Unidentified Taxa

Ba' ma-tci
Taxonomic notes: Hudson identified this taxon as a fungus but provided no information regarding its uses.

Bi ti
Taxonomic notes: Hudson described this plant as bulbous. Linguistic evidence suggests the possibility that this plant may have been a camas (*Camassia* spp.).
Adhesive: The root was used to prepare glue for adhering sinew to bows.

Binan'
Taxonomic notes: Hudson provided no descriptive information.
Seed food: The seeds were used to make a high quality pinole.

Bu ta' tce e'
Taxonomic notes: Hudson identified this fungus as "poison maranta" but did not specify any uses.

C na hai
Taxonomic notes: Hudson described this taxon as a bush growing in wet canyons.
Arrow: The "tough sticks" were used for arrows.

Can ka-li
Taxonomic notes: Hudson described this plant as a slim "arboreal" bush.
Arrow: The wood was popularly used for arrows.
Bow: The wood was used for bows.

Ci yo batsom

Taxonomic notes: Hudson identified this as a plant with a bulb.

Cleaning agent: The bulb was used as a disinfectant for baskets.

Insecticide: Baskets were washed with a solution prepared from this plant mixed with soap-root to kill weevils.

Poison: The bulb was considered poisonous.

Ka ka' wi no

Taxonomic notes: Hudson provided no information regarding the identity of this taxon.

Emetic: A root decoction was used as a fast-acting emetic.

Ka ki lec ("watery mucus")

Taxonomic notes: Hudson identified this as member of the algae order *Confervae* and reported that it was found in stagnant water. He did not identify any uses.

Ka si-bu

Taxonomic notes: Hudson identified this as member of the algae order *Confervae* found in stagnant water. He did not identify any uses.

Ka tsu ka-li

Taxonomic notes: Hudson described this as a plant that grows at the edge of water and reaches some 3.5 m in height.

Arrow: The shoots were used for arrows.

Lum ka-li

Taxonomic notes: Hudson identified this plant as "belladonna." Although the European Belladonna (*Atropa belladonna*) is not found in the study area, this name suggests it is a member of the family Solanaceae. Linguistic evidence suggests the possibility that this plant may be jimsonweed.

Antispasmodic: The plant was used to treat spasms.

Ma ta-bo' ka-li ("dry ground plant") and tsi-ma

Taxonomic notes: Hudson identified this plant as "shoestring weed," a name that is not associated in the literature with any of the taxa found in the study area. He described it as nettle-like in appearance and specified that it grew in rich, damp soils.

Cordage: The plant was used to produce a strong but rough fiber used for cordage and ropes. The stalks were collected after they died back and were beaten to separate the fibers, which were washed and twisted. It was considered an abundant emergency material that was easily worked.

Pi-du' bac
Taxonomic notes: Hudson described this taxon as a "mildew" found on old acorns.

Host plant: This mildew was used to produce a bluish paint used to make decorative markings on arrows.

Stan'-tci
Taxonomic notes: Hudson identified this as a fungus found on rotten logs. He provided no information regarding its uses.

Ta tce e'
Taxonomic notes: Hudson described this as a common mushroom, but did not describe its identifying characteristics.

Fungus food: The fungus was fried with tallow on hot frying stones or directly on coals.

Tca la' tce e'
Taxonomic notes: Hudson described this as a pure white mushroom.

Fungus food: It was fried with tallow on hot frying stones or directly on coals and eaten.

To tol tce e' ("stars falling from heaven")
Taxonomic notes: Hudson described this as a puffball mushroom, but did not provide additional information regarding its identity or uses.

Tsi tal' tce e'
Taxonomic notes: Hudson described this as a large mushroom.

Fungus food: It was considered edible.

Tsip
Taxonomic notes: Hudson described this as a white flowered plant.

Disinfectant: The plant was used as a disinfectant.

First aid: It was used to treat blisters.

Insecticide: Weevils were killed by washing baskets in a solution made from this plant and soaproot.

Poison: The root was considered poisonous.

Tso lom to
Taxonomic notes: Hudson provided no identifying information for this plant.

Febrifuge: The root was simmered in water and the resulting extract taken for fever.

Laxative: The root extract was also taken for constipation.

Unidentified shrub

<u>Taxonomic notes</u>: Hudson described this plant as a small deciduous shrub with straight, leaf-less shoots or twigs that never exceeded 6 mm in diameter (Hudson 1893).

<u>Basketry</u>: Bark from the shoots or twigs was the rarest and most desirable of the red-colored wefts used for patterned baskets.

6. Plant Technologies, Preparations, and Applications

Potter Valley Pomo ethnobotany, as reconstructed in the previous chapter, involved a prodigious repertoire of cultural plant knowledge. Members of the community utilized diverse local vascular plants, mushrooms, and algae, often modifying them through the act of collection or by preparing them in combinations or according to complex procedures. Sometimes they followed particular formulations or protocols to produce a single product from multiple plant or other natural and human resources. They also commonly used multiple plants, each differing in its effectiveness or desirability, for similar functions. In many cases, they prepared and employed plants in specific social contexts, some of which speak to the cultural and historical settings John Hudson and other observers documented over a century ago.

In this chapter, I describe a selection of the Potter Valley Pomo plant technologies, preparations, and applications mentioned more briefly in previous chapters. Organized topically, this chapter serves as a companion reference to the ethnobotanical information presented for each of the Potter Valley Pomo plants (Chapter 5). I discuss these ethnobotanical practices and contexts in as much ethnographical detail as historical sources permit. Through his personal relationships with members of the Northern Pomo community from Potter Valley, Hudson accessed certain aspects of their plant knowledge in detail and recorded precious information absent in other ethnographic and ethnobotanical treatments of Pomoan peoples. These data serve as the basis for the information presented in this chapter, unless otherwise noted.

Despite the breadth of Hudson's ethnobotanical records, the characteristic meagerness of his ethnographic documentation also resulted in conspicuous gaps. In order to complement and interpret Hudson's unpublished unpublished data, I draw on other early accounts containing information specifically about the Northern Pomo from Potter Valley (Barrett 1908a; H. M. Carpenter 1893a, b, 1899; Chestnut 1902; Gifford and Kroeber 1937; Hudson 1893, 1897, 1900a, b; Powers 1877; Stewart 1943). However, because many early ethnographers did not distinguish the Potter Valley Pomo or Northern Pomo from other Pomoan communities or language groups or published meager ethnobotanical information about them, many ambiguities remain.

Basic Technologies and Tools

Adhesives
The Potter Valley Pomo used resins and other plant exudates, especially from conifers, as adhesives. Sources included pines (*Pinus* spp.), white fir (*Abies concolor*), soaproot (*Chlorogalum pomeridianum*), and perhaps camas (*Camassia* spp.). Conifer resins were often heated to facilitate their application as adhesives. These materials were used in conjunction with cordage to

secure fishing and fowling hooks, to attach stone points to drill shafts, to attach stone axe heads to handles, and to attach feather fletching to arrows, among other applications. Additionally, adhesives were used to adhere sinew to bows, to mold finger grips at the base of arrows, and to fill patterned depressions carved in the exterior surfaces of flutes (cf. Barrett 1952). Glue used to apply sinew backing to bows was also made from soaproot and salmon skin.

Axes

An axe-like tool used to chop firewood was made by lashing a rough splinter of quartz or greenstone to a short ash (*Fraxinus* sp.) handle some 5 cm in diameter. The binding was typically California wild grape fiber (*Vitis californica*). This tool did not have the strength to cut fresh wood, being instead used with a lacerating motion to reduce deteriorated old logs into smaller pieces.

Blowing Tubes

Potter Valley Pomo woodworking was frequently accomplished with finely fashioned blowing tubes used to direct a stream of air onto hot coals and thereby burn wood in a controlled manner (see cover image). Used for careful hollowing and shaping, these instruments were both indispensable tools and handsome crafts in their own right. Blowing tubes consisted of a section of blue elderberry stalk (*Sambucus nigra* ssp. *caerulea*) some 45 cm in length. After removing the pith, an artist scraped the stalk smooth and wrapped the ends with animal sinew secured with conifer resin. The working end, from which air was emitted, was fitted with a perforated plug about 8 cm in length, made of hardwoods such as dogwood (*Cornus* spp.) or ash. The entire surface was polished with crushed soaproot, California buckeye (*Aesculus californica*) charcoal, and willow leaves (*Salix* spp.), as described below.

Cordages and Bindings

At least 12 plant materials were used to manufacture cordage or binding fibers (Table 17). The preferred material was iris (*Iris* spp.), which was substantially replaced by dogbane (*Apocynum cannabinum*) in the early nineteenth century because it required substantially less effort to manufacture. A strong but coarse fiber used for rope was produced from leather root (*Hoita macrostachya*). Milkweed (*Asclepias* spp.), stinging nettle (*Urtica dioica*), and horsetail (*Equisetum hyemale*) were also valued because their fine fibers produced durable cordages. Rough bindings and lashings were produced from a series of less desirable fibers, including willow, American sloughgrass (*Beckmannia syzigachne*), California hazelnut (*Corylus cornuta*), and California wild grape.

Digging Sticks, Picks, and Prying Devices

Digging sticks and prying devices were employed to unearth underground resources and as general-use implements. Due to the strength of its wood, mountain mahogany (*Cercocar-*

Table 17. Cordage plants, in order of preference.

Scientific Name	Common Name	Rank
Iris spp.	Iris	1
Apocynum cannabinum	Dogbane	2
Hoita macrostachya	Leather root	3
Asclepias spp.	Milkweed	4
Urtica dioica	Stinging nettle	5
Equisetum hyemale	Horsetail	6
Salix gooddingii	Willow	7
Beckmannia syzigachne	American sloughgrass	—
Corylus cornuta	California hazelnut	—
Salix lasiolepis	Arroyo willow	—
Unidentified (***ma ta-bo' ka-li***)	—	—
Vitis californica	California wild grape	—

Obs.: Preference ranks follow J. W. Hudson's unpublished data.

pus spp.) was a favorite for digging sticks used to obtain underground plant materials, such as sedge (*Carex* spp.) and alkali bulrush (*Bolboschoenus maritimus*) rhizomes, and bulb and corm foods. Additionally, pointed ash sticks were used to dig worms.

Drills

In order to perforate a variety of hard materials, such as shell and stone, rod drills with stone points were rotated between the palms in a similar manner to that used to produce fire. Drills made from sections of pithy woods such as creeping snowberry (*Symphoricarpos mollis*) measured approximately 30 to 40 cm in length and 1.5 cm in diameter. To the wider end, which made contact with the material being drilled, was affixed a stone point of jasper or chert. The binding material was animal sinew with conifer resin. The points were conical in shape so they bored from both sides. According to Hudson, there was no evidence of bow or pump drills among the Potter Valley Pomo until 1876, after which time they became common (Figure 27). In that year, a man known as "Old Blind George" purchased such an apparatus for three dollars from a Spanish jeweler in Ukiah, Mendocino County, and introduced it to the native people of Potter Valley (Hudson 1900b).

Fire Production

Fire production was accomplished with hand drills, utilizing a straight polished wooden shaft or spindle and a baseboard with a depression in the upper surface. The wide end of the spindle was inserted into the depression in the baseboard and the spindle was rotated vigorously between one's palms. Friction between the shaft and hearth created an ember that was used to ignite flammable tinders. Spindles were made from such woods as blue elderberry, fir, chamise (*Adenostoma fasciculatum*), and California lilac (*Ceanothus* spp.). Hearths were often made from relatively softer woods, including California buckeye and fir. Although diverse plant fibers could be used as tinder, important materials for the Northern Pomo and

Figure 27. Man using pump drill, Yokayo Rancheria. Photograph by H. W. Henshaw. Number BANC PIC 1978.008 M/X/P1 no. 16--PIC, from the C. Hart Merriam collection of Native American photographs, ca. 1890–1938, Bancroft Library, University of California, Berkeley.

other indigenous peoples in Mendocino County were powdered alder wood (*Alnus* spp.) and oak leaves (*Quercus* spp.) (Chestnut 1902).

Polishes

A variety of wooden objects, such as bowls, flutes, smoking pipes, arrows, and blowing tubes, were polished to improve their durability and aesthetic qualities. The technique described in greatest detail by Hudson involved the preliminary step of coating the surface with crushed soaproot. While still wet, damp buckeye charcoal was applied to the surface and rubbed with fresh willow leaves. Alternatively, horsetail was used alone as a fine-grained sandpaper, a technique that was also used to polish clamshell disks.

Straighteners

Rod implements, such as arrows and drills, were straightened, strengthened, and polished by alternately heating them and drawing them through a straightening tool made from thick sections of hardwood that were perforated and split. Preferred woods for these straighteners were manzanita (*Arctostaphylos* spp.), oak, and mountain mahogany.

Architecture and Furnishings

Thatched Houses

The permanent residences of the Potter Valley Pomo were dome-shaped semi-subterranean structures. Each thatched dwelling housed from one to five couples and their children. Flexible poles, frequently willow, were bent to form a frame over a circular pit measuring up to 4.5 m in diameter and about 30 cm in depth. According to Helen Carpenter (n.d.), these poles were not harvested with axes or cutting tools, but rather by building a fire at the base of the plant. The vertical poles were lashed with California wild grape fiber to a 25 cm hoop at the approximately 3 m high apex of the structure, thus forming a smoke hole. Thatching, which covered the entire exterior, was made from such insulating and water resistant fibers as brome (*Bromus* spp.), wild oats (*Avena* spp.), willow, or tule (*Schoenoplectus acutus* var. *occidentalis.*). Horizontal beams, often willow, were lashed at intervals of 60 to 90 cm. Small door openings, positioned on the south side of the structures, were covered with thatched mats, which could be repositioned to allow sufficient light to enter (H. M. Carpenter n.d.). Additionally, one or two small openings in the walls served as windows. Inside each house were several bed platforms. Permanent thatched residences were often accompanied by external shade roofs or awnings covered with cattail thatch (*Typha latifolia*) (cf. Barrett 1916; Peri et al. 1982).

In addition to permanent family dwellings, the Potter Valley Pomo employed a variety of structures for temporary residence or special purposes. Hudson described a thatched subterranean chamber that served as housing for the elderly or a "hibernary" for the elder women of a family. This structure was long and narrow, about 2 by 3.5 m, with a short stairway at one end covered with brush or tule. Hudson's illustrations of this structure may be found in Holmes (1902). One form of temporary shelter consisted of an alder framework covered with willow, Timothy canarygrass (*Phalaris angusta*), or other brush (cf. Loeb). Another temporary structure, employed during brief seasonal visits to the coast in the nineteenth century, was made from large slabs of coast redwood bark (*Sequoia sempervirens*) discarded by loggers. This structure (*hai-tca*) is described elsewhere as an early construction style of coastal Pomoan groups (Barrett 1916; Loeb 1926). Additionally, Hudson mentioned a form of wattle of unspecified architectural use, which consisted of bigleaf maple rods (*Acer macrophyllum*) interlaced with grasses and reeds.

Mats and Bedding

Essential furnishings in every home, plain-woven mats were used for bedding and floor coverings. Cattail stalks and leaves were a preferred material for household mats, but they were also made from brome and partially dried tule stalks collected after dying back in autumn. According to Barrett (1916), individual sleeping mattresses were constructed by digging small trenches in the floor and filling them with tule or grasses. Chestnut (1902) also mentioned the use of cattail down for bedding. Another form of matting, used for seating at ceremonial events and considered to be of great value, was a fine tule mat decorated with feathered acorn woodpecker scalps (*Melanerpes formicivorus*) sewn in four stripes.

Transportation

Watercraft

Tule balsas were the primary mode of water transportation employed by the Potter Valley Pomo, although they were only used when visiting areas with open fishing waters, such as Clear Lake. Lightweight and buoyant, balsas lasted for one or two years. Large quantities of mature tule stalks were easily collected in late autumn, when they were beginning to gray. Stalks were bound with California wild grape vines into five tapered rolls of variable lengths, often some 3 m long and 25 cm in diameter. These rolls were laid side by side with the outer ones elevated relative to the others so as to form a trough between them. The rolls were lashed together approximately 30 cm from one end and bent sharply upward to form a prow. The rolls were lashed throughout with a series of half hitches. Each major structural element of the balsa was named. The center roll, functioning as keel, was called **kom** ("fish gullet"). The pair of rolls on either side of the keel was called **ke'-ĕts** ("fish bladder"). The outer two rolls, functioning as gunwales, were called **da-ko'-ri** ("fenders"). The bow was called **yu-kal'** ("foaming"). A finished one-man balsa weighed less than its operator.

Balsas were propelled with spade-shaped paddles consisting of oak blades hafted to approximately 1.5 m ash poles. The operator sat in the middle of the balsa while paddling alternately on each side of the boat. Despite riding somewhat low in the water, tule balsas did not leak and operators did not get wet from waves. Hudson reported that the "floating poise" was "graceful, resembling a huge duck at its ease."

In addition to tule balsas, the Potter Valley Pomo used dugout canoes in the nineteenth century. Hudson reported that tule balsas were the only form of watercraft used by the Potter Valley Pomo prior to about 1850, when a punitive government expedition in the region constructed several dugout canoes from coast redwood, which were later obtained and copied by Pomoan peoples.

Carrying Devices

The Potter Valley Pomo carried loads with a variety of devices, some of which are described below, under basketry. Additionally, women routinely carried heavy loads with pack nets, consisting of dogbane netting with a 1 m square open mesh and a tumpline measuring about 6 cm in width and 1.5 m in length. The open netting was woven with fisherman's knots. A loaded pack net lay against one's back, suspended from the forehead by the tumpline, which was often decorated with clamshell disks.

Tumplines were frequently widest towards the center portion that crossed one's forehead. According to Helen Carpenter (n.d.), women and men used tumplines to carry all forms of heavy loads. As she described, carrying a large load for a considerable distance gave the bearer bloodshot eyes and a headache, and long-term use caused some older women to have disfigured heads with marked skull depressions.

In addition to burden baskets and mesh pack nets, utilitarian carrying baskets for firewood were constructed from a pair of wooden forks and suspended with a tumpline. Previously made from California wild grape, in the nineteenth century they were more frequently made from ash or oak.

Grooming

Clothing

Plant fibers were used to weave diverse items of clothing, including skirts, leggings, rain cloaks and hoods, hairnets, belts, baby wrappings, and diapers. Women's skirts, worn on special occasions, were fabricated from willow or tule fiber (cf. Chestnut 1902). Rain garments, including cloaks, skirts, aprons, and hoods, were woven from fibers from cattail, coast redwood, tule, and willow. Hairnets were made from dogbane and stinging nettle. Women tied their hair up under these hairnets, securing it with wooden pins. Infants were wrapped in cloth or gowns made from soft, insulating, and absorbent plant fibers. Preferred for this purpose were bull tule and dogbane. Other common materials were other species of tule, rush (*Juncus* spp.), cattail, cow parsnip (*Heracleum maximum*), and milkweed. Baby gowns, which were used for about two months before being discarded, were worn in conjunction with diapers and swaddling mats. Diapers were prepared from beaten, cleaned, and dried lichens or tule pith. Diapered infants were wrapped in soft cloth and covered completely with woven rush mats.

Hair

Men paid a great deal of attention to their head hair because it was considered a symbolic feature of manhood. The cultural importance of hair among the Potter Valley Pomo was evident to Hudson in the contrastive customs of expressing friendly affection through attention to one another's hair and mourning death by defiling one's own hair with resin and ash. According to Helen Carpenter (n.d.), ashes of the cremated deceased and conifer resin were mixed into a thick paste, little beads of which were adhered to small locks of bang hair (about 10 hairs to each lock). The result was a band of ashen beads about 4 cm tall that reached from ear to ear across the forehead.

Shampoo was made from crushed mature soaproot bulbs. Hair brushes were made from soaproot bulb fibers, as well as horsetail, common rush (*Juncus effusus*), Kellogg's yampah

It was the custom of the Po-ma tribes of Mendocino, Lake and Sonoma Counties to cremate their dead.

During the ceremony all belongings of the deceased were cast upon the pyre, also objects owned by friends which the deceased may have touched, in the endeavor to remove all trace of his earthly presence.

His name also dies and is discarded thereafter from the Pomoan language.

The spirit of the dead hovers for four days, to be assured of the sincere grief and observance of *da-bo-lin* on earth and his complete accoutrement for the long journey ahead.

On the fourth day of the ceremony four chosen men rake away the ashes and collect whatever bone, stone, shell and any object that has not been consumed, which they bury together and the earth is tramped down hard by the bare feet of any one present, amid crescendo of wailing.

When the cry ceases all engage in the interchange of presents brought for this function.

For six months thereafter the adult relatives of the deceased singe their hair close and smear pine pitch upon it as the symbol of grief.

Each day at sunset the grave is visited and prayers sung for "the one beyond".

The bereaved at home group together for wailing, which in former days could be heard for miles. As when one wailed they all wailed. This sunset wailing was a daily function.

– John W. Hudson

(*Perideridia kelloggii*), and angelica (*Angelica* spp.). In addition to shampooing and brushing, men frequently oiled and deloused their hair with redmaids (*Calandrinia ciliata*) or green oak gall. Juice from green oak galls was mixed with water and applied to invigorate the hair. Additionally, hair growth was promoted by rubbing a solution produced from oak gall charcoal into the scalp. Men also used this charcoal solution as a hair and beard dye. According to Chestnut (1902), a similar black dye was made by mixing the light-green juice from fresh galls with rusty iron nails.

Body Decorations

The Potter Valley Pomo adorned themselves with body paint, piercings, and other decorative items. Ceremonial decorations are presented below. Blue body paint was produced by crushing iris flowers in hot water. Jewelry was inserted in earlobes and nose septum piercings. Boys and girls had their earlobes perforated at puberty (cf. Barrett 1952). The process involved first cleansing the lobes and a pair of perforated wooden disks with a solution of angelica root. Each lobe was then held firmly between two perforated disks and pierced with a splint of wood. After healing, the perforations were enlarged by inserting stem segments of maidenhair fern (*Adiantum jordanii*), gradually increasing the number until reaching the desired size.

Men's ear plugs were made from approximately 8 cm stem sections of California sagebrush (*Artemisia californica*), elderberry, or snowberry. These were polished and the pith removed. Men of social distinction often decorated their ear plugs with shell pendants, which hung from strings that passed through the tube. Women's ear plugs, often their most valued possessions, were made from bleached blue heron ulnae bones (*Ardea herodias*) etched with banded designs. The larger ends of women's ear plugs were ornamented with basketry disks interwoven with red woodpecker scalp feathers and quail crest feathers (*Lophortyx californicus*). Woodpecker feathers were highly desired because they did not fade from exposure to sunlight. Green mallard duck scalp feathers (*Anas platyrhynchos*) were sometimes used as an alternative to woodpecker feathers.

> It was considered a badge of dignity and honorable services and its use restricted to grandfathers: to the eldest of a clan, to officials and to those that had wounded the enemy in battle. Its presence by widening the aliae of the nose and concealing the mouth corners by its polished pendants lent character and importance to a face.
>
> – John W. Hudson

Native doctors pierced men's nose septa with manzanita awls. The holes were then enlarged in the same manner as described above for ear piercings. In public, mature men wore in their septa approximately 8 cm rods made from abalone shell helixes (*Haliotis* spp.). At home, they usually wore approximately 5 cm sections of wormwood or sagebrush stem.

Fishing

Poisons

Poisons were used to stupefy fish and thereby facilitate their capture. The most common fish poisons were fresh crushed soaproot bulbs and turkey mullein leaves (*Croton setiger*). Hudson also mentioned the use moth mullein (*Verbascum blattaria*) for the same purpose, although he may have confused moth mullein with turkey mullein. Leaves and roots from Durango root (*Datisca glomerata*) were used alone in small pools or added to large pools in conjunction with soaproot and turkey mullein. Helen Carpenter (n.d.) described the use of soaproot bulbs to catch fish in the aftermath of a 1950 United States military massacre in Potter Valley (Chapter 3). With their food resources depleted, a group of Potter Valley Pomo dug soaproot bulbs very early in the season, when they were still very small. After removing the brown husks, each smooth bulb was held individually in the middle of a large pool of water and vigorously rubbed until foaming. This chore continued until the pool became a milky color and the fish began to rise to the surface, belly-up. The fish were then skimmed off the water with baskets.

Traps and weirs

Several forms of woven traps were used for fishing. One type was employed in conjunction with fish weirs to catch trout and salmon in low summertime waters. The weirs were assembled by driving willow pegs or rods vertically into a stream bed at the head of a pool. These were arranged in a V-shape to direct fish towards a single point downriver. Spaces between the pegs were closed by twining with willow shoots, leaving a 20 cm opening just below the surface of the water at the lowermost point. A narrow funnel-shaped trap was fastened to the downriver side of this gap. Made with a 2 to 3 cm mesh of willow rods, such traps were about 1 m long and 10 cm in diameter at the middle, with a flared mouth and a tapered end. As smaller fish swam downriver in search of an outlet in the weir, they entered the wide end of the trap. In conjunction with fish weirs, fishermen often perched on overhanging limbs to dispatch larger fish with spears.

Rigid open-twined conical fish traps were woven from the flexible shoots of such tough woody plants as dogwood, California hazelnut, and fragrant sumac (*Rhus aromatica*), as well as second-year shoots from California black oak (*Quercus kelloggii*), Nuttall's scrub oak (*Quercus dumosa*), and Oregon oak (*Quercus garryana*). The stems were prepared by stripping off any leaves and small branches. The straight shoots were bound at one end and gradually opened towards a rim, consisting of braided or coiled twigs, at the other end. This framework was reinforced at intervals with two rings of intertwined shoots, which were previously made pliable by heating in the fire until they steamed.

Dogbane pouch nets, shaped like grain sacks, were also used to trap fish, including suckers (family Catostomidae). The open end was spread with an arched willow rod and secured underwater with a vertical stake driven into the bottom of a pool.

Spears

Double pointed toggle spears were used to obtain salmon and steelhead (*Oncorhynchus* spp.). The shafts were made from Douglas fir saplings (*Pseudotsuga menziesii*) about 3.5 to 4.5 m in length and 4 cm in diameter. Lashed to one end of the shaft was a pair of approximately 30 cm tapered hardwood points, sometimes made from mountain mahogany, spread about 8 cm at their terminal ends (Figure 28). Each fork was mounted with a pair of 5 cm barbed deer horn points. The base of each point was fashioned with a socket to fit the hardwood prong and an eyehole, to which was affixed a dogbane cord. The struggling motion of a speared fish disengaged the barbed points from the prongs and the dogbane cord could then be used to retrieve the fish from the water (cf. Barrett 1952; Bennyhoff 1950; Mason 1902). Spear fishing was often conducted from platforms extending over waterways. For salmon, this was often done over deep pools at nighttime with the aid of firelight. Hudson speculated that these double pointed spears were derived relatively recently from an earlier single pointed design.

Hooks and Line

Gorge fish hooks were most commonly made of deer bone, but also of manzanita and oak wood. Splints of bone or wood, pointed at both ends and notched at the center, were tied to string and secured with a small amount of resin. Grasshoppers (order Orthoptera) were attached to each hook as bait. The weight of a grasshopper on the line permitted a long cast and held

Figure 28. Barbed fish spear points. Photograph by James R. Welch, 2011. Accession no. 1527, in the collections of Grace Hudson Museum, Ukiah.

the hook under the surface of the water at an appropriate depth. Fish swallowed these baited hooks lengthwise and a pull of the cord fixed them in horizontal position.

Fowling, Trapping, and Hunting

Fowling

Cranes (perhaps *Grus Canadensis* or *Ardea herodias*), turkey vultures (*Cathartes aura*), and California condors (*Gymnogyps californianus*) were caught with hooks. Fowling hooks were similar in style but slightly larger than those used for fishing. Fowling line, also slightly thicker than that used for fishing, was twisted loosely to avoid being cut by the bird's beak. Small fish were typically used as bait for cranes. For larger non-aquatic birds, a fowler often tied a baited hook to a tree limb in a strategic location. According to Barrett (1952), Pomoan groups caught vultures and condors for their feathers rather than for food.

Trapping

During the summer, deer were driven with fire into complex ridgetop traps consisting of a series of carefully positioned fences converging toward a series of snares downwind. The fires were set in chamise shrubs on the windward sides of these ridges. Deer snares consisted of a noose enclosed with netting. The noose was made with cordage consisting of two-thirds stinging nettle and one-third leather root fiber. Iris fiber was also employed. A small dogbane net was sewn to the noose loop along its edges. The whole apparatus was tied to a strong limb or shrub, such that when a deer's antlers struck the net, the noose was pulled over the animal's antlers or head. Trapped or snared deer were dispatched with approximately

2.5 m spears made from mountain mahogany. These were sharpened at both ends and fire-hardened. Also used for the same purpose was a wooden instrument approximately 1.2 m in length that was sharpened to a narrow stabbing point at one end and blunted at the other.

Hunting

Game animals were hunted with bows and arrows. Although hunting bows were made of a variety of woods, Pacific yew (*Taxus brevifolia*) was most highly valued (Chestnut 1902), California nutmeg (*Torreya californica*) was considered to make especially fine bows, and serviceberry (*Amelanchier alnifolia*) was valued for making strong bows. Also used were dogwood, California juniper (*Juniperus californica*), and an unidentified wood called **can ka-li** in Northern Pomo. Sinew backing was often applied to bows for improved strength and to prevent breaking (cf. Pope 1923). The sinew was affixed with glue produced by boiling soaproot with salmon skin and an unidentified plant called **bi ti**. Bow surfaces were rubbed with baked soaproot bulbs and soot or charcoal to give them an aged and blackened look. The Potter Valley Pomo produced three types of hunting arrows: war and big game arrows, small game arrows, and bird arrows. Each type was constructed in a different manner and with distinct plant materials (Table 18).

War and big game arrows had shafts made from light but rigid woods, such as mountain mahogany, American dogwood (*Cornus sericea*), cluster rose (*Rosa pisocarpa*), and marsh baccharis (*Baccharis douglasii*). Shoots from these plants were collected in autumn. They were first cleaned, straightened, and bound in bundles, before being stored to season the wood. A final polish was produced by rubbing with horsetail stalks or crushed green willow leaves. Colored markings in three colors were applied to the shafts to identify the owner and his community. A bluish paint was produced from old acorn mildew and an unidentified fungus (**pi-du' bac**). A red paint was produced from an unspecified local mineral. Black paint

Table 18. Arrow shafts plants, in order of preference.

Scientific Name	Common Name	Rank
Cercocarpus spp.	Mountain mahogany	1
Cornus spp.	Dogwood	2
Calycanthus occidentalis	Spicebush	3
Rosa californica	California wildrose	4
Baccharis douglasii	Marsh baccharis	5
Acer macrophyllum	Bigleaf maple	—
Artemisia californica	Wormwood or sagebrush	—
Baccharis salicifolia	Mule fat	—
Salix exigua	Sandbar willow	—
Salix sitchensis	Sitka willow	—
Salix spp.	Willow	—
Taxus brevifolia	Pacific yew	—
Unidentified (**c na hai**)	None	—
Unidentified (**can ka-li**)	None	—
Unidentified (**ka tsu ka-li**)	None	—

Obs.: Preference ranks follow J. W. Hudson's unpublished data.

was derived from charcoal. These markings were covered with Douglas fir resin varnish. Fine arrows had grooved finger grips at the base made from heated conifer resin. These were molded spirally with a loop of animal sinew cordage, which was pulled across the resin while twisting the shaft. Fletching was prepared from three lengthwise halves of falcon or hawk tail feathers, preferably Cooper's hawk (*Accipiter cooperii*). The feathers were secured to the shaft with animal sinew and Douglas fir resin. Approximately 8 cm foreshafts were fitted to the tip of war and big game arrow shafts. These was preferentially made from redberry (*Rhamnus* spp.) or mountain mahogany, but could also be made from serviceberry.

Small game arrows were less complex and were fashioned with somewhat less care than big game arrows. Their shafts were made from unspecified light and pithy woods and lacked the painted decorations and polish characteristic of big game arrows. Foreshafts were typically made of approximately 10 cm splints of bone or, alternatively, serviceberry or other unspecified hardwoods.

Bird arrows were lighter and more delicate than small game arrows. They had hardwood points made from oak, ash, and California lilac. Mounted on the shaft some 8 cm from the tip and at right angles to each other were pairs of hardwood splints that served to prevent the arrows from fully entering and thereby mutilating game birds.

Hunting techniques included the use of hunting calls, disguises, and fragrances. A favorite method for attracting deer of both sexes was to imitate the sound of a bleating fawn by holding a soft bindweed (*Calystegia* sp.) or ash leaf against the tongue and sucking. Deer were also hunted with masks that disguised hunters as their prey (cf. Barrett 1952). Stalking with a deer mask involved crawling slowly while exactly imitating a deer's movements. These masks were made of deer pelts with antlers made from California buckeye and ears made from buzzard feathers (presumably *Cathartes aura*). Attaching deer hair to the wooden antlers created the appearance of horn velvet. Lace lichen (*Ramalina menziesii*) inserted in the mouth imitated feed. Eyes were made from pieces of obsidian stone. Aromatic angelica root was chewed and applied to fetid fleshy parts of the mask. A piece of angelica root was also frequently placed inside the mask to help disguise odors. California bay leaves (*Umbellularia californica*) were heated over flames and rubbed on the mask for the same purpose.

Hunters also disguised their own odor with several aromatic plants. They applied infused or masticated vinegarweed (*Trichostema lanceolatum*) to their bodies and weapons. Hunters also fumigated themselves by standing over smoldering Douglas fir or California bay leaves and used

> The hunter crawls slowly in the presence of the game exactly imitating the deer's movements, as shaking of its head etc. One Indian hunter was once so absorbed and perfect in his show that a buck sprang him and gored him almost to death before his shouts brought help.
>
> – John W. Hudson

deodorants made from wormwood (*Artemisia californica*) and tuberous sanicle (*Sanicula tuberosa*). Another hunting preparation included chewing angelica root and pine seeds and casting the resultant quid into a fire. This produced a smoke that was believed to charm deer, making it easier to kill them.

Food Collection, Preparation, and Preservation

Beverages

A refreshing beverage was made from ripe manzanita fruits. Collected in July and August (Chestnut 1902), they were first parched, deseeded, and crumbled with a mortar and pestle. The resulting meal was often sweetened by mixing it at a ratio of 10 to one with baked and macerated fresh autumn willowweed leaves and stems (*Epilobium brachycarpum*). After seeping in water, the mixture was passed through a fine mesh strainer. The final product, clear amber in color, was consumed sparingly by dipping with one's fingers.

Salt

The Potter Valley Pomo obtained salt (*ce-e'*) from inland mines and from depressions in boulders close to the ocean shore that held the residue of evaporated spray. Inland mineral salt was mined from a deposit at the headwaters of Stony Creek (cf. Barrett 1952; McCarthy 1986; Stewart 1943), which involved a perilous journey into enemy territory. Hudson described this mineral salt as darkened by stains and vegetal impurities. After being ground in a stone mortar, cleaned, and sifted, it became light gray in color. This was, according to Hudson, pungent and inferior in flavor to sea salt cakes.

Evaporated sea salt collected from depressions in coastal bedrock was ground to a fine powder and combined in a proportion of 10 to one with powdered charcoal from a close grained wood, preferably California sagebrush or manzanita. Hudson reasoned that the charcoal prevented melting and recrystallization due to humidity. With increased trade activity during the nineteenth century, the salt mixture was made into durable cakes of uniform size, about 50 grams, which had a standard trade value. They were formed from slightly moist salt powder, which was kneaded and compressed between the palms and then dried in the sun for several days. Alternatively, they were baked in underground ovens or buried in hot ashes and coals. The finished product was black in color and disk-shaped, with thin edges, about 9 cm in diameter and 2.5 cm thick at the center. Salt cakes were nibbled or licked while eating game meat or salad foods. Only rarely were they crushed and sprinkled on food. According to Hudson, sea salt cakes contained small amounts of iodine and bromine, which gave them a unique flavor that was much preferred to commercially available salt. The Potter Valley Pomo also valued it for promoting the digestion of fatty foods.

Confections

A sweet "sugar," obtained by condensing sugar pine sap (*Pinus lambertiana*), was considered a rare delicacy. A similar confection was extracted from fresh conifer leaves (probably Douglas fir). Ripe California juniper fruits were toasted or baked and then ground to create a confection that was considered healthy. In the fall, sweet honey dew, an exudate produced by aphid infestation, was scraped or licked directly from the underside of madrone (*Arbutus menziesii*) leaves. Sweet nectar was sucked from the flowers of Indian warrior (*Pedicularis densiflora*). Morel mushrooms (*Morchella crassipes*) were also considered a sweet confection.

Pinole

The Potter Valley Pomo made pinole from parched and ground seeds from grasses and small flowering plants (Barrett 1952; Chestnut 1902). Many of the pinole seeds also belonged to the Northern Pomo plant category "seeds" (*ba ǎ*), as presented in Table 19. Women collected seeds from forbs and grasses with woven seed beaters and conical burden baskets. Seed beaters were shaped like large spoons, with approximately 25 cm diameter bowls and 25 cm long handles. They were used in meadows and fields to strike mature seeds from standing plants directly into burden baskets. The only example of open twine wickerwork among the Pomoan groups, seed beaters were fashioned from rush, willow, and oak. The seeds were parched by tossing them with hot coals in a basket, such that the ash and debris were carried away in the breeze (Figure 29). Pinole meal was eaten as a dry powder, often with a little salt (Chestnut 1902). It was also moistened and shaped into cakes or balls, but never baked (Barrett 1952).

Table 19. Plants associated with the native category "seeds" (*ba ǎ*).

Scientific Name	Common Name
Avena spp.	Wild oats
Balsamorhiza deltoidea	Deltoid balsamroot
Bromus carinatus	California brome
Clarkia amoena	Farewell to spring
Elymus elymoides	Squirreltail
Elymus triticoides	Beardless wildrye
Hemizonia congesta	Hayfield tarweed
Madia elegans	Common madia
Madia sativa	Coast tarweed
Ranunculus californicus	California buttercup
Rumex crispus	Curly dock
Rumex sp.	Dock

Figure 29. Woman parching seeds for pinole, Pinoleville Rancheria, 1901. Photograph by John W. Hudson. Negative no. CSA1777, The Field Museum, Chicago.

Baked Bulb or Corm Foods

Bulbs and corms of diverse liliaceous plants, known popularly as "Indian potatoes" in the late nineteenth century, were dug in summertime. In Northern Pomo, these foods were known as "bulbs and corms" (*bu*) or "baked bulbs and corms" (*ba tum bu*). They were cooked in underground ovens, as described below. The taxa associated in Hudson's data with the Northern Pomo category *bu* are presented in Table 20.

Table 20. Plants associated with the native category "bulbs and corms" (*bu*).

Scientific Name	Common Name
Brodiaea coronaria	Harvest clusterlily
Brodiaea terrestris	Dwarf clusterlily
Calochortus amabilis	Golden globelily
Calochortus luteus	Yellow mariposa
Calochortus pulchellus	Mount Diablo globelily
Calochortus superbus	Yellow mariposa
Calochortus venustus	Butterfly mariposa
Camassia leichtlinii	Common camas
Camassia quamash	Large camas
Dichelostemma capitatum	Bluedicks
Dichelostemma congestum	Ookow
Fritillaria affinis	Checker lily
Triteleia hyacinthina	White brodiaea
Triteleia laxa	Ithuriel's spear
Triteleia peduncularis	Long-rayed brodiaea

Underground Baking

Bulb foods, vegetable foods, and breads were baked in small underground pits. A fire was built in the pit to heat flat stones. Subsequently, half of the stones were removed and the fire was withdrawn. A layer of soil was then placed over the remaining half of the stones, followed by a layer of green leaves, frequently bigleaf maple, cow parsnip, soaproot, oak, or iris. The food to be cooked was placed on these leaves and then covered with additional layers of leaves. The remaining heated stones were placed on top and covered with a final layer of soil.

In a variation of the underground oven, small fish were often cooked between thick layers of green California grape leaves and hot steatite cobbles or other stones. The stones were headed in a fire. When they were sufficiently hot, they were removed and the embers were spread out. Grape leaves were spread over the embers, the fish were set on the leaves, more green leaves were spread over the fish, and the hot stones were placed on top. Cooking was completed in approximately one hour.

Breads and Mushes

The Potter Valley Pomo used ground acorns (family Fagaceae), California bay nuts, and buckeyes to prepare breads (*tcu-ni'*) and mushes (*to-o'*). Whereas acorns were available earlier in the fall, bay nuts and buckeyes were generally not gathered until November. Acorn mush was not only a daily staple, but also the only permitted food for girls during their four day reclusion at first menses and for boys during their four day ceremonial rites of passage ("man casting"). During the immediate post-partum period, mothers ate a restricted diet that included acorn mush. Table 21 presents a list of acorns in order of preference for use in mush. Buckeye mush was also consumed in considerable quantities during late fall and winter (H.M. Carpenter n.d.; Chestnut 1902). Although buckeyes produced a bland food (according to Hudson, "a colorless mess without grain, or savor"), they were abundant when few other plant foods were available and, according to some sources, could be stored for long periods (cf. Chestnut 1902; Loeb 1926). With its stronger flavor, bay nut bread was a welcome variation to the routine diet of acorn bread and made a desirable addition to salad foods, acorn mush, and acorn bread.

The oven, as it might be called, [...] and where the bread was now to be baked, was a scouped out place in the ground, a foot or more deep and two or more feet in diameter. A number of stones were in the bottom and on these a fire was kept burning until the stones and ground were well heated. The stones were then removed with hard wood sticks, and the earth covered with overlapping leaves, on these the bread was poured, more leaves covered the dough and on these the hot stones were laid, and the whole well covered with earth and allowed to remain for several hours.

– Helen M. Carpenter

Table 21. Acorn plants used for mush, in order of preference.

Scientific Name	Common Name	Rank
Notholithocarpus densiflorus	Tanoak	1
Quercus kelloggii	California black oak	2
Quercus douglasii	Blue oak	3
Quercus garryana	Oregon oak	4
Quercus lobata	Valley oak	5
Quercus agrifolia	Coast live oak	6
Quercus chrysolepis	Canyon live oak	7
Quercus dumosa	Nuttall's scrub oak	8
Chrysolepis chrysophylla	Giant chinquapin	9

Obs.: Preference ranks follow J. W. Hudson's unpublished data.

Acorns were harvested from the ground or detached from branches with hooked poles. They were then transported in burden baskets (Figure 30) to homes where they were hulled, dried and stored for later use (Figure 31). To crack their shells, acorns were held firmly one at a time on a pitted stone with the pointed end downward and struck with a hammer stone. Once broken, the shell was removed with one's fingers. Hudson commented that this final step caused many women to have perpetually worn and broken thumb nails. Worms

Figure 30. Closed plain-twined conical burden baskets, 1899. Photograph by A. O. Carpenter. Original in the collections of Grace Hudson Museum, Ukiah, California.

Figure 31. Hulling and drying acorns in the sun, Yokayo Rancheria, 1892. Photograph by H. W. Henshaw. Original in the collections of Grace Hudson Museum, Ukiah.

or larvae found inside were considered inedible and acorns containing them were discarded or processed in a special manner, described below. Prior to storage, acorn nut meats were dried, preferably in the sun, or smoked on racks over fire.

Acorns, bay nuts, and buckeyes were stored in elevated thatched granaries for later use. Granaries were often about 1 m in diameter, although various sizes were used (cf. Barrett 1916). They were woven with an open twine of dogwood or oak shoots and covered with a conical thatched lid. The largest type was used for acorns and buckeyes. Four or more granaries were positioned on a single platform, which measured approximately 2 by 3 m, supported by four 2.5 m poles. Ladders, about 2 m in height, provided access to granary platforms, which served as protection from rodents and were sometimes used for sleeping.

The day was fine and *Tsu-le sat* in the sun in front of the *sha* [house] to do some milling. On a flat stone that was for this express purpose, she placed a bottomless basket, which was some eight or nine inches in height and 15 inches in diameter. Into this she put a quantity of hulled acorns, and then with her legs resting across the top of the basket, proceeded to pound the acorns with a stone pestle until the whole was reduced to a meal, such was used in making the pinola. It would have been no easy task to read her thoughts as she patiently continued her work in this most uncomfortable position.

– Helen M. Carpenter

Acorns and buckeyes contain the poisonous compounds tannin and aesculin, respectively, which were removed through leaching or admixture with a special type of red earth (cf. Chestnut 1902; Gifford 1936). Before leaching, acorns were usually ground to a fine meal in a stone mortar (Figure 32). Grinding was facilitated with brushes made from soaproot husks, used to help control the accidental scattering of meal. In contrast, buckeyes were cooked prior to leaching. The large buckeye nuts were roasted for some three to 10 hours in underground ovens until they began to explode and force jets of steam to the surface. After hulling and discarding the bitter eyes, they were mashed in a wooden bowl until they resembled mashed potatoes (H. M. Carpenter n.d.).

The most common leaching method involved passing water through acorn or buckeye meal in a round sand depression at the margin of a stream (cf. Kroeber and Barrett 1962). To prevent sand from mixing with the meal, the basin was compressed or lined with a rush mat. A mound of acorn or buckeye meal was heaped in the center of the pit. The top of the mound was flattened or hollowed and filled with loose rush segments, which served to distribute the water evenly as it was poured onto the meal. Fresh water was poured through the rushes onto the mound until, in the case of acorns, the rusty colors of the tannins visibly disappeared from the leach waters and the astringent taste was eliminated. Excessive leaching was avoided

Figure 32. Woman pounding acorns. Original in the collections of Grace Hudson Museum, Ukiah.

because it caused the meal to lose its richness of flavor and nutritional content, which was attributed by the Potter Valley Pomo to the presence of sugars and fats. Prolonged leaching resulted in the visible escape of desirable acorn oils. When leaching was complete, the mass was left in the pit to dry until it had shrunk, cracked, and assumed a light bleached color. Dried in this manner, it could be stored for future use.

Another leaching method, used particularly for acorns contaminated by mold or other-wise considered inferior, involved placing whole hulled acorns in a loosely woven basket, which was submerged in a pool of water for a month or more (cf. Barrett 1952). This extended submersion was considered to satisfactorily eliminate both fungal contaminants and tannins. The nut meats swelled and cracked open in the process. The resultant mass was salted prior to cooking. Mush made in this manner was light tan in color, of a coarse consistency, and sweet to the taste (like hominy, according to Hudson). A similar leaching method involved submerging in running water a bag of ground acorn meal for about four days. This method resulted in reduced flavor due to loss of the acorn sugars and fats.

A final method used to remove tannins from acorns and, possibly, aesculin from buckeyes, involved adding a special type of red earth (*ma-po'*) before cooking (Figure 33). According to Hudson, the "friable reddish" earth was found in approximately 8 cm layers beneath the soil near the summits of ridges in the upper reaches of the Russian River. Infrequent in much of the Pomoan territories, red earth was found in large quantities in Potter Valley. Hudson described the "yawning supply pits" at the northern end of Potter Valley as especially productive, with many tons of cumulative production. He also speculated that red earth availability, whether through direct control of mines or through trade, was the single most important factor influencing the geographical distribution of the Northern Pomo population. Villages with control over productive and high quality red earth mines greatly benefited from them economically. As an indication of their cultural value, in Pomoan legend the first humans were created from red earth.

Chestnut (1902) provided a list of hypotheses to explain the Pomoan practice of adding red earth to breads and mushes, based on aesthetics, nutrition, food scarcity, spirituality, and medical health. However, Hudson's explanation that it was used to remove tannins, and possibly aesculin, is corroborated by recent research documenting the use of similar processes in the Mediterranean region (Johns and Duquette

A convenient place was found in the river bank for the basket to stand, where **Ka-weah-mah** could sit and look at the women who at once began scooping out pan shaped places in the sand, several feet back from waters edge. After these were made of the desired size, they were patted until smoothe as possible and then a layer of leaves was put in the bottom and around the sides. Into this the meal was poured and leveled down, and then began a water treatment to remove the unwholesome astringent qualities of the acorn. Water was carried in baskets and poured on the meal and as it drained off into the sand, more was added. [...] The meal is leached for two or three days and is then allowed to stand without any covering until thoroughly dry.

– Helen M. Carpenter

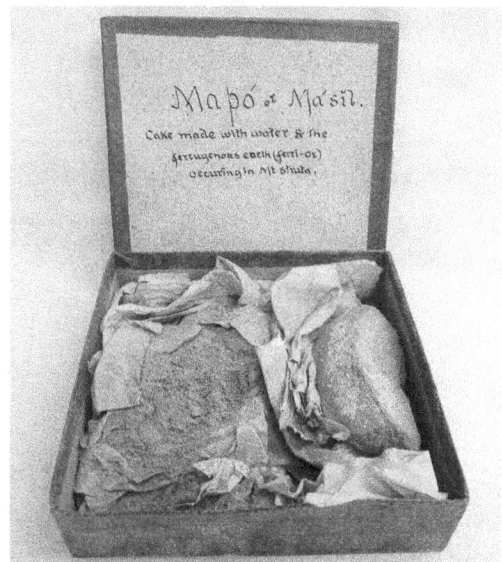

Figure 33. Red earth (*ma-po'*) collected by John W. Hudson in Potter Valley. Photograph by James R. Welch, 2011. In the collections of Grace Hudson Museum, Ukiah.

1991a, b). Varieties of acorns with lower tannin levels, such as tanoak (*Notholithocarpus densiflorus*), were preferably leached rather than treated with red earth. Red earth was used most frequently to prepare acorn meal bread, rather than mush, because it was considered more effective with the prolonged heat of underground baking. Small amounts of red earth were mixed with acorn or buckeye meal, at a ratio of about one to 20 (Hudson 1900a). Alternatively, an extract, prepared by passing water through red earth held in a basket filter, was added to the meal.

Batches of acorn meal were leached or mixed with red earth and cooked as needed, usually at least once each week. Acorn bread was baked in underground ovens, usually overnight. Acorn bread baked with red earth was very dark in color, dense, crumbly, and sweet to the taste (cf. Barrett 1952; Chestnut 1902). According to Hudson, it had a peculiar "alkaline" flavor that was greatly appreciated. It was often eaten with California bay nut bread to enhance its mild flavor.

Tsu-le [...] took a basket in which was some coarse meal made of acorns, and going to the river, dipped the basket into the water allowing some overflow and with the hand stirred the wet meal continuing the process until the whole was of the consistency of batter. Returning to the *sha*, the basket was placed near the now hot stone on the fire, and with a little twirling motion of the poker the stone fell into the batter and steamed and hissed for some little time before it was taken out and again placed on the fire. In the meantime the batter was stirred vigorously with the poker and then one of the other stones, fresh from the ashes was dropped into the mixture. This was repeated some three or four times before the pinola was "done to a turn."

– Helen M. Carpenter

For mush, acorn meal was usually cooked in a woven cooking basket with twice its volume of water. Cooking was accomplished by dropping heated stones into the batter and stirring constantly for some 10 to 20 minutes, while the mush simmered at about 65° to 80° C. The crusts that adhered to the cooking stones were considered a delicacy, often being reserved by the cook for a favored guest. Like many Pomoan foods, mush was preferred cool. According to Hudson, "cooled foods emphasize the flavor, encourage digestion and cannot injure teeth." It was served directly in the cooking basket or in smaller basketry bowls and eaten with one's index finger, which was dipped directly in the mush. In contrast, buckeye mush was eaten with a mussel shell (family Mytilidae). Mushes made from buckeye or less desirable types of acorns were often seasoned with salt or herbs.

California bay nuts were removed from storage as needed and roasted in hot embers to expel the volatile oils. They were then cracked, ground with a stone pestle, and salted for flavor and as a preservative. The result meal was oily and flavorful. Small cakes of bay nut meal were prepared by three methods. The first involved repeatedly heating the end of a hardwood stick or stone pestle and dipping it into the meal, which caused it to adhere to the instrument as it cooked. The cooked meal was scraped off and the process repeated. The accumulated meal was kneaded between the palms and formed into disk-shaped cakes. In the second method, the meal was spread thinly on a hot stone griddle, cut into squares, and left to cool. The third method involved spreading bay nut meal on a flat stone and repeatedly passing a flaming bundle of sticks over it until it cooked thoroughly. The finished product was a dark, crumbly loaf that Hudson reported resembled the flavor of peanuts. A single loaf was considered adequate ration for a day of travel. Difficult to chew, it was eaten cold with salt or could be softened by warming.

Flavorings

Bland foods, such as acorn mush and bread, were commonly supplemented with small quantities of parched seed flour from, for example, California compassplant (*Wyethia* spp.), farewell to spring (*Clarkia amoena*), and common madia (*Madia elegans*). Buckeye mush was often flavored with autumn willowweed and California bay leaves.

Basketry

The sophisticated art of Pomoan basketry involved a bewildering array of materials, weaves, and styles, many of which are well documented in the literature (e.g., Allen and Brown 1972; Barrett 1905, 1908b; Hudson 1893; Kroeber 1909; Kroeber 1922, 1925; Mason 1904; Merrill 1923; Ortiz 1993; Peri and Patterson 1976; Purdy 1902; Smith-Ferri 1998). Although some basketry plants have been documented elsewhere, Hudson's data permitted the identification of at least 42 fiber plants used by the Potter Valley Pomo in basketry (Table 22).

In addition, Hudson's data include information regarding diverse plants used in other aspects of basketry, such as dying and cleaning. The impressive diversity of basket forms woven by the Potter Valley Pomo included numerous utilitarian items, such as fish and bird traps, seed beaters, and baby cradles. Other basketry types employed in the daily routine included men's utility baskets, burden baskets, seed storage baskets, hopper-mortar baskets, winnowing and parching baskets, cooking baskets, and dry and wet storage baskets. Additionally, especially fine gift and ceremonial baskets were produced for special occasions.

Warp is the rigid foundation of a basket, often consisting of sturdy but flexible sticks. The most common Pomoan warp material was willow. Although Barrett (1908b) reported that only willows and California hazelnut were used for warp by the Northern Pomo, Hudson documented over 25 different Potter Valley Pomo warp plants (Table 23). Weft is a flexible fiber used as a cross-stitching. Hudson's data include over 31 different weft plants (Table 24).

Table 22. Basketry fiber plants with associated weaves and applications.

Scientific Name	Common Name	Wickerwork	Plain Twining	Diagonal Twining	Lattice Twining	Three-strand Twining	Three-strand Braiding	One-rod Coiling	Three-rod Coiling	Rims and lashings	Unspecified
Acer macrophyllum	Bigleaf maple		X	X	X			X	X		
Adiantum jordani	Maidenhair fern		?	?	?			X	X		
Alnus rhombifolia	White alder		X								
Apocynum cannabinum	Dogbane		?								
Avena spp.	Wild oats		?								
Beckmannia syzigachne	American sloughgrass										X
Carex spp.	Sedge		X	X	X	X	X	X	X		
Ceanothus foliosus	Wavyleaf ceanothus		X	X	X	X	X	X			
Ceanothus spp.	California lilac		X	X	X	X	X	X			
Cercis occidentalis	California redbud		X	X	X	X	X	X	X		
Cornus spp.	Dogwood		X	X	X	X	X	X			
Corylus cornuta	California hazelnut		X	X	X	X	X	X	X		
Equisetum hyemale	Horsetail		?	?	?			X	X		
Fraxinus sp.	Ash									X	
Juncus spp.	Rush	X	X								
Juniperus californica	California juniper										X
Picea sitchensis	Sitka spruce										X
Pinus contorta	Lodgepole pine										X
Pinus coulter	Coulter pine										X
Pinus lambertiana	Sugar pine										X
Pinus ponderosa	Ponderosa pine										X
Pinus sabiniana	California foothill pine										X
Prunus virginiana	Chokecherry										X
Pseudotsuga menziesii	Douglas fir									X	X
Pteridium aquilinum	Bracken fern		X	?	?	?	?	?	?		
Quercus dumosa	Nuttall's scrub oak		X								
Quercus garryana	Oregon oak		X								
Quercus kelloggii	California black oak		X								
Quercus spp.	Oak		X								X
Rhus aromatica	Fragrant sumac	X	X	X	X	X	X	X	X		
Salix exigua	Sandbar willow	X	X	X	X	X	X	X	?		
Salix gooddingii	Goodding's black willow	X	X	X	X	X	X	X	?		
Salix laevigata	Red willow	X	X	X	X	X	X	X	?		
Salix lasiolepis	Arroyo willow	X	X	X	X	X	X	X	?		
Salix sitchensis	Sitka willow	X	X	X	X	X	X	X	?		
Salix spp.	Willow	X	X	X	X	X	X	X	?	X	
Schoenoplectus acutus var. *occidentalis*	Tule		?	?	?	?	?	X	X		
Torreya californica	California nutmeg										X
Toxicodendron diversilobum	Poison oak							X	X		X
Typha latifolia	Common cattail		X								
Unidentified shrub	—		X	X	X	X	X	X	X		
Vitis californica	California wild grape									X	X

Obs.: Question marks (?) indicate ambiguity in Hudson's data.

Table 23. Basketry warp plants.

Scientific Name	Common Name	Comments
Acer macrophyllum	Bigleaf maple	One-rod coiling.
Alnus rhombifolia	White alder	Open twining.
Apocynum cannabinum	Dogbane	Plain-twined nets.
Avena spp.	Wild oats	Plain-twined mats.
Ceanothus foliosus	Wavyleaf ceanothus	Unspecified uses.
Ceanothus spp.	California lilac	One-rod coiling, plain twining.
Cercis occidentalis	California redbud	Coarse utilitarian baskets.
Cornus spp.	Dogwood	One-rod coiling, plain twining.
Corylus cornuta	California hazelnut	Coiling and twining.
Fraxinus sp.	Ash	Basket rims.
Juncus spp.	Rush	Plain-twined mats, open-twined traps.
Quercus dumosa	Nuttall's scrub oak	Open-twined traps.
Quercus garryana	Oregon oak	Open-twined traps.
Quercus kelloggii	California black oak	Open-twined traps.
Quercus spp.	Oak	Coarse utilitarian baskets, open twining.
Rhus aromatica	Fragrant sumac	One-rod coiling, twining.
Salix exigua	Sandbar willow	Coiling and twining.
Salix gooddingii	Goodding's black willow	Coiling and twining.
Salix laevigata	Red willow	Coiling and twining.
Salix lasiolepis	Arroyo willow	Coiling and twining.
Salix sitchensis	Sitka willow	Coiling and twining.
Salix spp.	Willow	Coiling and twining, coarse utilitarian baskets.
Schoenoplectus acutus var. *occidentalis*	Tule	Plain-twined mats.
Typha latifolia	Common cattail	Plain-twined mats.
Vitis californica	California wild grape	Coarse utilitarian baskets, rims.

Ta pi-ka (Sun basket). A saucer shaped basket about a foot in diameter, suspended by a flexible bail.

Its external mesh is fully interwoven with the scarlet pileum of the woodpecker (*Melanerpes formicivorus*), the rim finished with a row of shell wampum and quail plumes. Glistening shell pendants are interspersed on the brilliant red background of feathers.

It symbolizes the suns effulgence and productivity when used as a ceremonial salver for the fresh seed meal of the season.

The Sun basket was communal property, an evidence of tribal pride and orthodoxy, to use in a local ceremony or to be displayed on the center pillar in the *tca-ne* (assembly house) of another tribe observing a rite.

The importance of hospitalities of a Rancheria were demonstrated at the midsummer festival in the capacity of assembly chamber and the number of delegations from tribes each represented by its scarlet emblem gleaming in the fire light.

– John W. Hudson

Table 24. Basketry weft plants with fiber colors.

Scientific Name	Common Name	Color	Comments
Acer macrophyllum	Bigleaf maple	White	Patterns.
Adiantum jordani	Maidenhair fern	Black	Special purpose coil basketry.
Alnus rhombifolia	Alder	Unspecified	Open twining.
Apocynum cannabinum	Dogbane	Unspecified	Plain-twined nets.
Avena spp.	Wild oats	Unspecified	Plain-twined mats.
Beckmannia syzigachne	American sloughgrass	Unspecified	Unspecified uses.
Carex spp.	Sedge	Light	Twining and coiling, except open twining.
Cercis occidentalis	California redbud	Red	Patterns.
Corylus cornuta	California hazelnut	Black (dyed)	Ornamental coiled baskets.
Equisetum hyemale	Horsetail	Black (dyed)	Ornamental coiled baskets.
Juncus spp.	Rush	Unspecified	Open twining, plain-twined mats.
Juniperus californica	California juniper	Unspecified	Unspecified uses.
Picea sitchensis	Sitka spruce	Unspecified	Unspecified uses.
Pinus contorta	Lodgepole pine	Unspecified	Unspecified uses.
Pinus coulter	Coulter pine	Unspecified	Unspecified uses.
Pinus lambertiana	Sugar pine	Unspecified	Unspecified uses.
Pinus ponderosa	Ponderosa pine	Unspecified	Unspecified uses.
Pinus sabiniana	California foothill pine	Unspecified	Unspecified uses.
Pseudotsuga menziesii	Douglas fir	Unspecified	Unspecified uses.
Pteridium aquilinum	Bracken fern	Black (dyed)	Plain twining, other unspecified uses.
Quercus dumosa	Nuttall's scrub oak	Unspecified	Open-twined traps.
Quercus garryana	Oregon oak	Unspecified	Open-twined traps.
Quercus kelloggii	California black oak	Unspecified	Open-twined traps.
Quercus spp.	Oak	Unspecified	Coarse utilitarian baskets, open twining.
Rhus aromatica	Fragrant sumac	Red	Patterns.
Salix spp.	Willow	Black (dyed)	Open twining, other unspecified uses.
Schoenoplectus acutus var. *occidentalis*	Tule	Black (dyed)	Ornamental coils, plain-twined mats.
Torreya californica	California nutmeg	Unspecified	Patterns.
Typha latifolia	Common cattail	Unspecified	Plain-twined mats.
Unidentified shrub	None	Red	Patterns.
Vitis californica	California wild grape	Unspecified	Coarse utilitarian baskets, other unspecified uses.

Sedge rhizomes, which were intensively managed for optimal production, provided the most highly valued light-colored weft fibers for fine basketry styles. Other colored weft materials were used in patterned basketry. For example, spicebush (*Calycanthus occidentalis*) and fragrant sumac provided high quality burnt sienna and red weft fibers, respectively (Figure 34). Still other weft materials were dyed to attain darker colors, as described below.

The most thorough published accounts of Pomoan basketry weaves differ somewhat in how they classify weaving basketry techniques, although they all identify two basic categories, twining and coiling (Barrett 1905, 1908b; Hudson 1893; Kroeber 1909; Purdy 1902; Smith-Ferri 1998). Additionally, this literature identifies six twined weaves and two coiled weaves used by female basket weavers (Barrett 1908b). Male weavers only used two of these weaves for such utility baskets such as traps, burden baskets, and baby cradles. Table 25 com-

Figure 34. Basketry weft materials: tule, willow (stripped), willow, and redbud. Photograph by James R. Welch, 2011. In the collections of Grace Hudson Museum, Ukiah.

Table 25. Comparison of English and Northern Pomo basketry weave terms.

Weave		Northern Pomo term		Weave type	
English term					
Smith-Ferri (1998)	**Barrett (1908b) and Kroeber (1909)**	**Hudson (1893)**	**Purdy (1902)**	**Twine**	**Coil**
Wickerwork	Wicker work	—	—	X	
Plain twining	Plain twining	*bom toósh*	*bam-tush*	X	
Diagonal twining	Diagonal twining	*shu sétt*	*chu-set*	X	
Lattice twining	Lattice twining	*teé pe-kah*	*ti*	X	
Three-strand twining	Three-strand twining	*shỹ tsín*	*shat-sin*	X	
Three-strand braiding	Three-strand braiding	*shỹ tsín*	*shat-sin*	X	
One-rod coiling	Single-rod coiling	*tsỹ*	*tsai*		X
Three-rod coiling	Three-rod coiling	*bom tsoo woó*	*shi-bu*		X

pares English and Northern Pomo weave terminologies. The terminology employed here follows Hudson (1893), Mason (1900), and Smith-Ferri (1998).

Twining

Twined baskets were made with vertical warp rods interlaced with two or more flexible weft elements. Twining was either open or closed. Open twining was commonly used for fish traps, bird traps, and burden baskets (Figure 35). It was a coarse weave, made with peeled or unpeeled rods with visible spaces between them. The warp and weft fibers were generally the same material. Although in 1893 the Potter Valley Pomo usually used whole willow shoots, alder was more common in the past and continued to be used only for the strongest baskets. Men used open twining to make utility baskets (Barrett 1908b; Kroeber 1925). In contrast to open twining, closed twining was made with narrower fibers and tighter weaves, such that there were no visible spaces between strands. Closed twine baskets were used for carrying small items such as seeds, and could be made watertight for water storage and cooking. The

Figure 35. Open-twined utility basketry, 1899. At the center is a large conical burden basket. Represented clockwise, from top, are a plate-shaped utility basket, a woodpecker trap, a seed beater, a sitting baby cradle, and a collecting basket. Photograph by A. O. Carpenter. Original in the collections of Grace Hudson Museum, Ukiah.

fine weft fibers used in closed twining were selected and arranged with great care to create intricate patterns on basket exteriors. There were six distinct twined weaves: wicker, plain, diagonal, three-strand, three-strand braiding, and lattice.

Wickerwork was an open twine weave used only in the specific instance of the shallow basin of seed beaters. In this case, warp and weft weave elements were generally whole narrow rods, either peeled or unpeeled. In wickerware, differently than in the other twine weaves, none of the rods twisted against each other. Instead, they were arranged in an open, checker-like mesh of rods that passed alternately over and under one other.

Plain twining was among the most common Pomoan basketry weaves (Figure 36), being employed for cooking and storage baskets, burden baskets, hopper-mortar baskets, and winnowing and parching baskets (Hudson 1893; Purdy 1902). Its usual construction consisted of a radial rod foundation with two flexible weft fibers. Between each warp rod, the weft elements made a single or double twist against each other. Warp fibers for plain twining most often consisted of cleaned willow rods. The more flexible weft fibers included light-colored sedge fibers and red or black fibers from a variety of plants, which were used together to create patterns (Table 26). Larger plain-twined baskets had rims typically constructed of alder rods lashed with fir fibers (Hudson 1893). Plain twining was also used by men for crafting utility baskets (Barrett 1908b; Kroeber 1925).

Diagonal twining was a similar weave to plain twining, except that it was considered to produce especially graceful baskets with the smoothest exterior patterns. This weave was employed for baskets used for transporting, storing, winnowing and parching seeds, as well as for cooking (Barrett 1908b; Hudson 1893). They were constructed from the same types of plant fibers as plain-twined baskets, except that only the smallest, toughest, and most flexible warp fibers were selected. Different than plain twining, diagonal twining involved passing

Figure 36. Closed plain-twined baskets, 1899. Photograph by A. O. Carpenter. Original in the collections of Grace Hudson Museum, Ukiah.

Table 26. Basketry weaves with associated basket types and common plant materials.

Weave style	Basket types	Examples of common plant materials	Comments
Open twining	Burden baskets, fish traps, granaries, quail traps	White alder (*Alnus rhombifolia*)	Warp and weft.
		Willow (*Salix* spp.)	Warp and weft.
Wickerwork	Seed beaters	Willow (*Salix* spp.)	Warp and weft.
Plain twining	Conical burden baskets, cooking baskets, hopper-mortar baskets, storage baskets, winnowing baskets	Maidenhair fern (*Adiantum jordani*)	Black-colored weft for patterns.
		White alder (*Alnus rhombifolia*)	Rims.
		Sedge (*Carex* spp.)	Light-colored weft for patterns.
		California redbud (*Cercis occidentalis*)	Red weft for patterns.
		Douglas fir (*Pseudotsuga menziesii*)	Lashing for rim.
		Fragrant sumac (*Rhus aromatica*)	Red weft for patterns.
		Willow (*Salix* spp.)	Warp.
		Tule (*Schoenoplectus acutus* var. *occidentalis*)	Black weft for patterns.
		Unidentified shrub	Red weft for patterns.
Diagonal twining	Burden baskets, cooking baskets, winnowing and parching baskets	Same as for plain twining.	
Lattice twining	Cooking baskets, hopper-mortar baskets, storage baskets for liquids, winnowing and parching baskets	Same as for plain twining.	
Three-strand twining	Burden baskets, storage baskets	Sedge (*Carex* spp.)	Weft.
		Willow (*Salix* spp.)	Warp.
Three-strand braiding	Burden baskets, storage baskets	Sedge (*Carex* spp.)	Weft.
		Willow (*Salix* spp.)	Warp.
One-rod coiling	Unspecified	Same as plain twining.	
Three-rod coiling	Unspecified	Same as plain twining.	

weft elements alternately over and under two warp rods at a time such that with each pass, the stich was offset by one warp rod (Barrett 1908b; Hudson 1893). As Hudson explained in his unpublished manuscripts, it is "the art of progressively enclosing pairs of upright warp rods within a pair of horizontal weft tapes, which pass each other in spaces alternating those just below them."

Also similar to plain twining, three-strand twining employed three weft elements, which were passed over two rods at a time and under one. It was most frequently used for the limited purposes of starting basket bottoms or finishing rims (Barrett 1908b). In these instances, cleaned willow rods were often used as warp elements and sedge fiber for weft elements. Closed and open variations were used by women for burden and storage baskets and by men for utility baskets (Barrett 1908b; Hudson 1893; Kroeber 1909, 1925). In another variation similar to three-strand twining, three-strand braiding involved three alternately overlapping weft elements. It was used for the same purposes and basket types as three-strand twining (Barrett 1908b).

Lattice twining was a complex weave, incorporating a combination of twining and coiling, and required approximately twice the investment of time than plain twining (Hudson 1893; Kroeber 1909). It was used for cooking baskets, winnowing and parching baskets, hopper-mortar baskets, and watertight baskets used to store liquids (Hudson 1893). Similar in all other ways to plain twining, lattice twining incorporated both rigid weft elements and flexible weft strands. The weft rods, positioned perpendicular to radial warp rods, generally covered only limited portions of a basket. With each stitch, each flexible weft element passed around a radial warp rod on the inside of the basket and around a coiled weft rod on the outside, creating the appearance of twining on the interior and coiling on the exterior (Barrett 1908b; Purdy 1902). The additional layer of weft rods served to give a basket additional strength. Men also used a variation of lattice twining with vertical and horizontal structural rods for baby cradles (Barrett 1908b).

Coiling

The second basic category of weaves was coiling, which consisted of spiraled warp rods stitched together with flexible weft fibers. The spiral began in the center of the base and built upon itself continuously to the rim. There were two coiling weaves, one-rod and three-rod.

One-rod coiling consisted of a single coiled warp rod, said to simulate the coil of a rattlesnake (Hudson 1893). Willow was the most typical warp material because it could be obtained in considerable lengths with consistent diameter. One-rod coiled baskets were often intricately patterned with the same weft fibers employed in closed twined baskets. Decorative feathers were occasionally incorporated into the weave for gift and ceremonial baskets (Barrett 1908b) (Figure 37). Nineteenth and early twentieth century curios collectors sought this style of Pomoan basketry above all others (cf. Bibby 1996).

Figure 37. One-rod coiled baskets with feather ornamentation, 1899. Photograph by A. O. Carpenter. Original in the collections of Grace Hudson Museum, Ukiah.

The feathered baskets are all for beauty, luxury, the family jewels.

The decoration is as the fancy dictates. Around the top, or in patches, many are entirely overlaid with feathers in patterns, as smoothe as the breast of a bird.

And care is taken in the selection of feathers that do not fade. The yellow of the larks breast and the red of the black birds wing soon lose their beauty, while the color lasts as the feather from the green head of the mallard duck, the brown from the wood duck, the lemon yellow from the woodpeckers throat and the bright red from his head.

Perhaps the greatest evidence of the basket-makers delicate artistic sense, and one least understood and appreciated, is in their use of the hair-like red feathers from the woodpeckers scalp. These are sparsely placed in very fine baskets the object being to give a red glow when the basket is held at arms length.

The bulb of each feather is bitten to loosen the natural glue and held in place on the basket with three stitches. The feather might be broken off but it could never be pulled out.

Quail crests and fine *ka'-ya* [clamshell beads] finish the rim. And often dainty pendants of very small *ka'-ya* and polished arrow-head shaped bits of abalone shell are woven in rows around.

– John W. Hudson

Three-rod coiling was similar to one-rod coiling, except that a bundle of three smaller warp fibers was used instead of one single coiled rod. Although three-rod coiling was especially labor-intensive, the final result appeared somewhat similar to one-rod coiling (Hudson 1893). The primary difference was that three-rod coiling permitted more intricate designs, making it the most highly esteemed basketry weave in Pomoan society (Purdy 1902). Three-rod coil gift or ceremonial baskets were also frequently decorated by incorporating feathers into the weave (Barrett 1908b).

Dyes, Paints, and Designs

Paints and dyes for general use were prepared from diverse plants and minerals. A red stain of unknown application was obtained from popcorn flower (*Plagiobothrys fulvus*). The expressed juice of foothill larkspur flower petals (*Delphinium hesperium*) was used as a blue paint. Iris flowers crushed in hot water were applied as body paint. A black paint for general use was made from California buckeye and willow charcoal. Scorched but not burnt California bay nut meats were used as a black paint for one's face and eyebrows.

Fibers, especially the fine weft fibers used to produce patterns on the exteriors of baskets, were often dyed to produce desirable colors. Six different processes were used to achieve fine black basketry fibers. The first began by removing the bark from the material to be dyed. Each cleaned fiber strand was evenly painted with charcoal paste, possibly made from California buckeye or willow. They were then placed in the bottom of a pit with willow ash and covered with moist soil for about 80 hours. If removed too early, the color was dark brown instead of the desired glossy black. If left in the pit too long, the charcoal and ash mixture destroyed the fiber material. In the second method, the fibers were submerged for an even longer period of time in the mud of a mineral spring. Third, they were buried with damp wood ashes for 16 to 18 hours. Fourth, the fiber material was soaked for one day in a mixture of water, powdered charcoal, and crushed blue elderberry or California black oak leaves. Fifth, the fibers were soaked in acorn leach water mixed with hematite or a rusty nail. Sixth, they were buried with crushed acorn shells.

A variety of other techniques were used to color objects used in ceremony, contests, and hunting. A red dye produced from alder bark was used for leather root and milkweed fibers in women's dance headbands. This may have been accomplished by smoking the fiber with white alder wood (Chestnut 1902). The preferred technique for decorating game pieces, flutes, and arrows involved tightly wrapping the item with strips of dogwood, California redbud (*Cercis occidentalis*), or California wild grape fibers and exposing the surface to heat until it turned black. Removing bark wrappings revealed a negative pattern on the object. Alternatively, moist clay was applied instead of strips of bark. As mentioned above, the backs of hunting bows were treated with a mixture of soot and soaproot bulb glue to give them a permanent black finish. Arrows were often marked with a bluish paint obtained from acorn mold.

Pottery and Vessels

Wooden Vessels
A variety of wooden vessels were shaped from oak knots, especially those found in the trunks of California black oak trees. Knots were removed by making peripheral cuts with an obsidian blade followed by blows with a hardwood hammer.

Clay Vessels
Hudson described in some detail a series of clay vessels and objects fashioned by the Potter Valley Pomo. Platter-shaped blue clay vessels were somewhat common. They were not fired, but rather dried in the sun, after which they were painted in their entirety or in patterns with a pigment made from a red mineral mixed with soaproot glue. Although these blue clay vessels were commonly used to hold water and rarely used for cooking, Hudson considered their chief function to be symbolic.

Hai' pi-ka' (of-wood cut-tear-off). [...] the enclosed cellular tissue was removed by blowpipe (*hŏ pi-du'-tin*) and shell scraper, and the exterior reduced to the hard wood. Interlacing fibres gave durability, thin walls lightness while the smooth interior and bowl-like shapes afforded vessels for many uses and range of sizes from a drinking cup to a 20 gallon tub. [...] Contrary to usual Indian custom, *hai' pi-ka'* were not considered personal property to be destroyed at the owners death, but were passed down as heirlooms and often became aesthetic by generations of handling.

– John W. Hudson

Also fashioned from clay, animal figurines were usual play items for children (cf. Barrett 1952; Loeb 1926). Another type of clay figurine, often painted in patterns and inlayed with clamshell disks, was given to young women upon reaching puberty or marrying. Symbolic of female domestic activities and marital duties, these typically were made in the form of miniature conical burden baskets filled with fine seed meal or pine sugar. Similar figurines are mentioned in a Pomoan legend recorded by Hudson, in which New Woman, upon her emergence into the world, is given clay representations of a pestle, a grinding hopper, a sifter, and a pot. Another type of clay figurine was used to assist in conception. Shaped like the torso of a pregnant woman, these were secretly suspended over the beds of childless women and, when discovered, were accepted graciously (cf. Loeb 1926). Hanging these fertility charms over the beds of elderly women was considered an excellent form of humor.

Field activities during the wet season were very limited and moon phases often obscured, a traveler keeping tab daily with his *hai pĕm'* (sticks carried). Such important dates as *da cu-we'-na* (next new moon, time of low tide and gathering sea products), or *du-wĭ da'xa-la'* (wane of moon, time for trapping) were warm weather dates. Reference to *da ma-to'* (full moon), or to other phases by addition or subtraction of nights were not uncommon terms.

– John W. Hudson

The day, *ma-tcĭ'* (earth passing) began at sunrise, *da-tcau'* (light-flies), was marked at noon, *ma-tcĭ di-le'* (day middle) and closed at unset, *da-tco ma'* (lightless earth). In the deep Poman valleys the hours of sunrise and sunset and comparative periods of morn and afternoon differed in villages according to their relation to E.W. horizons. Noon only was the same everywhere and was a base for definitive appointments. This meridian time was fixed by the *pă-cĭt'hai* (shadow pole), a simple but fairly accurate sundial that stood presumably in every community and at isolated homes.

– John W. Hudson

Hudson described a final form of pottery based on inference from his inspection of sherds found near old burials. This evidence led him to conclude that the Potter Valley Pomo previously made clay vessels for grain storage that were nearly 30 cm in diameter, with flat bottoms and slightly constricted rims. He proposed that they were formed by molding clay on the inner surface of wooden bowls and that they were used with lids. Several of the remnants he inspected were scored on the exterior surface with geometric and curved lines.

Counting and Timekeeping

Counting was employed in marking the calendar and making trade calculations. Smaller numbers, often registered with notches in wood, were calculated with a system based on multiples of eight. Larger numbers were tabulated using a vigesimal system, whereby multiples of 20 were temporarily recorded with combinations of distinctive feathers and sticks. This system, which easily accommodated numbers into the many thousands, was used to keep track of important dates associated with ceremonial events, lunar phases, and astronomical events. For example, 1492 was represented by the sum of three long sticks (1200), 14 short rods (280), one split feather (10), and two straws (2).

Shadow pole sundials were made from straight and smooth conifer sapling, such as pine, some 3.5 to 6 m long. Set into the earth, they stood vertically near the entry to the assembly house, which was located on the structure's southern side. Lashed across the top end was a short wooden crossbar. At midday, a shadow pole cast its shadow to the north, across a white stone set into the structure's earthen roof in line with the base of the pole and the North Star.

Contests and Games

Implements of botanical origin were employed in diverse games and contests. Games were often competitive and frequently involved large wagers (Aginsky and Aginsky 1950). Several such pastimes are described here, although it is not a comprehensive list. Juggling, dice play-ing, and running races are just a few of the Potter Valley Pomo games not discussed here due to insufficient information.

Racket and Ball Games

Men and women played a game that somewhat resembled lacrosse. Each mixed gender team of 10 or more people chose a captain (cf. Culin 1975; Loeb 1926; Powers 1872). The game was started by an umpire tossing a ball between the captains, who tried to catch it with rackets. The goal was to throw the ball between opposing posts positioned some 150 m apart. For-feiture resulted from such fouls as tripping, striking, and roughhousing. The rackets, often made from dogwood, ash, or oak, were constructed by bending the end of an approximately 1.2 m stick into a hoop, which was closed with netting made from iris fiber cordage. Game balls measuring approximately 6 cm in diameter were made from knots of California bay wood. Another game resembling shinny, or hockey, was played using shinny sticks, often made from manzanita, and wooden balls made from oak knots. According to some sources, this game closely resembled the ball and racket game described above (Barrett 1952; Loeb 1926).

Contest Shooting

Separate arrow shooting contests were held for distance and accuracy. Hudson reported that distance shooters often cleared 180 m (cf. Loeb 1926). Distance contests involved such large wagers that they could result in financial ruin. For this reason, the arrows employed were made with the same high degree of care as those used for warfare or large game hunting. Distance contest arrows were predominantly made from a sage plant, most likely wormwood (*Artemisia ludoviciana*), because it was considered the lightest and most rigid of arrow materials. Each arrow had an approximately 5 cm polished fore-shaft and red-shafted flicker feather (*Colaptes cafer*) fletching. Accuracy contests, also called hoop shooting, employed targets placed at a distance of some 18 to 30 m from the archers (cf. Loeb 1926). Targets consisted of a plain-twined tule mat with an ap-proximately 2.5 cm wooden ring positioned at its center. Contestants were allocated five points for hitting inside the ring and two points for meeting the target outside the ring. The first to earn 10 points won the game. Like all fine arrows, those used in accuracy contests had both a main shaft and a foreshaft. The main shafts were made from moderately dense woods, such as big-leaf maple or cluster rose. Foreshafts were made from mountain mahogany.

Dolls

Young girls played with dolls made from approximately 40 m splints of Fremont's cotton-wood (*Populus fremontii*), 10 cm wide at the top and tapering down to a point. They were dressed with skirts from soft common rush fiber. Hair, mouths, and navels were applied with charcoal paint and eyes were represented with clamshell disks.

Hoop Game

In this game, four players stood at the corners of a square field, some 18 m across. In sequence, each rolled a hoop to the next player. The object of the game was to throw a lance through the hoop while it was moving. When a player missed the hoop, he left the game and a substitute took his place. The last player to remain in the game received a wager pool. The lances were made from approximately 2.5 m lengths of willow and the hoops from circular bundles of dogbane cordage.

Stave Games

Women played stave games, also called the "game without bickering" (***xa-dai***), on woven mats placed between them. Each of the two or more players was allotted 12 plain or black counting rods at the beginning of the game. Examples of counting rods in the collections of the Grace Hudson Museum were made from wormwood (Figure 38). A player grasped six playing staves in both hands and cast them upon the mat. Fashioned from California buckeye or willow, staves were approximately 30 cm long, rounded on one side, and flat on the other (Figure 39). The rounded sides were decorated with charred patterns. After a player cast, the arrangement of upturned flat or rounded surfaces determined the number of counting rods won. In a game between two players, counting rods were won from each other. When three

Figure 38. Wormwood game counters. Photograph by James R. Welch, 2011. Accession no. 1398A, in the collections of Grace Hudson Museum, Ukiah.

Figure 39. Women's gambling staves. Photograph by James R. Welch, 2011. Accession no. 1558, in the collections of Grace Hudson Museum, Ukiah.

or more people played, counters were initially won from the bank, which was stocked with 24 rods at the beginning of the game, and then from other opponents. The name "game without bickering" derives from a legend in which the game was given to women by the mythical being **Ka-tai'**, who forbade disagreements and wagers between members of the same sex. Nevertheless, Hudson reported that at the time of his research women enthusiastically bet even their last possessions in this game.

Boat Racing

Special tule balsas were crafted for boat races held in the open waters of Clear Lake and other regions the Potter Valley Pomo visited. Racing balsas were longer, narrower, and more tightly bound than regular balsas. According to Hudson, boat racers reached speeds of about 10 kilometers per hour (a "six mile gait").

Musical Instruments

Acorn Strings

Strings of acorn shells were held in the mouth by one end and rapidly spun to produce musical notes (cf. Barrett 1952; Loeb 1926).

Bullroarers and Clappers

Swung in circles to produce a thunderous sound, bullroarers were made from approximately 8 by 30 cm staves of manzanita, Fremont's cottonwood, and oak wood (cf. Barrett 1952). Northern Pomoans considered the sound to be the voice of the thunder deity (Loeb 1926). Used in conjunction with bullroarers, split-stick clappers were made of manzanita, Fremont's cottonwood, and elderberry wood. Inside the assembly house during thunder dance ceremonies, clappers were slapped to represent the sound of lightening, followed by the roar of a bullroarer to suggest thunder.

A' la hai' tcil. Thunder Ceremony or ceremony for rain and praying. All assemble in the *tca-ne* [assembly house] at dusk, about May first, except the four Thunder stick whirlers and Lightening clappers. At a signal from *Yum-ta*, the high priest, the *tsi lo ma dim* (drummer) springs on his drum and starts long roll with his heels, at which the *tsa hai dim* (lightening stick clapper) strikes a loud slap with his sticks and then the four thunder stick wielders stationed at the four cardinal points of the *tca-ne* begin o whirl their sticks, which uproar continues for two minutes to attract the Gods attention. When silent again, *Yum-ta* offers a prayer.

– John W. Hudson

Flutes

Flutes or whistles with four finger holes were made from elderberry stalk sections. These were understood to have been invented by the legendary being Robin (*Turdus migratorius*) to charm worms out of the ground. Considered the patron of flutists, Robin only bored four flute holes because he lacked available fingers. A Robin's "signature" design was carved with obsidian blades on the surface of flutes between finger holes and filled with pine resin (Figure 40). Crushed green willow leaves were rubbed on the exterior surface to give it a final polish. Although Loeb (1926) furnished contradictory data, Hudson reported that this type of flute was used by hereditary *kuk' su* doctors, who practiced divination and brought health in the autumn season (cf. Barrett 1917b).

Figure 40. John W. Hudson illustration of "Robin's signature" design. Drawing from John W. Hudson's fieldnotes.

Foot Drums

Large drums were installed at the back of assembly houses. Made from Fremont's cottonwood, these were shaped like inverted canoes. Measuring some 2.5 m long, 60 cm wide, and 30 cm high, they were suspended with ropes over a shallow pit filled with leaves. Drummers stood on top of the drums, making sounds with their heels that could be heard at great distances.

Mouth Bows

Consisting of a small wooden bow with a taught string, mouth bows were secured at the center between one's teeth and played by striking the string and the ends of the bow with one's fingers. Hudson reported that the instrument was a "favorite with lovers" and produced a "soft pleasing variety of notes." Mouth bows were made from dogwood, willow, and other light woods (cf. Barrett 1952; Loeb 1926).

Trade and Currency

Magnesite

The Potter Valley Pomo participated in regional trade networks and recognized certain standards for trade and exchange. As Hudson described, magnesite cylinders (*po'*) were the "coin and treasure most highly valued, the 'gold' basis of Keyan finance," referring to a Pomoan group from Clear Lake that dominated the largest mining reserves of magnesite in the region.

Although most magnesite in the region came from Clear Lake, there were several small deposits in lower Potter Valley, mined by the residents of the settlement *Po'-mo po'-ma* ("red magnesite mine people"). Magnesite clumps, some as large as boulders, were broken apart by baking in underground ovens, which also served to bring out the mineral's reddish colors. The stone was shaped by chipping with jasper flakes, followed by abrasion with wet sandstone. Drilling long cylinders was quite laborious, the difficulty increasing substantially with the depth of the hole. Finished cylinders were polished with horsetail followed by animal hide (Figure 41). The quality of the red coloration rather than size served as the principal basis for a cylinder's value. Nevertheless, some of the most valuable cylinders were quite enormous, reaching 1.5 m in length and 30 cm in width, as reported by Hudson. One example of such a

Po had a monetary potency beyond shell coin (*ka'-ya*). It could purchase the most precious possessions, condone a man-killing and where known abroad was enhanced in value, even beyond Sacramento basin and to the shores of San Francisco Bay. *Po* is now rarely seen in an Indians hands, for it is hoarded by the orthodox for one purpose only: to accompany and serve the dead in its future abode above (*xa-li'*).

– John W. Hudson

Barter was conducted by medium of salt cakes [...] from the ocean and flakes of obsidian (*ka-tca*) from the interior for weapons. Tribes near the mouth of the river introduced strings of small white sea shell (*Olivella*) as a trading wampum; a money (*xal*) of standard size and value that represented wealth and exacted counting into the hundreds. It was perhaps centuries prior to the appearance of a white-man (Sir Francis Drake, 1579) on their coast, that they had invented tools of stone for shaping and boring the larger shells (*Saxidomus*) for financial and ornamental purposes and whose multiplicity extended the counting system into thousands.

– John W. Hudson

Figure 41. Magnesite cylinder (po'). Photograph by James R. Welch, 2011. Accession no. 1346, in the collections of Grace Hudson Museum, Ukiah.

piece was valued at 5000 clamshell disk beads. Magnesite disks (*po ka-wi*), used as currency and decoration, were made from the smaller castoff fragments from cylinder manufacture. Produced by similar procedure to that described below for clamshell disks, magnesite disks were many times more valuable.

Clamshell Disks

All Pomoan peoples once used clamshell disks as a form of currency. However, by 1893 only the Potter Valley Pomo continued to manufacture and use them (Hudson 1893). The raw materials were obtained at Bodega Bay, Sonoma County. The local Bodega Miwok permitted Pomoan groups to dig California butterclam (*Saxidomus nutalli*) and Heart Cockle (*Clinocardium nuttallii*) shells free of charge (Loeb 1926). Clamshell disks were roughly chipped from whole shells and perforated with drills while held with one's feet in split elderberry stave clamps. They were then strung in approximately 18 cm lengths on resilient willow shoots or rush flower stalks. These served as axles to support the clamshell disks as they were rolled with one's hands on a stone slab to wear off the rough edges. A final polish was accomplished by rubbing with horsetail followed by buckskin.

Used as a standard form of exchange, clamshell disks were given in payment for services, such as certain ceremonial roles in male puberty rites, and to obtain economically valuable items (Hudson 1893; Peri and Patterson 1976). For example, coils of rush rhizome fibers had a commercial value of about 20 clamshell disks each. Fine black fibers from alkali bulrush rhizomes and maidenhair fern were even more highly valued, commanding approximately 100 clamshell disks per coil. Coils of fine red weft fibers from such plants as California redbud and fragrant sumac were typically valued at about 17 clamshell disks. These fiber coils had standard sizes for trade between indigenous groups throughout the region north of the San Francisco Bay, west of the Sacramento basin, and south of Eel River basin. Hanks of dogbane fiber were also separated into small bundles and finished with braided ends. These traded for between 10 and 19 clamshell disks each.

Warfare

Many of the weapons used for large game hunting, described above, were also used in warfare. For example, a club-ended stabbing spear was particularly feared. Also, big game bows made from California juniper were esteemed for use in warfare. Men wore special body armor and headdresses during war. Armor providing an excellent barrier to spears and arrows was worn only rarely by the Potter Valley Pomo, being more common among hostile Yuki groups to the north (Figure 42). It was fashioned from fir and mountain mahogany rods measuring approximately 1 cm in diameter. These were hardened through exposure to fire and bound together firmly, side by side, with tightly twisted cord of iris or stinging nettle. Shredded soaproot husks were affixed to the interior as a soft lining. Visually impressive warfare headdresses consisted of an approximately 5 cm wide woven dogbane band supporting a row of upright

Figure 42. "Firelog Joe" wearing armor, Hopland Rancheria, 1892. Photograph by A.O. Carpenter. Original in the collections of Grace Hudson Museum, Ukiah.

eagle tail feathers. Some were decorated with shell ornaments, clamshell disks, or downy feathers.

Archery was a sport of the savage youth, an art taught him from the time he could string his toy splint of willow and improvised rude shafts of the horseweed. At the age of breech-clouts he could shoot rapidly and with considerable accuracy with the small game bow and had imbibed much of the theory of those mighty weapons used by his elders.

In some cases he followed his captain to war in the capacity of slinger, or from his ambush behind the firing line he noted the course of the enemies arrows and during a lull would dash forth and collect such shafts as were not injured beyond repair.

On his return home the renovation of such spoils was a matter of much pride and ambition.

– John W. Hudson

Medicines and Poisons

Hudson documented at least 75 plants used as medicines, remedies, health aids, or poisons. This section highlights those used for medicinal applications with the greatest numbers of documented plant taxa: women's health, first aid, laxatives, analgesics, gastrointestinal aids, remedies for sexually transmitted diseases, and poisons.

Women's Health and Childbirth

At least 14 plants were considered relevant to women's health (Table 27). At first menses, young women spent four days in seclusion with a restricted diet of acorn mush. There, her female associates prepared her to return to the community by bathing her in tepid water perfumed with sprigs of California sagebrush and soaproot. Menstruating women used soft fiber padding as belts or napkins. Preferred materials were common rush, lace lichen, tule, and cattail.

Immediately after giving birth and expulsion of the afterbirth, attendants bathed mothers in the hip area with water infused with California sagebrush and gave them a lichen napkin

Table 27. Taxa important for women's health, indicating associated conditions or events.

Scientific Name	Common Name	First Menses	Menstruation	Pregnancy	Birth	Nursing
*Allium bolanderi**	Bolander's onion			X		
Artemisia californica	California angelica	X			X	
Asclepias eriocarpa	Kotolo milkweed					X
Asclepias fascicularis	Mexican whorled milkweed					X
Chlorogalum pomeridianum	Soaproot		X			
*Eschscholzia californica**	California poppy					X
Juncus effusus	Common rush		X			
*Madia elegans**	Common madia			X		
Matricaria discoidea	Pineapple weed		X			
Mimulus aurantiacus	Bush monkeyflower					X
Ramalina menziesii	Lace lichen		X			
Schoenoplectus acutus var. *occidentalis*	Tule		X			
Schoenoplectus acutus var. *occidentalis*	Common tule		X			
*Triteleia hyacinthina**	White brodiaea			X		
Typha latifolia	Common cattail	X				

Obs.: Asterisks (*) indicate taxa considered harmful to women's health. This list does not include foods prescribed for an expectant mother immediately before birth, including acorn mush, baked bulbs, and fresh greens.

Ka-wĭ ba-a'-dĭn (child production). [...] At home the event was prepared for by experienced kin. The expedience of a head presentation was understood and to assure this condition certain exercises were begun several weeks before confinement. That most popular with Poman women was called "*ka-wĭ ko-di' ba-an ka-kebi-cul'-cu yŏ-mal-hu'n*" (infant easy born properly by hillside descending), in which she struts down a slope, with erect body and jolting steps to promote gravitation of the foetal head. A vegetable and fish diet was observed and at premonitory symptoms was given a laxative of *Taraxacum* leaves or bark of *Rhamnus californica* (*hŏ mi-tă'*). With wide spread feet the assistant kneels and sits upon the floor. The triangular space between her thighs was filled with a cushion of lichen (*ku-tci'*, *Ramalina reticulata*) and covered with a greased buckskin to receive the infant.

– John W. Hudson

(cf. Barrett 1952). After the newborn was fitted with a broad umbilical bandage, its umbilicus was tied several centimeters from the body with Fremont's cottonwood fiber thread and severed with an obsidian blade. The wound was dressed with a strong California sagebrush infusion and bound with a flat smooth pebble about 4 cm across. While recuperating after giving birth, a woman would recline in a warm place, eating a meatless diet of acorn mush, baked bulbs, and salad foods. During this time, she also avoided expressly avoided eating Bolander's onion (*Allium bolanderi*), common madia, and white brodiaea (*Triteleia hyacinthina*). To assure abundant breast milk and to treat soreness, a recent mother's breasts were frequently cleansed with a warmed California sagebrush solution and massaged.

First Aid

Sores and wounds were treated with the fresh leaves of ladies' tobacco (*Pseudognaphalium californicum*) or an infusion of hound's tongue (*Cynoglossum grande*) or Coast Range mulesears (*Wyethia glabra*). Persistent sores were treated with a powder made from fringed redmaids. Cuts and infected sores were also treated with an infusion made from ash bark and threenerve goldenrod (*Solidago velutina*) mixed with a special mud found near Potter Valley. Boils were treated with a poultice of fresh poison oak (*Toxicodendron diversilobum*) or cooked and mashed death camas bulb (*Toxicoscordion venenosum*). Blisters were treated with an unidentified plant called **tsip** in Northern Pomo.

Laxatives and Purgatives

Among the purgatives were boiled Fendler's meadowrue seeds (*Thalictrum fendleri*), madrone leaf honeydew, Durango root infusion, and possibly yarrow (*Achillea millefolium*). Toasted toyon root (*Heteromeles arbutifolia*) was considered a mild laxative. Also used to treat constipation were condensed sugar pine pitch, an infusion prepared from young inner bark or, alternatively, chewing older bark from cascara buckthorn (*Frangula purshiana*), and a root extract from an unidentified plant called **tso lom to** in Northern Pomo. Additionally, at the first signs of labor, expectant mothers were given laxatives made from California coffeeberry bark (*Frangula californica*) or common dandelion greens (*Taraxacum officinale*).

Analgesics

Several plants were used to treat toothache, including shooting star (*Dodecatheon hendersonii*), California bay, California poppy (*Eschscholzia californica*), and American mistletoe (*Phoradendron villosum*). Internal pain was treated with California sagebrush and bush monkeyflower (*Mimulus aurantiacus*), which were used in combination with massage and fomentation. Headache was treated with shooting star leaves mixed with California bay oil. Cooked and mashed death camas bulbs were applied externally to reduce the pain associated with strains and bruises.

Gastrointestinal Aids

The plants used as gastrointestinal aids and to treat nausea, upset stomach, or indigestion included yarrow, cascara buckthorn, and fragrant sumac. Abdominal pains or colic were treated with California sagebrush or bush monkeyflower in combination with massage or a steam bath or, alternatively, an infusion of Durango root. An infusion of blazingstar (*Mentzelia* sp.) was used for biliousness.

Sexually Transmitted Diseases

Most of the documented remedies for sexually transmitted diseases were used for gonorrhea. These included dogwood bark, man-root seeds (*Marah* sp.), whole boiled rosilla plant (*Helenium puberulum*), an infusion of Fendler's meadowrue root, and an infusion of stinging nettle root. Additionally, unspecified sexually transmitted infections were treated with ground manzanita seeds, which were mixed with red paint and coyote dung and hair.

Poisons

The bulbs of several plants were considered harmful. These include two unidentified plants called **ci yo batsom** and **tsip** in Northern Pomo, firecracker brodiaea (*Dichelostemma idamaia*), and death camas. Additionally, California nutmeg was employed by sorcerers (**katan'**) to cause irritation, pain, and blindness.

Narcotics and Stimulants

A variety of plants produced altered states of mind. Those used in healing, divination, and ceremonialism are discussed in subsequent sections. Red larkspur (*Delphinium nudicaule*) was used to cause sleep. The roots were chewed to achieve a calm state. They were also used during competitions to cause an opponent to become drowsy. In such cases, the dried and powdered root was blown into the opponent's face.

Men commonly smoked tobacco (*Nicotiana* spp.) for pleasure and ceremony, thanking Coyote (**Du-wi'**) when smelling new tobacco or lighting a pipe. It was inhaled deeply in order to cause an elevated psychological state. The strength of the tobacco varied according to how it was collected and prepared. According to Hudson, wooden smoking pipes postdate stone pipes (cf. Barrett 1952). Wooden smoking pipes were made from a single section of pithy ash wood. After hollowing and rough shaping with an ember and blowing tube, the exterior was inlaid with abalone shell fragments. This was accomplished by repeatedly charring the surface and scraping it out with an obsidian tool to create depressions for the shell. The surface was polished by rubbing with horsetail. A finished pipe was tubular in shape and from approximately 10 to 35 cm long. Its bowl was 2.5 cm or more deep. A small piece of charcoal was dropped into the bowl before filling the pipe to prevent the tobacco from passing through the stem. In a strong wind, the burning tobacco could be secured with a finger, a chip of wood or a piece of stone. Men often reclined while smoking, elevating the pipe at a sharp angle.

Curing

There were two principal types of healers or "doctors" among the Northern Pomo. Sucking doctors (*ma tu'*) worked independently, and were often the first to be called to a patient to make a diagnosis (cf. Freeland 1923; Loeb 1926). In contrast, outfit doctors (also, singing or rattle doctors) were members of secret societies and were frequently called upon after a sucking doctor to bring about or finish a cure. Whereas outfit doctors were almost always men, sucking doctors were also frequently women. Another contrast between the two was that sucking doctors tended to acquire their power through dreams, whereas outfit doctors learned from older doctors (Gifford 1926). Both types collected payment in clamshell beads for their services.

Sucking Doctors

Sucking doctors employed a variety of divination and curing techniques. Jimsonweed root (*Datura* spp.) was taken in decoction and tobacco was smoked to facilitate divination. According to Helen Carpenter (n.d.), illness was often attributed to a person having heard the voice of some inanimate object or superhuman creature. A sucking doctor began a diagnosis by cutting the patient and sucking some of the blood. The doctor then sought to find the exact thing that spoke to the patient. In cases caused by superhuman creatures, this involved fashioning an effigy based on the patient's recollection. In all other cases, the doctor showed the patient various objects until the patient's alarmed reaction or physical convulsion suggested the correct object had been found. Greater severity of reaction increased the certainty that the object was correctly identified. Once made or located, the effigy was destroyed.

Tsi pa' ka-li tci ya'. Buteo borealis. Red tailed hawk. Patron saint of doctors. Familiarly called *Tci ya*.

Di yăn di yăn'. Accipiter cooperi. Coopers hawk.

Di yăn di yăn' caught a bull snake and ate it. He swelled up and became very ill. His brother *Tci ya*, the great doctor, came and "scolded him bad" for presuming to imitate him (*Tci ya*) in catching snakes. *Tci ya* always sings four songs before eating a snake and everybody knows *Di yăn di yăn'* cannot sing at all. Then *Tci ya* sang and danced around *Di yăn di yăn'* and wound a bull snake around his own neck "to doctor him by" and assured his little brother that he was not only cured but henceforth could eat any of the snakes with impunity.

– John W. Hudson

When I was a little boy I went with an old Medicine man to capture a rattle snake. We went to a certain pile of boulders where the doctor sat upon the ground and commenced singing in a low tone and shaking his rattle [...]. After he had kept this up about ten minutes a rattlers head appeared in a hole near by. The snake gazed intently at the doctor then very slowly crept out and finally lay near the doctor's knees. The doctor then thrust a forked stick over the snake's neck and slipping his hand down the stick grasped the snake behind its head. He then sewed up the snakes lips with his bone needle and *ma cu'* [*Apocynum*] thread, and pried open the corners of its jaws with a small bone and loosened the two fangs at their roots. He slipped a thread loop around the fangs and easily extracted them. The fangs were cleansed and kept for scarifying neuralgic patients. The snake was carried home in a sack and kept for treatments of patients. The fat of rattlers [...] is very potent in medicine paint, or ointments.

– John W. Hudson

Sucking doctors also used sets of pegs and miniature bows and arrows made from poison oak during curing sessions. The bows and arrows were painted with four red bands that signified the four cardinal directions. These were used to drive the disease or ailment towards the patient's feet, where four painted pegs were planted in the ground to dissipate the ailment as it passed from his feet. These paraphernalia were made new for each treatment and destroyed by the doctor's assistant at the end of the ceremony. Sucking doctors often wore headgear supported by hairnets (Barrett 1952).

Outfit Doctors

Outfit doctors accomplished their work through singing with the aid of rattles. They also utilized charms and other instruments in their work, such as feathers, minerals, snake heads, and bones. The rights and skills of outfit doctors were hereditary and demanded a great deal of time and effort on the part of the student in order to be mastered (Wilson and Hills 1968).

Bear Doctors

Important ceremonial figures in many parts of indigenous California (Barrett 1917b), bear doctors were believed to turn themselves into grizzly bears (*Ursus horribilis*). Bear doctor was a secret office among the Potter Valley Pomo, carrying the duty to punish offenses not otherwise addressed by legal sanctions, such as stealing, inhospitality, and wife or child abuse. The office was hereditary and sometimes passed to women. The only person who was said to know the identity of a bear doctor and the location of his mountain den was the village chief. A bear doctor's functions required cunning, strength, and decisive skill, as failure led to disgrace and death. According to

Loeb (1926), bear doctors were believed capable of miraculous behaviors and thought to use this power to kill, causing them to be subject to aggression by other community members.

Bear doctors wore tanned bearskins that completely covered the body except for the face, hands, and feet. According to Barrett (1917b), they also wore fine woven nets covered with shredded soaproot fiber, which completely covered the body and mask. Face masks were made from oak rods woven with open twining. They also could wear ceremonial rod armor similar to the kind used in warfare.

Spirituality

The supernatural essence of goodness (*xa*) was the primary spiritual medium among the Potter Valley Pomo. *Xa* manifested in a number of material substances, including mineral objects with a "sexual aspect," the down and guide feathers of predatory birds, such as hawks (order Falconiformes), owls (order Falconiformes and family Accipitridae), and eagles (*Aquila chrysaetos* or *Haliaeetus leucocephalus*), and the crests, beaks and tails of birds that dig out "preternatural foods," such as woodpeckers (*Melanerpes formicivorus* and *Dryocopus pileatus*), owls, and eagles. *Xa* also became

Xa, manifestations of the supernatural spirits (*tcă xa-lĭ*) left on earth from the beginnings and investing certain peculiar objects with supernatural attributes. [...] *Xa* is the genius of procreation, acquisition, alien to human activities (*xa co'-i*), but a spiritual concomity of men whose aid may be engaged through prayer and possession of its symbols (*xa-nu'*). *Xa* is summoned by sexual contact, is the mystery of conception and gestation, leaves its stamp on the buttocks of new born till erased by cognoscence; places an indelible mark on the skin of a favored mortal and absorbs the dead as it ascends to *xa-lĭ'* (supernatural regions). [...] *Xa* is the inspiration of song (*bĕn'-xa*), the rhythmic impulse of song-dance ceremonies, the buoyancy of regalia (*tăt' xa*) and the stimulus of fingers tapping upon the flute. It is the celestial, beneficent influence as opposed to the terrestrial demon of disaster, pain (*xa-ŏ'*) which ever attends the fortunes of man.

– John W. Hudson

apparent through omens, apparitions, and such abnormalities as albinism and other physical deformities.

The spiritual attributes of *xa* were also to be found in the aromatic juices of five highly esteemed plants: American trail plant (*Adenocaulon bicolor*), angelica, sweetcicely (*Osmorhiza* sp.), Fendler's meadowrue, and leather root. Hudson referred to these plants as "psychic" (*xa-nu'*). American trail plant was used to anoint gamblers for good luck and to purify

Xa-nu. A fetish, or charm-stone, believed of supernatural origin and attributes. A visible, tangible token from the procreative spirits (*Xa*) so planted in the path of a favored mortal that he may find it, treasure and invoke its succor in times of stress. Fetishes are of either sex. The potent, aggressive male (*tsa-xa*) of phallic shape and function, as the source of magical influence must be respectfully and intelligently directed by its human host, whether hunter, gambler or warrior. […] The passive female fetish (*xa-ne*) of vulvar aspect is latent till conjoined with a *tca-xa* and if mutually adapted the pair constitute a *xa-nu* of indominable cogency. The sagacity, skill or riches (*xal*) of man is attributed to his secret possession of well mated fetishes.

– John W. Hudson

a body in preparation for cremation. Angelica juice, expressed from the roots by chewing, was applied to the head and upper body to cleanse and remove odors. Four days after the birth of a child, mothers and fathers purified themselves and dispelled "earthly evils" with applications of angelica root juice. However, mothers avoided all of the psychic plants during the first few days after giving birth. Like American trailplant, angelica was also used to ceremonially purify dead bodies. Angelica was also ritually smoked to prevent snakebite, bring success in gambling and hunting, and to cure a variety of ailments. Sweetcicely was used similarly to bring luck in competitions and in hunting. An infusion of Fendler's meadowrue root was used as an ointment for pallbearers.

Ceremonialism

Ceremonial Accoutrements

Northern Pomo ceremonialism, as described by early ethnographers, involved a diverse set of accoutrements, many of which were specific to certain rites or varied according to context (Barrett 1917a; Kroeber 1907; Loeb 1931).

Men's dance headgear consisted of hairnets with milkweed forehead bands interwoven with clamshell disks and California quail crest feathers. Women's ceremonial dance headbands were also made from milkweed fiber with a strip of mink hide (*Mustela vison*) tied behind the head. These were ornamented with clamshell disks, each fixed with a projecting 5 cm oak rod wound with milkweed fiber dyed with alder bark. Pendants composed of flicker quill sections and quail crest feathers hung from the tip of each rod so that they vibrated with the dance rhythm. Bleached milkweed or dogbane fiber was used to craft weighty ceremonial belts that ranked among the most valuable of possessions among the Northern Pomo. These were tightly woven with six weft elements and about 10 warp elements, and decorated with clamshell disks and brightly colored bird feathers. According to Loeb (1926), such belts were often given by a groom's family to his bride's family.

Kuksu Rites and Ceremonies

Adolescent boys were tested in rites held at their "first signs of lust." Associated with the Kuksu (*kuk'su*) religion (Barrett 1917a; Curtis 1924; Loeb 1926), these rites involved seclusion for four days or more in the sweathouse, during which time the boys ate only acorn mush. Part of these rites included a ceremony called "man casting." During nighttime sweat ceremonies, men disguised as "devils" tested the boys' strength and endurance by throwing them into the air and catching them before they fell. The ceremonial role of these "devils" was hereditary and their primary purpose

The devils [...] are hideously dressed with top knots of feathers and their bodies painted with stripes. A broad stripe of red paint across the face covering mouth, nose and cheeks. Another stripe of blue clay covers the forehead. A ring of blue clay around the biceps and also below thee elbows. A ring of red paint above the elbows and around the wrists. These colors are repeated in the same way on the legs. A broad chevron reaches from each deltoid down to the umbilicus of blue clay. [They also wear a] broad red belt.

– John W. Hudson

was to perform these rites for adolescent boys. Upon occasion, a bad-tempered boy might be intentionally dropped so that he might suffer mild injury as a lesson. The devils carried ceremonial batons made from madrone wood and ornamented with eagle feathers affixed to the handle. Dancing around the candidates, they held the feather batons while singing and advising initiates to treat others well as adults. They thrust the batons in candidates' faces, reminding them that rudeness will bring an unfathomably treacherous future. At the conclusion of these rites, the boys were sent away to collect food, firewood, and clamshell disks to pay the devils for conducting the ceremony.

Some Kuksu ceremonies were held in assembly houses (also called roundhouses or ceremonial houses), large semisubterranean structures used for dancing and cult activities (Barrett 1916; W. H. Holmes 1902; Kroeber 1925). These earth-covered buildings were often from 12 to 18 m in diameter. Stewart (1943) reported there was just one assembly house in Potter Valley, located in the village of *Ca-nĕl'*. For Kuksu ceremonies, a tall wooden pole was raised in front of the assembly house (Barrett 1917a). Such poles were made from straight white fir and pine saplings some 15 cm in diameter and about 15 m in length, harvested from a crowded grove. To the narrow pole tips were attached two long ropes made of dogbane decorated with downy feathers from double-crested cormorant (*Phalacrocorax auritus*), geese, and gulls (*Larus* spp.). With the aid of people standing along its full length, the wide end of a ceremonial pole was set in a pit in the ground and it was lifted into vertical position. As it was raised, two "maids" (virgins) kept the feathered flags from touching the ground. When the pole was vertical, the flags hung to just above the ground. During the ceremony, a series of men, including native sucking doctors (*ma tu'*), climbed the pole in turn while onlookers pelted them with acorn meal, sweet cakes, and other edible delicacies (cf. Barrett 1952). The second night after being raised, the pole was secretly removed and hidden until the following year.

Sweathouses

Sweathouses (or men's houses), found in every Pomoan community, were semi-subterranean structures of smaller size but somewhat similar construction to assembly houses (Figure 43). They were usually about 4.5 to 6 m in diameter (cf. Kroeber 1925). According to most reports, the heat used for sweating on a daily basis came from fire, not from steam (Barrett 1952; Curtis 1924; Loeb 1926). Used daily, the lodge was the focal point of men's activities. Men are reported to have spent a great deal of time sleeping and gambling inside sweathouses (Barrett 1916; Loeb 1926). According to Hudson, herbal steam baths of California sagebrush and bush monkeyflower were also used to treat certain health conditions, such as colic.

Figure 43. Men's sweathouse, Yokayo Rancheria, 1897. Photograph by V. K. Chestnut. Original in the collections of Grace Hudson Museum, Ukiah.

Mythology

Plants figure prominently in several legends recorded by Hudson and Carpenter, being employed in diverse manners by mythological or legendary beings and, in some cases, being given by these beings to humanity. For example, in an unnamed legend Quail Woman and the mythical being *Ce ta ta* exchanged a series of royal gifts before their marriage. She gave *Ce ta ta* a clamshell disk belt and various baskets. He gave Quail Woman a dogbane headband, a necklace, and two milkweed blankets. The first blanket had four quail crest feather stripes and the second had four red woodpecker scalp feather stripes.

"Poma Genesis"

Throughout native California and among Pomoan peoples, Coyote was a mythological being responsible for human creation and other beneficial legendary events (Barrett 1906; Powers 1872). Differing in some respects from mythological Coyote beings in other native cultures in California and western North America (Mourning Dove 1990; Nabhan 2013), Coyote was for the Pomoan peoples a creative force and trickster. Exhibiting some of these attributes, the California valley coyote (*Canis latrans* ssp. *ochropus*) was considered by the Potter Valley Pomo to be a rare and sacred animal, but nevertheless of poor repute because it was foolish and forgetful.

In the legend Poma Genesis, Coyote (*Du-wi'*) attempted three times to create the first people from branches and mud before finally succeeding. In each attempt he began with a framework of ash forks, which he stuck into the ground. In the first unsuccessful attempt, he smeared blue clay over the forks in the shape of a bear. The next day he overslept and, finding his work ruined by the sun, urinated on it. Before his second unsuccessful attempt, he urinated twice on Coyote Cairn, located on the pass between Potter Valley and the Eel River, to the north. As he did so, he exclaimed, "Luck to one passing here." Since that moment, twin springs (*ka-be tcu'-tca ka*) have flowed down each side of the pass. Coyote then tried to create people a second time using white clay mixed with urine and sap from California wild grape and milkweed. He again overslept the next day and, finding his work again ruined by the sun, urinated on it. In the third unsuccessful attempt, Coyote tried a mixture of red clay, urine, and sap from California wild grape and milkweed. The following day he again overslept and, finding his work cracked and peeling by the sun, urinated on it. In the fourth attempt, Coyote used mud made from red earth (*ma-po'*). He plastered it on the forks, which also had the form of a bear, but with shorter arms and a thumb, and urinated on it. This time it began to move about. The next day, Coyote noticed that his creations were women and commented, "All I have to do is bore a few holes." Then, reconsidering, he collected tree limbs with emerging lateral branches, called *tsa* ("penis") in Northern Pomo. He trimmed the lateral branches suitable lengths, stating that "Such pegs won't come loose." He repeated the plastering process, this time fashioning the hands after the front feet of lizards. When he returned, the people were alive, huddling together in the corner of the sweathouse.

"La-moo and Ka-watth"

In the legend "*La-moo* and *Ka-watth*", Coyote pitted Gopher (*La-moo*) and Mole (*Ka-watth*) against each other in a race to build the largest mountain (H. M. Carpenter n.d.). At the end of the race, Coyote and the two contestants waited for seven days in a sweathouse on Mount San Hedrin, Mendocino County. While they waited, Coyote arranged 23 cm alder twigs, each with hawk wing feathers carefully tied to one end, side by side on the sweathouse floor. Gopher lost the race and was transformed into abundant acorns, buckeyes, and clovers (*Trifolium* spp.) to "feed the people for all time to come." Mole won the race and became a man. Coyote proclaimed him headman, saying "This […] is your country, here the acorn and buckeye shall flourish, here shall grow luxuriant clover, for your future use […]."

7. Final Remarks

The culturally and demographically transformative injustices suffered by the Pomoan community from Potter Valley in the decades leading up to John Hudson's anthropological study continued after his death. Some eighty years after being dislocated from Potter Valley by non-indigenous settlers, they were again removed from traditional lands by the 1958 Rancheria Act, which revoked federal recognition of Pomoan rights to most of their remaining small parcels of land. Descendants of the Potter Valley Pomo and members of the Pomoan communities at Pinoleville, Guidiville, and Redwood Valley were again compulsorily removed from their homes and forced to seek refuge elsewhere.

Termination of the Potter Valley Rancheria also resulted in cancellation of the tribe's federal status. All the land that remained for them were the original four hectares they purchased with private funds in 1892 (Potter Valley Tribe 2010), now located amidst the valley's residences and farms. Regaining its tribal status in the 1993, the Potter Valley Tribe has recently sought to obtain additional lands in Potter Valley and their other former territories. They acquired parcels in Redwood Valley in 2003, Ukiah in 2005, Potter Valley in 2006 (Figure 44),

Figure 44. Agricultural project on land purchased in 2006 by the Potter Valley Tribe, Potter Valley, 2011. Photograph by James R. Welch.

Fort Bragg in 2009, and along the Eel River in 2012 (Potter Valley Tribe 2011; Ukiah Daily Journal Staff 2012). Although the Potter Valley Tribe is now small, serving a population of 31 people in 2013, it seeks to increase its associations with other tribes and stimulate youth education of their native culture and environment through the recuperation and stewardship of these traditional Potter Valley Pomo lands.

Also having endured the revocation of their land rights and tribal status following the Rancheria Act, the Pinoleville community, which includes many descendants of the Potter Valley Pomo, reorganized in 2006 as the Pinoleville Tribe. Although this group retained the Pinoleville Indian Reservation, a portion of its original land near Ukiah, the tribe now pursues full rights to their revoked traditional lands (The Pinoleville Tribe 2011). Accompanying this effort, the Pinoleville Native Plants Project planted a native plant reserve and organized the ethnobotanical guide *Native Plants Used by Native Pomos* to promote the preservation of plants and plant knowledge of importance to Pomoan peoples (Pinoleville Native Plants Project 2004; The Pinoleville Tribe 2003).

These ongoing initiatives by descendants of the Potter Valley Pomo and neighboring Pomoan communities illustrate the challenges involved in conserving cultural ecological knowledge and retaining access to traditional landscape resources in the present era. They also highlight that the dynamic ethnobotanical tradition Hudson documented continues today. As the Potter Valley, Pinoleville, and other local Pomoan tribes invest in ethnobotanical conservation and ecological restoration projects, the value of Hudson's historical research gains new applied value and, potentially, renewed appreciation by members of Pomoan communities and the general public. The relevance of his research remains largely unexplored due to the previous inaccessibility of his plant data. Nevertheless, its enormous contemporary potential is evident in some of his most significant contributions, including his robust data sets regarding local plants used for food, medicine, and artistry.

For example, my reconstructed Potter Valley Pomo ethnobotany includes 42 taxa used in Potter Valley Pomo basketry, which is substantial considering that just 29 taxa are recorded elsewhere for all Pomoan groups, including the communities that spoke Northern Pomo (Moerman 1998, 2011). Pomoan basketry is famous for its technical and aesthetic excellence, being among the most sought after and highly valued indigenous art traditions worldwide from Hudson's era to the present (Abel-Vidor et al. 1996; Bibby 1996; Cohodas 1997). The cultural and artistic values evident in Pomoan basketry makers' ongoing craft suggest that Hudson's ethnobotanical data related to basketry fibers, dyes, and treatments may have immediate value to specialists.

Some of the ambiguities and omissions resulting from Hudson's amateur research methods and abbreviated documentary style suggest potentially productive lines of inquiry for future research. For example, Hudson recorded extensive information about the Pomoan practice of removing tannins from acorns using local deposits of red earth (**ma-po'**), excavated from shallow pits high on the ridges surrounding Potter Valley. Similar geophagical practices have been documented elsewhere in the world (Johns and Duquette 1991a, b), but scant information is available about this practice among native peoples in California (cf. Barrett 1952; Chestnut 1902; Hudson 1900a). Specifically, the locations and specific geological characteristics of this resource remain unknown, as do its potential dietary implications and potentials.

Another subset of Hudson's data with notable potential for contemporary research is his Northern Pomo linguistic data for native and introduced California plants. Although linguists studied Northern Pomo vocabulary and grammar in recent decades (O'Connor 1990, 1992; Oswalt 1964), only a few living individuals now passively speak Northern Pomo. Thus, Hudson's linguistic data, which cover numerous plant taxa undocumented elsewhere, have great potential for biolinguistic research into the early relationship between Pomoan peoples and the Northern California landscape.

The contemporary relevance of Hudson's ethnobotanical study is not limited to its specific artistic or scholarly applications. Today Potter Valley is largely residential and agricultural, with many vineyards, pear orchards, and cattle farms (Figure 45). The local community participates in timely debates about natural resource management in and around the valley, especially with regard to watershed resource management (CEED 2002; Potter Valley Ir-

Figure 45. Potter Valley, California, 2011. Photograph by James R. Welch.

rigation District 2011; Regional Water Quality Control Board 2005; Yoshiyama and Moyle 2010). With their focus on environmental issues at local and regional scales, these discussions benefit from data on the cultural values of landscape resources. The value of Pomoan ethnobotanical knowledge for cultural resource conservation in areas threatened by development activities was demonstrated by pioneering studies coordinated by David W. Peri in the 1980s (Peri and Patterson 1979; Peri et al. 1980; Peri et al. 1982; Peri et al. 1985a; Peri et al. 1983, 1985b; Theodoratus et al. 1975). With similar potential for informing environmental controversies in Potter Valley and elsewhere, Hudson's data on indigenous landscape management, foodways, ethnomedicine, and cultural practices remain extremely relevant more than a century after they were collected.

Afterword

As I grew up in the Ukiah-Potter Valley area, it was hard to keep in touch with the native ways of my ancestors. Pomo tribes in Mendocino County had long been broken up and their members scattered. Some adapted to the rapidly changing world of northern California; others were left to live in poverty on reservations, or worse. I was mostly concerned with developing my own life, avoiding the many pitfalls of native life in the area, making a living, starting a family.

It was only after I was given the task of reviving the government and spirit of the Potter Valley Tribe that I began to look earnestly at the importance of natural resources, their importance to us, and our responsibility to them. Our ancestors had lived for thousands of years in many villages in the Potter Valley area; by the time I was a youth we had declined in members to a few and in our land base to a 10-acre piece purchased in 1892 by 14 Indians—including my grandmother and other relatives. As our tribe began the uphill climb of gaining federal recognition to increasing our land base, the importance of the earth and our resources was always there. I began to see that future generations might never develop the love for hunting, food gathering and being outdoors in natural settings.

We are now in the information age with data and bits of history whizzing through our lives. Are we leaving knowledge behind? We forget the knowledge of where food and shelter comes from, how important the earth is as our home, and the practices of the past. This is the role of books such as *Sprouting Valley*, keeping the traditional use of plants and our living resources alive, and telling our stories in scientific terms, for all those who want both information and knowledge. We have used this publication in the scientific, political and educational realms; environmental reviews, cultural resource studies, justification for land acquisition, and in our attempts to keep such knowledge available for our youth. As our task of reviving traditional ecological knowledge proceeds, we should not forget to thank those who tell the stories and those who chronicle the past.

Salvador Rosales, Chairperson
Potter Valley Tribe
Ukiah, California
April 9, 2013

References Cited

Abbott, Isabella A., and George J. Hollenberg. 1976   *Marine Algae of California*. Stanford University Press, Stanford.

Abel-Vidor, Suzanne, Dot Brovarney, and Susan Billy. 1996   *Remember Your Relations: The Elsie Allen Baskets, Family, and Friends*. Heyday Books, Ukiah, CA.

Abrams, LeRoy, and Roxana Ferris. 1960   *Illustrated Flora of the Pacific States*, Vol. 4. Stanford University Press, Stanford.

Aginsky, Bernard W. 1939   Population Control in the Shanel (Pomo) Tribe. *American Sociological Review* 4(2):209–216.

Aginsky, Bernard W., and Ethel G. Aginsky. 1950   The Pomo: A Profile of Gambling Among the Indians. *Annals of the American Academy of Political and Social Science* 269:108–113.

Allen-Diaz, Barbara, Richard Standiford, and Randall D. Jackson. 2007   Oak Woodlands and Forests. In *Terrestrial Vegetation of California*, eds. Michael G. Barbour, Todd Keeler-Wolf, and Allan A. Schoenherr, pp. 313–338. University of California Press, Berkeley.

Allen, Elsie, and Vinson Brown. 1972   *Pomo Basketmaking: A Supreme Art for the Weaver*. Naturegraph, Healdsburg, CA.

Anderson, M. Kat. 1993   Native Californians as Ancient and Contemporary Cultivators. In *Before the Wilderness: Environmental Management by Native Californians*, eds. Thomas C. Blackburn and M. Kat Anderson, pp. 151–174. Ballena Press, Menlo Park, CA.

Anderson, M. Kat. 1999   The Fire, Pruning, and Coppice Management of Temperate Ecosystems for Basketry Material by California Indian Tribes. *Human Ecology* 27(1):79–113.

Anderson, M. Kat. 2002   An Ecological Critique. In *Forgotten Fires: Native Americans and the Transient Wilderness*, eds. Omer Call Stewart, Henry T. Lewis, and M. Kat Anderson, pp. 37–64. University of Oklahoma Press, Norman.

Anderson, M. Kat. 2005   *Tending the Wild: Native American Knowledge and the Management of California's Natural Resources*. University of California Press, Berkeley.

Arora, David. 1986   *Mushrooms Demystified: A Comprehensive Guide to the Fleshy Fungi*. Ten Speed Press, Berkeley.

Baird, Joseph A. 1962   *Grace Carpenter Hudson (1865–1937): Oil Paintings and Sketches, Including Works on Loan from C. Frederick Faude*. California Historical Society, San Francisco.

Baldwin, Bruce G., Douglas H. Goldman, David J. Keil, Robert Patterson, and Thomas J. Rosatti, eds. 2012   *The Jepson Manual: Vascular Plants of California*, second edition. University of California Press, Berkeley.

Barbour, Michael G., and Richard A. Minnich. 2000   California Upland Forests and Wood-lands. In *North American Terrestrial Vegetation*, eds. Michael G. Barbour and William D. Billings, pp. 161–202. Cambridge University Press, Cambridge.

Barrett, Samuel Alfred. 1905   Basket Designs of the Pomo Indians. *American Anthropologist, New Series* 7(4):648–653.

Barrett, Samuel Alfred. 1906   A Composite Myth of the Pomo Indians. *Journal of American Folklore* 19(72):37–51.

Barrett, Samuel Alfred. 1908a   *The Ethno-Geography of the Pomo and Neighboring Indians.* University of California Publications in American Archaeology and Ethnology, Vol. 6, No. 1. University of California Press, Berkeley.

Barrett, Samuel Alfred. 1908b   *Pomo Indian Basketry.* University of California Publications in American Archaeology and Ethnology, Vol. 7, No. 3. University of California Press, Berkeley.

Barrett, Samuel Alfred. 1916   Pomo Buildings. In *Holmes Anniversary Volume: Anthropological Essays Presented to William Henry Holmes in Honor of his 70th Birthday*, pp. 1–17. J. W. Bryan Press, Washington, DC.

Barrett, Samuel Alfred. 1917a   *Ceremonies of the Pomo Indians.* University of California Publications in American Archaeology and Ethnology, Vol. 12, No. 10. University of California Press, Berkeley.

Barrett, Samuel Alfred. 1917b   *Pomo Bear Doctors.* University of California Publications in American Archaeology and Ethnology, Vol. 12, No. 11. University of California Press, Berkeley.

Barrett, Samuel Alfred. 1936   The Army Worm: A Food of the Pomo Indians. In *Essays in Anthropology in Honor of Alfred Louis Kroeber*, pp. 1–5. University of California Press, Berkeley.

Barrett, Samuel Alfred. 1952   *Material Aspects of Pomo Culture.* Bulletin of the Public Museum of the City of Milwaukee, Vol. 20, Parts I–II. Public Museum of the City of Milwaukee, Milwaukee.

Barrows, David Prescott. 1900   *The Ethno-botany of the Coahuilla Indians of Southern California.* The University of Chicago Press, Chicago.

Bauer Jr., William J. 2009   *We Were All Like Migrant Workers Here: Work, Community, and Memory on California's Round Valley Reservation, 1850–1941.* University of North Carolina Press, Chapel Hill.

Bean, Lowell John, and Harry W. Lawton. 1993   Some Explanations for the Rise of Cultural Complexity in Native California with Comments on Proto-Agriculture and Agriculture. In *Before the Wilderness: Environmental Management by Native Californians*, eds. Thomas C. Blackburn and M. Kat Anderson, pp. 1–47. Ballena Press, Menlo Park, CA.

Bean, Lowell John, and Dorothea Theodoratus. 1978 Western Pomo and Northeastern Pomo. In *Handbook of the North American Indians*, Vol. 8: California, ed. Robert F. Heizer, pp. 289–305. Smithsonian Institution, Washington, DC.

Bendix, Jacob. 2002 Pre-European Fire in California Chaparral. In *Fire, Native Peoples, and the Natural Landscape*, ed. Thomas R. Vale, pp. 269–293. Island Press, Washington, DC.

Bennyhoff, James A. 1950 *California Fish Spears and Harpoons.* University of California Anthropological Records, Vol. 9, No. 4. University of California Press, Berkeley.

Benson, Todd. 1991 The Consequences of Reservation Life: Native Californians on the Round Valley Reservation, 1871–1884. *Pacific Historical Review* 60(2):221–244.

Benson, William. 1981 The Stone and Kelsey Massacre. In *The Way We Lived: California Indian Stories, Songs, and Reminiscences*, ed. Malcolm Margolin, pp. 166–173. Heyday Books, Berkeley.

Berlin, Brent. 1992 *Ethnobiological Classification: Principles of Categorization of Plants and Animals in Traditional Societies.* Princeton University Press, Princeton.

Best, Catherine. 1996 *A Flora of Sonoma County: Manual of the Flowering Plants and Ferns of Sonoma County, California.* California Native Plant Society, Sacramento.

Bibby, Brian. 1996 *The Fine Art of California Indian Basketry.* Heyday Books, Berkeley.

Bocek, Barbara R. 1984 Ethnobotany of Costanoan Indians, California, Based on Collections by John P. Harrington. *Economic Botany* 38(2):240–255.

Boynton, Searles R. 1989 *The Painter Lady: Grace Carpenter Hudson.* Sun House Guild, Ukiah, CA.

Calflora. 2012 Calflora: Information on California Plants for Education, Research and Conservation. The Calflora Database, a non-profit organization, Berkeley. Available at: http://www.calflora.org (verified 30 July 2012).

California Indian Assistance Program. 1994 *Field Directory of the California Indian Community.* Department of Housing and Community Development, State of California, Sacramento.

Carpenter, Aurelius O., and Percy H. Millberry. 1914 *History of Mendocino and Lake Counties, California.* Historic Record Company, Los Angeles.

Carpenter, Helen M. 1893a Among the Diggers of Thirty Years Ago, Part I. *The Overland Monthly* 21(122):146–155.

Carpenter, Helen M. 1893b Among the Diggers of Thirty Years Ago, Part II. *The Overland Monthly* 21(124):389–399.

Carpenter, Helen M. 1899 Frontier Facts. *The Overland Monthly* 34(200):150–151.

Carpenter, Helen M. n.d. *Be-Lo-Ki.* Unpublished manuscript, located in the collections of the Grace Hudson Museum, Ukiah, CA.

CEED (The Center for Environmental Economic Development). 2002   A River in the Balance: Benefits and Costs of Restoring Natural Water Flows to the Eel River. Friends of the Eel River, Redway, CA.

Chestnut, Victor King. 1902   *Plants Used by the Indians of Mendocino County, California.* Contributions from the U.S. National Herbarium, Vol. 7. Government Printing Office, Washington, DC.

Clifford, James. 1983   On Ethnographic Authority. *Representations* 2:118–146.

Cohodas, Marvin. 1997   *Basket Weavers for the California Curio Trade.* University of Arizona Press and the Southwest Museum, Tuscon.

Colson, Elizabeth. 1974   *Autobiographies of Three Pomo Women.* Archaeological Research Facility, University of California, Berkeley.

Conn, Steven. 2004   *History's Shadow: Native Americans and Historical Consciousness in the Nineteenth Century.* University of Chicago Press, Chicago.

Cook, Sherburne Friend. 1939   Smallpox in Spanish and Mexican California, 1770–1845. *Bulletin of the History of Medicine* 12:182–187.

Cook, Sherburne Friend. 1956   *The Aboriginal Population of the North Coast of California.* University of California Anthropological Records, Vol. 16, No. 3. University of California Press, Berkeley.

Coville, Frederick V. 1897   The Technical Name of the Camas Plant. *Proceedings of the Biological Society of Washington* 11:61–65.

Crawford, Elizabeth M. 2000   *The Writer Lady: Helen Carpenter and the Pomos of Be-Lo-Ki.* Visual Identity, Ukiah, CA.

Culin, Stewart. 1975   *Games of the North American Indians.* Dover, New York.

Curtis, Edward S. 1924   *The North American Indian,* Vol. 14: The Kato, the Wailaki, the Yuki, the Pomo, the Wintun, the Maidu, the Miwok, the Yokuts. E. S. Curtis, Seattle.

Davis, E. Wade. 1995   Ethnobotany: An Old Practice, a New Discipline. In *Ethnobotany: Evolution of a Discipline,* eds. Richard E. Schultes and Siri von Reis, pp. 40–51. Dioscorides Press, Portland, OR.

Dixon, Roland B., and Alfred L. Kroeber. 1903   The Native Languages of California. *American Anthropologist, New Series* 5(1):1–26.

Dixon, Roland B., and Alfred L. Kroeber. 1919   *Linguistic Families of California.* University of California Publications in American Archaeology and Ethnology, Vol. 16, No. 3. University of California Press, Berkeley.

Dorsey, George A. 1901   Recent Progress in Anthropology at the Field Columbian Museum. *American Anthropologist, New Series* 3(4):737–750.

Eames, Ninetta. 1897   The California Indian on Canvas. *Frank Leslie's Popular Monthly* 43:380–387.

Eversole, Barbara. 1979   National Register of Historic Places Inventory-Nomination Form: The Sun House and Hudson-Carpenter Park. Sun House Guild, Report No. 5482-0001-0000, Ukiah, CA.

Fernald, Merritt Lyndon. 1900   The Representatives of *Scirpus maritimus* in America. *Rhodora* 2(24):239–241.

Forbes, Jack D. 1969   *Native Americans of California and Nevada*. Naturegraph, Healdsburg, CA.

Fowler, Cynthia, and Dana Lepofsky. 2011   Traditional Resource and Environmental Management. In *Ethnobiology*, eds. E. N. Anderson, Deborah Pearsall, Eugene Hunn, and Nancy J. Turner, pp. 285–304. Wiley-Blackwell, Hoboken, NJ.

Freeland, Lucy Shepard. 1923   *Pomo Doctors and Poisoners*. University of California Publications in American Archaeology and Ethnology, Vol. 20, No. 4. University of California Press, Berkeley.

Gifford, Edward Winslow. 1923   *Pomo Lands on Clear Lake*. University of California Publications in American Archaeology and Ethnology, Vol. 20, No. 5. University of California Press, Berkeley.

Gifford, Edward Winslow. 1926   *Clear Lake Pomo Society*. University of California Publications in American Archaeology and Ethnology, Vol. 18, No. 2. University of California Press, Berkeley.

Gifford, Edward Winslow. 1936   Californian Balanophagy. In *Essays in Anthropology Presented to A. L. Kroeber in Celebration of his Sixtieth Birthday, June 11, 1936*, ed. Robert H. Lowie, pp. 87–98. University of California Press, Berkeley.

Gifford, Edward Winslow. 1967   *Ethnographic Notes on the Southwestern Pomo*. University of California Anthropological Records, Vol. 25. University of California Press, Berkeley.

Gifford, Edward Winslow, and Alfred L. Kroeber. 1937   *Culture Element Distributions: IV Pomo*. University of California Publications in American Archaeology and Ethnology, Vol. 37, No. 4. University of California Press, Berkeley.

Goodrich, Jennie, Claudia Lawson, and Vana Parrish Lawson. 1996   *Kashaya Pomo Plants*. Heyday Books, Berkeley.

Gruber, Jacob W. 1970   Ethnographic Salvage and the Shaping of Anthropology. *American Anthropologist* 72:1289–1299.

Halpern, Abraham M. 1964   A Report on a Survey of Pomo Languages. In *Studies in California Linguistics*, ed. William Bright, pp. 88–93. University of California Press, Los Angeles.

Hawksworth, Frank G., and Robert F. Scharpf. 2007   Spread of European Mistletoe (*Viscum album*) in California, U.S.A. *European Journal of Forest Pathology* 16(1):1–5.

Heizer, Robert Fleming. 1973   *Collected Documents on the Causes and Events in the Bloody Island Massacre of 1850*. Publications of the University of California Archaeological

Research Facility, Vol. 10. Archaeological Research Facility, University of California, Berkeley.

Hickman, James C., ed. 1993   *The Jepson Manual: Higher Plants of California*. University of California Press, Berkeley.

Hitchcock, Charles Leo, Arthur Cronquist, Marion Ownbey, and J. W. Thompson. 1959   *Vascular Plants of the Pacific Northwest, Part 4: Ericaceae through Campanulaceae*. University of Washington Press, Seattle.

Holmes, Karen. 2006   Crossing Boundaries: The Life and Times of A. O. Carpenter. In *Aurelius O. Carpenter: Photographer of the Mendocino Frontier*, eds. Marvin A. Schenck, Karen Holmes, and Sherrie Ann Smith-Ferri, pp. 13–32. Grace Hudson Museum and Sun House, Ukiah, CA.

Holmes, William Henry. 1902   *Anthropological Studies in California*. Annual Report of the Smithsonian Institution Board of Regents for 1900, pp. 155–196. Government Printing Office, Washington, DC.

Hrusa, Fred and Calflora. 2001   California Plant Synonyms (XWALK). The Calflora Database, a non-profit organization, Berkeley. Available at: http://www.calflora.org/xwalk/index.html (verified 29 July 2012).

Hudson, John W. 1893   Pomo Basket Makers. *The Overland Monthly* 21(126):561–578.

Hudson, John W. 1897   Pomo Wampum Makers. *The Overland Monthly* 30(176):101–108.

Hudson, John W. 1900a   Preparation of Acorn Meal by Pomo Indians. *American Anthropologist, New Series* 2:775–776.

Hudson, John W. 1900b   A So-called Aboriginal Tool. *American Anthropologist, New Series* 2:782.

ICE MAPS (Interactive California Environmental Management, Assessment, and Planning System). 1997   California Vegetation: Mendocino County. California Natural Resources Agency, Sacramento. Available at: http://ceres.ca.gov (verified 20 January 2012).

IPNI (International Plant Names Index). 2012   The International Plant Names Index. Available at: http://www.ipni.org (verified 29 July 2012).

James, George W. 1901   *Indian Basketry and How to Make Indian and Other Baskets*, third edition. Henry Malkan, Los Angeles.

Jepson Flora Project. 2012a   Jepson eFlora. The Jepson Herbarium, Berkeley. Available at: http://ucjeps.berkeley.edu/IJM.html (verified 29 July 2012).

Jepson Flora Project. 2012b   The Jepson Online Interchange: California Floristics. The Jepson Herbarium, Berkeley. Available at: http://ucjeps.berkeley.edu/interchange (verified 29 July 2012).

Jepson, Willis Linn. 1909   *A Flora of California*, Vol. 1. Cunningham, Curtis & Welch, San Francisco.

Jepson, Willis Linn. 1925   *A Manual of the Flowering Plants of California*. University of California Press, Berkeley.

Jepson, Willis Linn. 1936   *A Flora of California*, Vol. 2. University of California Press, Berkeley.

Johns, Timothy, and Martin Duquette. 1991a   Detoxification and Mineral Supplementation as Functions of Geophagy. *American Journal of Clinical Nutrition* 53:448–456.

Johns, Timothy, and Martin Duquette. 1991b   Traditional Detoxification of Acorn Bread with Clay. *Ecology of Food and Nutrition* 25:221–228.

Kaplan, Victoria D. 1977   A Biographical Sketch of John Wilz Napier Hudson and Grace Carpenter Hudson. In *The Hudson-Carpenter Estate and Its Collection*, ed. David W. Peri, pp. 41–55. Ukiah City Council, Ukiah, CA.

Kasch, Charlie. 1947   The Yokayo Rancheria. *California Historical Society Quarterly* 26:209–215.

Kniffen, Fred B. 1939   *Pomo Geography*. University of California Publications in American Archaeology and Ethnology, Vol. 36, No. 6. University of California Press, Berkeley.

Kroeber, Alfred L. 1907   *The Religion of the Indians of California*. University of California Publications in American Archaeology and Ethnology, Vol. 4, No. 6. University of California Press, Berkeley.

Kroeber, Alfred L. 1909   California Basketry and the Pomo. *American Anthropologist, New Series* 11(2):233–249.

Kroeber, Alfred L. 1911   *The Languages of the Coast of California North of San Francisco*. University of California Publications in American Archaeology and Ethnology, Vol. 9, No. 3. University of California Press, Berkeley.

Kroeber, Alfred L. 1922   *Elements of Culture in Native California*. University of California Publications in American Archaeology and Ethnology, Vol. 13, No. 8. University of California Press, Berkeley.

Kroeber, Alfred L. 1925   *Handbook of the Indians of California*. Smithsonian Institution, Bureau of Ethnology, Vol. 78. Government Printing Office, Washington, DC.

Kroeber, Alfred L., and Samuel Alfred Barrett. 1962   Acorns: Staple Food of California Indians. University of California, Berkeley. 28 minute film.

Kuhnlein, Harriet V., and Nancy J. Turner. 1986   Cow-parsnip (*Heracleum lanatum* Michx.): An Indigenous Vegetable of Native People of Northwestern North America. *Journal of Ethnobiology* 6(2):309–324.

Lanson, Lucienne T., and Patricia L. Tetzlaff. 2006   *Grace Hudson, Artist of the Pomo Indians: A Biography*. Donning Company, Virginia Beach, VA.

Lewis, Henry T. 1973. *Patterns of Indian Burning in California: Ecology and Ethnohistory*. Ballena Press, Ramona, CA.

Lewis, Henry T. 2002   An Anthropological Critique. In *Forgotten Fires: Native Americans and the Transient Wilderness*, eds. Omer Call Stewart, Henry T. Lewis, and M. Kat Anderson, pp. 17–36. University of Oklahoma Press, Norman.

Lewis, Henry T., and Theresa A. Ferguson. 1999   Yards, Corridors, and Mosaics: How to Burn a Boreal Forest. In *Indians, Fire, and the Land: In the Pacific Northwest*, ed. Robert Boyd, pp. 164–184. Oregon State University Press, Corvallis.

Loeb, Edwin M. 1926   *Pomo Folkways*. University of California Publications in American Archaeology and Ethnology, Vol. 19, No. 2. University of California Press, Berkeley.

Loeb, Edwin M. 1931   The Religious Organizations of North Central California and Tierra Del Fuego. *American Anthropologist* 33(4):517–556.

Lum, Kwei-Lin. 1975   Gross Patterns of Vascular Plant Species Diversity in California. Master's Thesis (Ecology), University of California, Davis.

Mabberley, David J. 1987   *The Plant Book: A Portable Dictionary of the Higher Plants*. Cambridge University Press, Cambridge.

Mason, Otis Tufton. 1900   The Hudson Collection of Basketry. *American Anthropologist, New Series* 2(2):346–353.

Mason, Otis Tufton. 1902   *Aboriginal American Harpoons: A Study of Ethnic Distribution and Invention*. Government Printing Office, Washington, DC.

Mason, Otis Tufton. 1904   *Aboriginal American Basketry: Studies in a Textile Art without Machinery*. Government Printing Office, Washington, DC.

McCarthy, Helen. 1986   Salt Pomo: An Ethnogeography. *Journal of California and Great Basin Anthropology* 8(1):24–36.

McCarthy, Helen. 1993   Managing Oaks and the Acorn Crop. In *Before the Wilderness: Environmental Management by Native Californians*, eds. Thomas C. Blackburn and M. Kat Anderson, pp. 213–228. Ballena Press, Menlo Park, CA.

McLendon, Sally. 1973   *Proto Pomo*. University of California Publications in Linguistics, Vol. 71. University of California Press, Berkeley.

McLendon, Sally. 1993   Collecting Pomoan Baskets, 1889–1939. *Museum Anthropology* 17(2):49–60.

McLendon, Sally, and Robert L. Oswalt. 1978   Pomo: Introduction. In *Handbook of the North American Indians*, Vol. 8: California, ed. Robert F. Heizer, pp. 274–288. Smithsonian Institution, Washington, DC.

McMurray, Susan R., and Elizabeth A. Tharp. 1977   The Hudson-Carpenter Collection of Manuscripts. In *The Hudson-Carpenter Estate and Its Collection*, ed. David W. Peri, pp. 148–192. Ukiah City Council, Ukiah, CA.

Merrill, Ruth E. 1923   *Plants Used in Basketry by the California Indians*. University of California Publications in American Archaeology and Ethnology, Vol. 20, No. 13. University of California Press, Berkeley.

Moerman, Daniel E. 1998   *Native American Ethnobotany*. Timber Press, Portland, OR.

Moerman, Daniel E. 2010   *Native American Food Plants: An Ethnobotanical Dictionary*. Timber Press, Portland, OR.

Moerman, Daniel E. 2011   Native American Ethnobotany: A Database of Foods, Drugs, Dyes and Fibers of Native American Peoples, Derived from Plants. University of Michigan, Dearborn, MI. Available at: http://herb.umd.umich.edu (verified 3 December 2011).

Mourning Dove. 1990   *Coyote Stories*. Bison Books, Winnipeg, MB.

Munz, Philip A., and David D. Keck. 1973   *A California Flora with Supplement*. University of California Press, Berkeley.

Nabhan, Gary Paul. 2013   The Wild, the Domesticated, and the Coyote-Tainted: The Trickster and the Tricked in Hunter-Gatherer versus Farmer Folklore. In *Explorations in Ethnobiology: The Legacy of Amadeo Rea*, eds. Marsha Quinlan and Dana Lepofsky, pp. 129–140. Society of Ethnobiology, Denton, TX.

Newmaster, Steven G., Ragupathy Subramanyam, Rebecca F. Ivanoff, and Nirmala C. Balasubramaniam. 2006   Mechanisms of Ethnobiological Classifications. *Ethnobotany* 18:4–26.

Nuttall, Thomas. 1842   *The North American Sylva*, Vol. 1. J. Dobson, Philadelphia.

O'Connor, Mary Catherine. 1990   Third-person Reference in Northern Pomo Conversation: The Indexing of Discourse Genre and Social Relations. *International Journal of American Linguistics* 56(3):377–409.

O'Connor, Mary Catherine. 1992   *Topics in Northern Pomo Grammar*. Garland Press, New York.

Ortiz, Beverly R. 1993   Contemporary California Indian Basketweavers and the Environment. In *Before the Wilderness: Environmental Management by Native Californians*, eds. Thomas C. Blackburn and M. Kat Anderson, pp. 195–212. Ballena Press, Menlo Park, CA.

Oswalt, Robert Louis. 1964   The Internal Relationships of the Pomo Family of Languages. In *Actas y Memorias del XXXV Congreso Internacional de Americanistas, Mexico*, Vol. 2, pp. 413–427.

Palmer, Lyman L. 1880   *History of Mendocino County, California, Comprising its Geography, Geology, Topography, Climatography, Springs and Timber*. Alley, Bowen and Company, San Francisco.

Peri, David W. 1985   Pomoan Plant Resource Management. *Ridge Review* 4(4):5–9.

Peri, David W., and Scott M. Patterson. 1976   The Basket is in the Roots, That's Where It Begins. *Journal of California Anthropology* 3(2):17–32.

Peri, David W., and Scott M. Patterson. 1979   Ethnobotanical Resources of the Warm Springs Dam: Lake Sonoma Project Area, Sonoma County, California. U.S. Army Corps of Engineers, Report No. DACW07-78-C-0040, San Francisco.

Peri, David W., Scott M. Patterson, and Jennie Goodrich. 1980   History of the Transplanting of Sedge, Angelica and Lomatium, Warm Springs Dam, Lake Sonoma Project. Elgar Hill, Environmental Planning and Analysis, Sausalito, CA.

Peri, David W., Scott M. Patterson, Jennie Goodrich, Elgar Hill, and Richard N. Lerner. 1982 Ethnobotanical Mitigation, Warm Springs Dam-Lake Sonoma, California. U.S. Army Corps of Engineers, San Francisco.

Peri, David W., Scott M. Patterson, and Susan L. McMurray. 1985a The Makahmo Pomo: An Ethnographic Survey of the Cloverdale (Makahmo) Pomo. U.S. Army Corps of Engineers, San Francisco.

Peri, David W., Scott M. Patterson, Shirley Silver, and Richard N. Lerner. 1983 The Dry Creek Pomo. U.S. Army Corps of Engineers, San Francisco.

Peri, David W., Scott M. Patterson, Shirley Silver, and Richard N. Lerner. 1985b Mihilakawna Pomo of Dry Creek. U.S. Army Corps of Engineers, San Francisco.

Pinoleville Native Plants Project. 2004 *Native Plants Used by Native Pomos.* Pinoleville Indian Reservation, Ukiah, CA.

Plover, Nora N. 1934 Grace Hudson: Artist and Hostess, a Personality Portrait. *Redwood Empire Women* 11(2):11–13.

Pope, Saxton T. 1923 *A Study of Bows and Arrows.* University of California Publications in American Archaeology and Ethnology, Vol. 13, No. 9. University of California Press, Berkeley.

Potter Valley Irrigation District. 2011 Land Stewardship Proposal for Eel River Watershed. Potter Valley Irrigation District, Potter Valley.

Potter Valley Tribe. 2010 Environmental Assessment of Tribal Lands. Tribal Environmental Office, Potter Valley Tribe, Ukiah, CA.

Potter Valley Tribe. 2011 Land Stewardship Plan for the PG&E Stewardship Council, Eel River Planning Unit, Mendocino County, California. Tribal Environmental Office, Potter Valley Tribe, Ukiah, CA.

Powell, John Wesley. 1880 *Introduction to the Study of Indian Languages, with Words Phrases and Sentences to be Collected.* Government Printing Office, Washington, DC.

Powers, Stephen. 1872 The Northern California Indians, No. VI: The Pomo and Cahto. *The Overland Monthly* 9(6):498–507.

Powers, Stephen. 1875 Aboriginal Botany. *Proceedings, California Academy of Sciences* 5:373–379.

Powers, Stephen. 1877 *The Tribes of California.* Contributions to North American Ethnology, Vol. 3. Government Printing Office, Washington, DC.

Purdy, Carl. 1902 *Pomo Indian Baskets and their Makers.* C. M. Davis Company, Los Angeles.

Regional Water Quality Control Board. 2005 Watershed Planning Chapter. Regional Water Quality Control Board, North Coast Region, Santa Rosa, CA.

Robbins, Wilfred W., John P. Harrington, and Barbara Freire-Marreco. 1916 *Ethnobotany of the Tewa Indians.* Government Printing Office, Washington, DC.

Sarris, Greg. 1994 *Mabel McKay: Weaving the Dream.* University of California Press, Berkeley.

Schneider, Khal. 2010   Making Indian Land in the Allotment Era: Northern California's Indian Rancherias. *The Western Historical Quarterly* 41(4):429–450.

Sentinel Archaeological Research. 2007   Potter Valley Tribe of Pomo Indians: A Cultural and Historical Overview. Potter Valley Tribe, Ukiah, CA.

Shelton, Delight Corbett. 1986   *From Acorns to Oaks: A Potter Valley History, 1855 to 1985.* Delight Corbett Shelton, Potter Valley, CA.

Smith-Ferri, Sherrie Ann. 1998   Weaving a Tradition: Pomo Indian Baskets from 1850 through 1996. Ph.D. Dissertation (Anthropology), University of Washington, Seattle.

Smith-Ferri, Sherrie Ann. 2006   You'll Have Lots of Work When the Indians are Done Picking Hops: A. O. Carpenter's Native American Photographs. In *Aurelius O. Carpenter: Photographer of the Mendocino Frontier,* eds. Marvin A. Schenck, Karen Holmes, and Sherrie Ann Smith-Ferri, pp. 97–109. Grace Hudson Museum and Sun House, Ukiah, CA.

Smith, Galdys L., and Clare R. Wheeler. 1992   *A Flora of the Vascular Plants of Mendocino County, California.* University of San Francisco, San Francisco.

Smith, S. Galen. 1995   New Combinations in North American *Schoenoplectus, Bolboschoenus, Isolepis,* and *Trichophorum* (Cyperaceae). *Novon* 5(1):97–102.

Stewart, Omer Call. 1943   *Notes on Pomo Ethnogeography.* University of California Publications in American Archaeology and Ethnology, Vol. 40, No. 2. University of California Press, Berkeley.

Swezey, Sean L. 1978   Barrett's Armyworm: A Curious Ethnographic Problem. *The Journal of California Anthropology* 5(2):256–262.

Tavares, Isabelle I. 1997   A Preliminary Key to *Usnea* in California. *Bulletin of the California Lichen Society* 4(2):19–23.

The Pinoleville Tribe. 2003   Native Plants Garden. *Pinoleville Tribal Times* 2003(1):6.

The Pinoleville Tribe. 2011   Pinoleville Pomo Nation. The Pinoleville Tribe, Ukiah, CA. Available at: http://www.pinoleville-nsn.us (verified 2 December 2011).

The Plant List. 2012   The Plant List, Version 1. Available at: http://www.theplantlist.org (verified 29 July 2012).

Theodoratus, Dorothea, David W. Peri, Clinton M. Blount, and Scott M. Patterson. 1975   An Ethnographic Survey of the Mahilkaune (Dry Creek) Pomo. U.S. Army Corps of Engineers, Report No. DACW07-75-C-0022, San Francisco.

Thompson, Robert A. 1896   *Russian Settlement in California, Fort Ross, Sonoma County.* Sonoma Democrat Publishing Company, Santa Rosa, CA.

Timbrook, Jan. 2007   *Chumash Ethnobotany: Plant Knowledge among the Chumash People of Southern California.* Heyday Books, Berkeley.

Timbrook, Jan, John R. Johnson, and David D. Earle. 1993   Vegetation Burning by the Chumash. In *Before the Wildernes: Environmental Management by Native Californians,* eds. Thomas C. Blackburn and Kat Anderson, pp. 117–149. Ballena Press, Menlo Park, CA.

Turner, Nancy J., Iain J. Davidson-Hunt, and Michael O'Flaherty. 2003   Living on the Edge: Ecological and Cultural Edges as Sources of Diversity for Social-Ecological Resilience. *Human Ecology* 31(3):439–461.

Turner, Nancy J., Robin Smith, and James T. Jones. 2005   'A Fine Line between Two Nations': Ownership Patterns for Plant Resources among Northwest Coast Indigenous Peoples. In *Keeping It Living: Traditions of Plant Use and Cultivation on Northwest Coast of North America*, eds. Douglas Deur and Nancy J. Turner, pp. 151–180. University of Washington Press, Seattle.

Ukiah Daily Journal Staff. 2012   Potter Valley Tribe to Get 700 Acres of Eel River Property. In *The Ukiah Daily Journal*, 5 October 2012 edition, Ukiah, CA.

USDA (United States Department of Agriculture) and NRCS (Natural Resources Conservation Service). 2012   The PLANTS Database. National Plant Data Team, Greensboro, NC. Available at: http://plants.usda.gov (verified 29 July 2012).

Vale, Thomas R. 2002   The Pre-European Landscape of the United States: Pristine or Humanized? In *Fire, Native Peoples, and the Natural Landscape*, ed. Thomas R. Vale, pp. 1–39. Island Press, Washington, DC.

Vellinga, E. C. 2000   Notes on *Lepiota* and *Leucoagaricus*: Type Studies on *Lepiota magnispora*, *Lepiota barsii*, and *Agaricus americanus*. *Mycotaxon* 76:429–438.

Walker, Richard. 1992   Community Models of Species Richness: Regional Variation of Plant Community Species Composition on the West Slope of the Sierra Nevada, California. Master's Thesis (Geography), University of California, Santa Barbara.

Watson, Ebenezer Bliss, and R. L. Pendleton. 1916   *Soil Survey of the Ukiah Area, California.* Government Printing Office, Washington, DC.

Weiser, Andrea, and Dana Lepofsky. 2009   Ancient Land Use and Management of Ebey's Prairie, Whidbey Island, Washington. *Journal of Ethnobiology* 29:161–166.

White, Richard E. 1980   *Land Use, Environment and Social Change: The Shaping of Island County, Washington.* University of Washington Press, Seattle.

Wilson, Birbeck, and Caroline L. Hills. 1968   *Ukiah Valley Pomo Religious Life, Supernatural Doctoring, and Beliefs: Observations of 1939–1941.* University of California Archaeological Survey, Vol. 72. University of California Press, Berkeley.

Yanovsky, Elias. 1936   *Food Plants of the North American Indian.* U.S. Department of Agriculture, Washington, DC.

Yoshiyama, Ronald M., and Peter B. Moyle. 2010. Historical Review of Eel River Anadromous Salmonids, with Emphasis on Chinook Salmon, Coho Salmon and Steelhead. Center for Watershed Sciences, University of California, Davis.

List of Primary Taxa by Use Category

Abortifacient
- *Anthemis* sp.
- *Phoradendron villosum*

Adhesive
- *Abies concolor*
- *Camassia leichtlinii*
- *Camassia quamash*
- *Chlorogalum pomeridianum*
- *Pinus ponderosa*
- *Pinus* spp.
- *Pseudotsuga menziesii*
- Unidentified (***bi ti***)

Analgesic
- *Artemisia californica*
- *Dodecatheon hendersonii*
- *Eschscholzia californica*
- *Mimulus aurantiacus*
- *Phoradendron villosum*
- *Toxicoscordion fontanum*
- *Toxicoscordion micranthum*
- *Toxicoscordion venenosum*
- *Umbellularia californica*

Antidiarrheal
- *Achillea millefolium*
- *Eschscholzia californica*
- *Rumex crispus*
- *Rumex* sp.

Antihemorrhagic
- *Aralia californica*
- *Artemisia californica*
- *Polygala californica*

Antirheumatic
- *Navarretia squarrosa*
- *Toxicoscordion fontanum*
- *Toxicoscordion micranthum*
- *Toxicoscordion venenosum*

Antispasmodic
- Unidentified (***lum ka-li***)

Architecture
- *Acer macrophyllum*
- *Alnus rhombifolia*
- *Avena barbata*
- *Avena fatua*
- *Bolboschoenus robustus*
- *Bromus carinatus*
- *Bromus diandrus*
- *Cornus glabrata*
- *Cornus sericea*
- *Phalaris angusta*
- *Quercus agrifolia*
- *Quercus* spp.
- *Salix* spp.
- *Schoenoplectus acutus* var. *occidentalis*
- *Sequoia sempervirens*
- *Typha latifolia*

Arrow
- *Baccharis douglasii*
- *Baccharis salicifolia*
- *Calycanthus occidentalis*
- *Cornus glabrata*
- *Cornus sericea*
- *Rosa californica*
- *Rosa pisocarpa*
- *Salix sitchensis*
- *Taxus brevifolia*
- Unidentified (***c na hai***)
- Unidentified (***can ka-li***)
- Unidentified (***ka tsu ka-li***)

Asthma remedy
- *Artemisia californica*

Basketry

Acer macrophyllum
Adiantum jordani
Alnus rhombifolia
Apocynum cannabinum
Beckmannia syzigachne
Bolboschoenus maritimus
Calycanthus occidentalis
Carex barbarae
Carex mendocinensis
Ceanothus foliosus
Ceanothus spp.
Cercis occidentalis
Cornus glabrata
Cornus sericea
Corylus cornuta
Equisetum hyemale
Fraxinus sp.
Juncus effusus
Juncus exiguus
Juncus laccatus
Juniperus californica
Picea sitchensis
Pinus contorta
Pinus coulteri
Pinus lambertiana
Pinus ponderosa
Pinus sabiniana
Pinus spp.
Prunus virginiana
Pseudotsuga menziesii
Pteridium aquilinum
Quercus spp.
Rhus aromatica
Salix exigua
Salix gooddingii
Salix laevigata
Salix lasiolepis
Salix sitchensis

Salix spp.
Schoenoplectus acutus var. *occidentalis*
Torreya californica
Toxicodendron diversilobum
Unidentified shrub
Vitis californica

Beverage

Arctostaphylos manzanita
Clinopodium douglasii
Epilobium brachycarpum
Heracleum maximum
Pseudotsuga menziesii

Bow

Amelanchier alnifolia
Taxus brevifolia
Torreya californica
Unidentified (**can ka-li**)

Bread

Arctostaphylos manzanita
Chrysolepis chrysophylla
Dichelostemma capitatum
Dichelostemma congestum
Epilobium brachycarpum
Fritillaria affinis
Microseris laciniata
Notholithocarpus densiflorus
Perideridia kelloggii
Quercus agrifolia
Quercus chrysolepis
Quercus douglasii
Quercus dumosa
Quercus garryana
Quercus kelloggii
Quercus lobata
Quercus spp.
Typha latifolia
Umbellularia californica

Brush or broom
Angelica californica
Angelica tomentosa
Chlorogalum pomeridianum
Equisetum hyemale
Juncus effusus
Juncus exiguus
Juncus laccatus
Perideridia kelloggii

Bulb or corm food
Brodiaea coronaria
Brodiaea terrestris
Calochortus amabilis
Calochortus luteus
Calochortus pulchellus
Calochortus superbus
Calochortus venustus
Camassia leichtlinii
Camassia quamash
Dichelostemma capitatum
Dichelostemma congestum
Erythronium californicum
Fritillaria affinis
Taraxia ovata
Triteleia hyacinthina
Triteleia laxa
Triteleia peduncularis

Burn dressing
Achillea millefolium

Cathartic
Anthemis sp.
Rhus aromatica
Sambucus nigra ssp. *caerulea*

Ceremony
Abies concolor
Apocynum cannabinum
Arbutus menziesii
Artemisia californica
Cercocarpus betuloides

Cercocarpus ledifolius
Hoita macrostachya
Juncus effusus
Juncus exiguus
Juncus laccatus
Pinus spp.
Umbellularia californica

Cleaning agent
Angelica californica
Angelica tomentosa
Artemisia californica
Chlorogalum pomeridianum
Umbellularia californica
Unidentified (**ci yo batsom**)

Clothing
Apocynum cannabinum
Asclepias eriocarpa
Asclepias fascicularis
Bolboschoenus robustus
Heracleum maximum
Juncus effusus
Juncus exiguus
Juncus laccatus
Ramalina menziesii
Salix gooddingii
Salix lasiolepis
Salix spp.
Schoenoplectus acutus var.
occidentalis
Sequoia sempervirens
Typha latifolia
Urtica dioica

Cold remedy
Eriodictyon californicum

Colorant
Aesculus californica
Alnus rhombifolia
Cercis occidentalis
Chlorogalum pomeridianum

Cornus glabrata
Cornus sericea
Delphinium hesperium
Iris douglasiana
Iris macrosiphon
Pinus spp.
Plagiobothrys fulvus
Quercus kelloggii
Quercus spp.
Salix spp.
Sambucus nigra ssp. *caerulea*
Toxicodendron diversilobum
Umbellularia californica
Vitis californica

Communication

Adenostoma fasciculatum

Confection

Arbutus menziesii
Juniperus californica
Morchella sp.
Pedicularis densiflora
Pinus lambertiana
Pseudotsuga menziesii

Container

Heracleum maximum
Quercus kelloggii
Quercus spp.

Cooked green

Brassica nigra
Chlorogalum pomeridianum
Lathyrus jepsonii
Lomatium utriculatum
Lupinus bicolor
Lupinus formosus
Nemophila menziesii
Raphanus sativus
Rumex sp.
Sonchus asper
Trifolium variegatum

Vicia americana

Cooking

Acer macrophyllum
Chlorogalum pomeridianum
Fraxinus sp.
Heracleum maximum
Iris douglasiana
Iris macrosiphon
Juncus effusus
Juncus exiguus
Juncus laccatus
Quercus spp.
Schoenoplectus acutus var.
    occidentalis
Vitis californica

Cordage

Apocynum cannabinum
Asclepias eriocarpa
Asclepias fascicularis
Beckmannia syzigachne
Corylus cornuta
Equisetum hyemale
Hoita macrostachya
Iris douglasiana
Iris macrosiphon
Unidentified (**ma ta-bo' ka-li**)
Salix gooddingii
Salix lasiolepis
Urtica dioica
Vitis californica

Counterirritant

Artemisia californica

Decoration

Adenostoma fasciculatum
Adiantum jordani
Angelica californica
Angelica tomentosa
Apocynum cannabinum
Arctostaphylos manzanita

Artemisia californica
Asclepias eriocarpa
Asclepias fascicularis
Bromus diandrus
Calochortus luteus
Calochortus superbus
Calochortus venustus
Cercocarpus betuloides
Cercocarpus ledifolius
Chlorogalum pomeridianum
Juncus effusus
Juncus exiguus
Juncus laccatus
Pseudotsuga menziesii
Quercus spp.
Sambucus nigra ssp. *caerulea*
Symphoricarpos mollis
Umbellularia californica

Dermatological aid
Anemopsis californica

Disinfectant
Calandrinia ciliata
Scrophularia californica
Unidentified (**tsip**)

Diuretic
Cornus glabrata
Cornus sericea
Iris douglasiana
Iris macrosiphon

Divination and doctoring
Abies concolor
Angelica californica
Angelica tomentosa
Datura stramonium
Equisetum hyemale
Toxicodendron diversilobum

Emetic
Datisca glomerata
Taraxia ovata

Thalictrum fendleri
Unidentified (**ka ka' wi no**)
Wyethia glabra

Emollient
Artemisia californica

Eye medicine
Marah sp.
Ranunculus orthorhynchus

Febrifuge
Artemisia californica
Sanicula tuberosa
Trichostema lanceolatum
Unidentified (**tso lom to**)

Fiber (unspecified)
Sambucus nigra ssp. *caerulea*

Fire
Abies concolor
Adenostoma fasciculatum
Aesculus californica
Alnus rhombifolia
Ceanothus spp.
Cornus glabrata
Cornus sericea
Quercus spp.
Sambucus nigra ssp. *caerulea*

First aid
Calandrinia ciliata
Cynoglossum grande
Fraxinus sp.
Pseudognaphalium californicum
Solidago velutina
Toxicodendron diversilobum
Toxicoscordion fontanum
Toxicoscordion micranthum
Toxicoscordion venenosum
Unidentified (**tsip**)
Wyethia glabra

Fishing
Apocynum cannabinum

Arctostaphylos manzanita
Cercocarpus betuloides
Cercocarpus ledifolius
Chlorogalum pomeridianum
Cornus glabrata
Cornus sericea
Corylus cornuta
Croton setiger
Datisca glomerata
Juncus effusus
Juncus exiguus
Juncus laccatus
Lomatium utriculatum
Phoradendron villosum
Pseudotsuga menziesii
Quercus dumosa
Quercus garryana
Quercus kelloggii
Quercus spp.
Rhus aromatica
Salix spp.
Verbascum blattaria

Flavoring
Clarkia amoena
Croton setiger
Epilobium brachycarpum
Madia elegans
Madia sativa
Plantago major
Umbellularia californica
Wyethia angustifolia

Food (unspecified)
Plantago major

Fowling
Arctostaphylos manzanita
Ceanothus spp.
Fraxinus sp.
Quercus spp.

Fragrance
Artemisia californica
Pseudotsuga menziesii
Sanicula tuberosa
Trichostema lanceolatum

Fruit food
Amelanchier alnifolia
Arbutus menziesii
Arctostaphylos manzanita
Carpobrotus chilensis
Crataegus gaylussacia
Fragaria chiloensis
Fragaria vesca
Gaultheria shallon
Heteromeles arbutifolia
Prunus subcordata
Prunus virginiana
Ribes californicum
Ribes divaricatum
Rosa californica
Rosa pisocarpa
Rubus leucodermis
Rubus parviflorus
Rubus spectabilis
Rubus ursinus
Sambucus nigra ssp. *caerulea*
Solanum xanti
Umbellularia californica
Vaccinium ovatum
Vaccinium parvifolium
Vitis californica

Fungus food
Armillariella mellea
Leucoagaricus americanus
Unidentified (**ta tce e'**)
Unidentified (**tca la' tce e'**)
Unidentified (**tsi tal' tce e'**)

Gaming and competition
Acer macrophyllum

Aesculus californica
Apocynum cannabinum
Arctostaphylos manzanita
Artemisia californica
Cercocarpus betuloides
Cercocarpus ledifolius
Cornus glabrata
Cornus sericea
Delphinium nudicaule
Fraxinus sp.
Iris douglasiana
Iris macrosiphon
Juncus effusus
Juncus exiguus
Juncus laccatus
Populus fremontii
Quercus spp.
Ramalina menziesii
Rosa pisocarpa
Salix spp.
Schoenoplectus acutus var.
    occidentalis
Umbellularia californica

Gastrointestinal aid
Achillea millefolium
Artemisia californica
Datisca glomerata
Frangula purshiana
Mentzelia sp.
Mimulus aurantiacus
Rhus aromatica
Sambucus nigra ssp. *caerulea*

Hair treatment
Quercus spp.

Host plant
Fraxinus sp.
Heracleum maximum
Quercus spp.
Unidentified (**pi-du'bac**)

Hunting
Adenostoma fasciculatum
Aesculus californica
Amelanchier alnifolia
Angelica californica
Angelica tomentosa
Apocynum cannabinum
Calystegia sp.
Cercocarpus betuloides
Cercocarpus ledifolius
Cornus glabrata
Cornus sericea
Fraxinus sp.
Hoita macrostachya
Iris douglasiana
Iris macrosiphon
Pinus spp.
Rhamnus crocea
Rhamnus ilicifolia
Rosa californica
Rosa pisocarpa
Urtica dioica

Insecticide
Calandrinia ciliata
Chlorogalum pomeridianum
Perideridia kelloggii
Quercus spp.
Unidentified (**ci yo batsom**)
Unidentified (**tsip**)

Laxative
Achillea millefolium
Arbutus menziesii
Datisca glomerata
Frangula californica
Frangula purshiana
Heteromeles arbutifolia
Pinus lambertiana
Taraxacum officinale
Thalictrum fendleri

Unidentified (*tso lom to*)

Legend

Aesculus californica
Allium dichlamydeum
Allium spp.
Alnus rhombifolia
Asclepias eriocarpa
Asclepias fascicularis
Bolboschoenus maritimus
Carex barbarae
Carex mendocinensis
Chlorogalum pomeridianum
Fraxinus sp.
Nicotiana attenuata
Nicotiana quadrivalvis
Osmorhiza sp.
Quercus spp.
Sequoia sempervirens
Umbellularia californica
Vitis californica

Leprosy treatment

Fraxinus sp.
Solidago velutina

Matting or bedding

Avena barbata
Avena fatua
Bolboschoenus robustus
Bromus carinatus
Juncus effusus
Juncus exiguus
Juncus laccatus
Phalaris angusta
Ramalina menziesii
Salix gooddingii
Schoenoplectus acutus var.
    occidentalis
Trifolium spp.
Typha latifolia
Woodwardia fimbriata

Medicine (unspecified)

Alnus rhombifolia
Angelica californica
Angelica tomentosa
Aralia californica
Artemisia californica
Equisetum hyemale
Eriodictyon californicum
Marah sp.
Quercus spp.
Toxicodendron diversilobum

Mush

Aesculus californica
Arctostaphylos manzanita
Chrysolepis chrysophylla
Microseris laciniata
Notholithocarpus densiflorus
Quercus agrifolia
Quercus chrysolepis
Quercus douglasii
Quercus dumosa
Quercus garryana
Quercus kelloggii
Quercus lobata
Quercus spp.

Music

Arctostaphylos manzanita
Cornus glabrata
Cornus sericea
Populus fremontii
Quercus spp.
Salix spp.
Sambucus nigra ssp. *caerulea*

Narcotic

Delphinium nudicaule

Nut food

Araucaria araucana
Corylus cornuta
Pinus lambertiana

Pinus sabiniana
Pinus spp.
Pseudotsuga menziesii
Torreya californica
Umbellularia californica

Packing or carrying
Apocynum cannabinum
Fraxinus sp.
Quercus kelloggii
Quercus spp.
Vitis californica
Woodwardia fimbriata

Padding or toweling
Asclepias eriocarpa
Asclepias fascicularis
Juncus effusus
Juncus exiguus
Juncus laccatus
Ramalina menziesii
Schoenoplectus acutus var.
     occidentalis

Panacea
Artemisia californica
Salix lasiolepis

Pediatric aid
Populus fremontii

Poison
Dichelostemma ida-maia
Torreya californica
Toxicoscordion fontanum
Toxicoscordion micranthum
Toxicoscordion venenosum
Unidentified (**ci yo batsom**)
Unidentified (**tsip**)

Polish
Aesculus californica
Chlorogalum pomeridianum
Equisetum hyemale
Pseudotsuga menziesii

Salix spp.

Psychiatric aid
Datura stramonium
Osmorhiza sp.

Root food
Aralia californica
Perideridia kelloggii
Sanicula tuberosa
Sonchus asper
Tragopogon porrifolius
Typha latifolia

Salad food
Agoseris apargioides
Agoseris grandiflora
Allium bolanderi
Allium dichlamydeum
Allium spp.
Amsinckia lycopsoides
Angelica californica
Angelica tomentosa
Asclepias eriocarpa
Asclepias fascicularis
Bolboschoenus robustus
Calandrinia ciliata
Claytonia perfoliata
Erodium cicutarium
Foeniculum vulgare
Geranium dissectum
Heracleum maximum
Lathyrus vestitus
Lupinus bicolor
Lupinus formosus
Lupinus nanus
Microseris laciniata
Nuphar polysepala
Oenanthe sarmentosa
Perideridia kelloggii
Plagiobothrys fulvus
Platystemon californicus

Pseudotsuga menziesii
Raphanus sativus
Schoenoplectus acutus var.
    occidentalis
Sonchus asper
Taraxacum officinale
Tauschia kelloggii
Tragopogon porrifolius
Trifolium ciliolatum
Trifolium fucatum
Trifolium gracilentum
Trifolium microdon
Trifolium obtusiflorum
Trifolium spp.
Trifolium variegatum
Trifolium willdenovii
Trifolium wormskioldii
Typha latifolia
Wyethia angustifolia
Yabea microcarpa

Salt
    Aesculus californica

Sea vegetable
    Macrocystis pyrifera
    Porphyra sp.

Seed food
    Achyrachaena mollis
    Anemopsis californica
    Avena barbata
    Avena fatua
    Balsamorhiza deltoidea
    Bromus carinatus
    Calycadenia multiglandulosa
    Ceanothus foliosus
    Elymus elymoides
    Elymus triticoides
    Festuca temulenta
    Hemizonia congesta
    Iva axillaris

Madia elegans
Madia sativa
Perideridia kelloggii
Plagiobothrys fulvus
Ranunculus californicus
Ranunculus occidentalis
Rumex crispus
Rumex sp.
Trichostema lanceolatum
Unidentified (**binan'**)

Smoking
    Eriodictyon californicum
    Fraxinus sp.
    Nicotiana attenuata
    Nicotiana quadrivalvis
    Symphoricarpos mollis
    Vitis californica

Snakebite remedy
    Asclepias eriocarpa
    Asclepias fascicularis
    Heracleum maximum
    Perideridia kelloggii

Spirituality
    Adenocaulon bicolor
    Angelica californica
    Angelica tomentosa
    Hoita macrostachya
    Lomatium utriculatum
    Osmorhiza sp.
    Thalictrum fendleri

STD remedy
    Arctostaphylos manzanita
    Cornus glabrata
    Cornus sericea
    Helenium puberulum
    Marah sp.
    Thalictrum fendleri
    Urtica dioica

Stimulant
    Calandrinia ciliata
Timekeeping
    Pinus spp.
Tool
    Abies concolor
    Acer macrophyllum
    Aesculus californica
    Arctostaphylos manzanita
    Ceanothus cuneatus
    Ceanothus spp.
    Cercocarpus betuloides
    Cercocarpus ledifolius
    Cornus glabrata
    Cornus sericea
    Fraxinus sp.
    Quercus agrifolia
    Quercus spp.
    Sambucus nigra ssp. *caerulea*
    Symphoricarpos mollis
    Taxus brevifolia
    Umbellularia californica
Trade
    Apocynum cannabinum
    Carex barbarae
    Carex mendocinensis
    Juncus effusus
    Juncus exiguus
    Juncus laccatus
    Salix spp.
Ulcer remedy
    Heracleum maximum
War
    Abies concolor
    Arctostaphylos manzanita

Cercocarpus betuloides
Cercocarpus ledifolius
Chlorogalum pomeridianum
Iris douglasiana
Iris macrosiphon
Juniperus californica
Salix exigua
Urtica dioica
Vitis californica
Watercraft
    Arctostaphylos manzanita
    Bolboschoenus robustus
    Fraxinus sp.
    Quercus spp.
    Schoenoplectus acutus var.
        occidentalis
    Sequoia sempervirens
Women's health
    Allium bolanderi
    Artemisia californica
    Asclepias eriocarpa
    Asclepias fascicularis
    Chlorogalum pomeridianum
    Eschscholzia californica
    Juncus effusus
    Juncus exiguus
    Juncus laccatus
    Madia elegans
    Matricaria discoidea
    Mimulus aurantiacus
    Ramalina menziesii
    Schoenoplectus acutus var.
        occidentalis
    Triteleia hyacinthina
    Typha latifolia

List of Primary Taxa by Family

Adoxaceae
    Sambucus nigra ssp. *caerulea*

Agaricaceae (Fungi)
    Leucoagaricus americanus

Agavaceae
    Camassia quamash
    Camassia leichtlinii
    Chlorogalum pomeridianum

Aizoaceae
    Carpobrotus chilensis

Alliaceae
    Allium bolanderi
    Allium dichlamydeum
    Allium spp.

Anacardiaceae
    Rhus aromatica
    Toxicodendron diversilobum

Apiaceae
    Angelica californica
    Angelica tomentosa
    Foeniculum vulgare
    Heracleum maximum
    Lomatium utriculatum
    Oenanthe sarmentosa
    Osmorhiza sp.
    Perideridia kelloggii
    Sanicula tuberosa
    Tauschia kelloggii
    Yabea microcarpa

Apocynaceae
    Apocynum cannabinum
    Asclepias eriocarpa
    Asclepias fascicularis

Araliaceae
    Aralia californica

Araucariaceae
    Araucaria araucana

Asteraceae
    Achillea millefolium
    Achyrachaena mollis
    Adenocaulon bicolor
    Agoseris apargioides
    Agoseris grandiflora
    Anthemis sp.
    Artemisia californica
    Baccharis douglasii
    Baccharis salicifolia
    Balsamorhiza deltoidea
    Calycadenia multiglandulosa
    Eriophyllum lanatum
    Helenium puberulum
    Hemizonia congesta
    Iva axillaris
    Madia elegans
    Madia sativa
    Matricaria discoidea
    Microseris laciniata
    Pseudognaphalium californicum
    Solidago velutina
    Sonchus asper
    Taraxacum officinale
    Tragopogon porrifolius
    Wyethia angustifolia
    Wyethia glabra

Bangiaceae (Algae)
    Porphyra sp.

Betulaceae
    Alnus rhombifolia
    Corylus cornuta

Blechnaceae
    Woodwardia fimbriata

Boraginaceae
    Amsinckia lycopsoides
    Cynoglossum grande

Eriodictyon californicum
Nemophila menziesii
Plagiobothrys fulvus
Brassicaceae
    Brassica nigra
    Cardamine californica
    Raphanus sativus
Calycanthaceae
    Calycanthus occidentalis
Caprifoliaceae
    Symphoricarpos mollis
Convolvulaceae
    Calystegia sp.
Cornaceae
    Cornus glabrata
    Cornus sericea
Cucurbitaceae
    Marah spp.
Cupressaceae
    Juniperus californica
    Sequoia sempervirens
Cyperaceae
    Bolboschoenus maritimus
    Bolboschoenus robustus
    Carex barbarae
    Carex mendocinensis
    Schoenoplectus acutus var.
        occidentalis
Datiscaceae
    Datisca glomerata
Dennstaedtiaceae
    Pteridium aquilinum
Equisetaceae
    Equisetum hyemale
Ericaceae
    Arbutus menziesii
    Arctostaphylos manzanita
    Gaultheria shallon
    Vaccinium ovatum

Vaccinium parvifolium
Euphorbiaceae
    Croton setiger
Fabaceae
    Cercis occidentalis
    Hoita macrostachya
    Lathyrus jepsonii
    Lathyrus vestitus
    Lupinus bicolor
    Lupinus formosus
    Lupinus nanus
    Trifolium ciliolatum
    Trifolium fucatum
    Trifolium gracilentum
    Trifolium microdon
    Trifolium obtusiflorum
    Trifolium spp.
    Trifolium variegatum
    Trifolium willdenovii
    Trifolium wormskioldii
    Vicia americana
Fagaceae
    Chrysolepis chrysophylla
    Notholithocarpus densiflorus
    Quercus agrifolia
    Quercus chrysolepis
    Quercus douglasii
    Quercus dumosa
    Quercus garryana
    Quercus kelloggii
    Quercus lobata
    Quercus spp.
Geraniaceae
    Erodium cicutarium
    Geranium dissectum
Grossulariaceae
    Ribes californicum
    Ribes divaricatum

Iridaceae
> *Iris douglasiana*
> *Iris macrosiphon*

Juncaceae
> *Juncus effusus*
> *Juncus exiguus*
> *Juncus laccatus*

Lamiaceae
> *Clinopodium douglasii*
> *Marrubium vulgare*
> *Trichostema lanceolatum*

Laminariaceae (Algae)
> *Macrocystis pyrifera*

Lauraceae
> *Umbellularia californica*

Liliaceae
> *Calochortus amabilis*
> *Calochortus luteus*
> *Calochortus pulchellus*
> *Calochortus superbus*
> *Calochortus venustus*
> *Erythronium californicum*
> *Fritillaria affinis*

Loasaceae
> *Mentzelia* sp.

Melanthiaceae
> *Toxicoscordion fontanum*
> *Toxicoscordion micranthum*
> *Toxicoscordion venenosum*

Montiaceae
> *Calandrinia ciliata*
> *Claytonia perfoliata*

Morchellaceae (Fungi)
> *Morchella* sp.

Nymphaeaceae
> *Nuphar polysepala*

Oleaceae
> *Fraxinus* sp.

Onagraceae
> *Clarkia amoena*
> *Epilobium brachycarpum*
> *Taraxia ovata*

Orobanchaceae
> *Castilleja exserta*
> *Pedicularis densiflora*

Papaveraceae
> *Eschscholzia californica*
> *Platystemon californicus*

Phrymaceae
> *Mimulus aurantiacus*

Physalacriaceae (Fungi)
> *Armillariella mellea*

Pinaceae
> *Abies concolor*
> *Picea sitchensis*
> *Pinus contorta*
> *Pinus coulteri*
> *Pinus lambertiana*
> *Pinus ponderosa*
> *Pinus sabiniana*
> *Pinus* spp.
> *Pseudotsuga menziesii*

Plantaginaceae
> *Plantago major*

Poaceae
> *Avena barbata*
> *Avena fatua*
> *Beckmannia syzigachne*
> *Bromus carinatus*
> *Bromus diandrus*
> *Elymus elymoides*
> *Elymus triticoides*
> *Festuca temulenta*
> *Phalaris angusta*

Polemoniaceae
> *Navarretia squarrosa*

Polygalaceae
  Polygala californica
Polygonaceae
  Rumex crispus
  Rumex sp.
Primulaceae
  Dodecatheon hendersonii
Pteridaceae
  Adiantum jordani
Ramalinaceae (Fungi)
  Ramalina menziesii
Ranunculaceae
  Delphinium hesperium
  Delphinium nudicaule
  Ranunculus californicus
  Ranunculus canus
  Ranunculus occidentalis
  Ranunculus orthorhynchus
  Thalictrum fendleri
Rhamnaceae
  Ceanothus cuneatus
  Ceanothus foliosus
  Ceanothus spp.
  Frangula californica
  Frangula purshiana
  Rhamnus crocea
  Rhamnus ilicifolia
Rosaceae
  Adenostoma fasciculatum
  Amelanchier alnifolia
  Cercocarpus betuloides
  Cercocarpus ledifolius
  Crataegus gaylussacia
  Fragaria chiloensis
  Fragaria vesca
  Heteromeles arbutifolia
  Prunus subcordata
  Prunus virginiana
  Rosa californica

Rosa pisocarpa
Rubus leucodermis
Rubus parviflorus
Rubus spectabilis
Rubus ursinus
Salicaceae
  Populus fremontii
  Salix exigua
  Salix gooddingii
  Salix laevigata
  Salix lasiolepis
  Salix sitchensis
  Salix spp.
Sapindaceae
  Acer macrophyllum
  Aesculus californica
Saururaceae
  Anemopsis californica
Scrophulariaceae
  Scrophularia californica
  Verbascum blattaria
Solanaceae
  Datura stramonium
  Nicotiana attenuata
  Nicotiana quadrivalvis
  Solanum xanti
Taxaceae
  Taxus brevifolia
  Torreya californica
Themidaceae
  Brodiaea coronaria
  Brodiaea terrestris
  Dichelostemma capitatum
  Dichelostemma congestum
  Dichelostemma ida-maia
  Triteleia hyacinthina
  Triteleia laxa
  Triteleia peduncularis

Typhaceae
>	*Typha latifolia*

Urticaceae
>	*Urtica dioica*

Viscaceae
>	*Phoradendron villosum*

Vitaceae
>	*Vitis californica*

Undetermined
>	*Ba' ma-tci*
>	*Bi ti*
>	*Binan'*
>	*Bu ta' tce e'*
>	*C na hai*
>	*Can ka-li*
>	*Ci yo batsom*
>	*Ka ka' wi no*
>	*Ka ki lec'*
>	*Ka si-bu'*
>	*Ka tsu ka-li*
>	*Lum ka-li*
>	*Ma ta-bo' ka-li*
>	*Pi-du'bac*
>	*Stan'-tci*
>	*Ta tce e'*
>	*Tca la' tce e'*
>	*To tol tce e'*
>	*Tsi tal' tce e'*
>	*Tsip*
>	*Tso lom to*
>	Unidentified shrub

www.ingramcontent.com/pod-product-compliance
Lightning Source LLC
Chambersburg PA
CBHW080248030426
42334CB00023BA/2741